AF713185

Why Informal Workers Organize

Why Informal Workers Organize

Contentious Politics, Enforcement, and the State

CALLA HUMMEL

OXFORD
UNIVERSITY PRESS

OXFORD
UNIVERSITY PRESS

Great Clarendon Street, Oxford, OX2 6DP,
United Kingdom

Oxford University Press is a department of the University of Oxford.
It furthers the University's objective of excellence in research, scholarship,
and education by publishing worldwide. Oxford is a registered trade mark of
Oxford University Press in the UK and in certain other countries

© Calla Hummel 2021

The moral rights of the author have been asserted

All rights reserved. No part of this publication may be reproduced, stored in
a retrieval system, or transmitted, in any form or by any means, without the
prior permission in writing of Oxford University Press, or as expressly permitted
by law, by licence or under terms agreed with the appropriate reprographics
rights organization. Enquiries concerning reproduction outside the scope of the
above should be sent to the Rights Department, Oxford University Press, at the
address above

You must not circulate this work in any other form
and you must impose this same condition on any acquirer

Published in the United States of America by Oxford University Press

198 Madison Avenue, New York, NY 10016, United States of America

British Library Cataloguing in Publication Data

Data available

Library of Congress Control Number: 2021937204

ISBN 978–0–19–284781–2

DOI: 10.1093/oso/9780192847812.001.0001

Printed and bound by
CPI Group (UK) Ltd, Croydon, CR0 4YY

Cover image: Calla Hummel

Links to third party websites are provided by Oxford in good faith and
for information only. Oxford disclaims any responsibility for the materials
contained in any third party website referenced in this work.

Acknowledgments

Hundreds of people helped with this project and I am deeply indebted to all of them. First, this project only exists because of the incredible people who work on the streets and put in extra hours to organize their colleagues and demand a better life. I am grateful to the dozens of street vendors in Bolivia and Brazil who decided to trust me, talk with me, and teach me. I am especially grateful to the people who took the time to explain how the markets work, how to sell in them, and how to interact with officials as a street vendor. I am grateful to the public servants who took time out of their very busy schedules to answer my questions and let me observe their work. I am deeply thankful for the many frank conversations that elected officials and administrators had with me about trying to balance the overwhelming demands of their jobs and their sense of what was right and fair. I especially appreciate the people who invited me on patrol or to their stalls and shared coca with me when we worked long hours.

In addition to the street vendors and officials whose words are in this project, my work in La Paz and São Paulo would not have gone very far without the help of Cecilia Salazar, Luciana Molina Barragán, Luciana Itikawa, Amaru Villanueva, Jorge Derpic, Amy Kennemore, Sam Serrano, Linda Farthing, Christof Bex, and Sara Shariari. I am very lucky to have you as colleagues. Many thanks to Jenny, Silvia, Amira, Ceci, and everyone else who is part of La Paz Rugby Feminino, as well as Lu, Renata, William, Ana, Marcela, and everyone who has gone to a queercore show with me.

I was lucky to be part of amazing networks in Miami and Austin while writing this book. Raúl Madrid has been and continues to be an ideal mentor and encouraged and helped me with this project before we had ever met. I look up to you as a scholar and a person. Javier Auyero, Mike Findley, Wendy Hunter, Kurt Weyland, and Scott Wolford contributed to this project in more ways than I can count. Each encouraged me to work on this project in their courses I took as a novice graduate student, and each provided invaluable feedback that brought this undertaking from an off-the-wall idea to a fully formed research project. My colleagues at the University of Miami have been an incredible support network and have helped transform this project from a dissertation into a book. Mike Touchton, Merike Blofield, and Sallie Hughes have been part of many substantive discussions. Greg Koger, Louise

Davidson-Schmich, Jennifer Connolly, Joe Uscinski, Laura Gómez-Mera, and Costa Pischedda have provided moral support as well as general advice and a fantastic social network. I am especially indebted to my writing group buddies Kathryn Nowotny, Marisa Omori, Catherine Newell, Dexter Callander, Melissa Scott, and Judith Williams and to the UM Humanities Writing Group for letting a social scientist crash their sessions.

I have benefited from scholars who kept me going with feedback and encouragement over the years. Thank you to Andy Baker, Ximena Velasco Guachalla, and Carew Boulding for sharing data and code and then armfuls of moral support. Many, many thanks to Alisha Holland, John Gerring, Cathy Boone, Diana Kapiszewski, Skip Lupia, Candelaria Garay, Bethany Albertson, Scott Moser, John Patty, Maggie Penn, David Rueda, Shelby Grossman, Sally Roever, and Dan Brinks for support and advice. I am also indebted to my undergraduate mentors Angelina Godoy, Lisa Glidden, and Tuna Kuyucu, who helped me develop the very early stages of this project. I benefited immensely from all of the faculty at the University of Texas, as well as IQMR, ICPSR, and EITM, and I appreciate all of your time and effort.

None of us can write books without academic buddies. Thank you to Dana El Kurd, Kim Guiler, Rodolfo Disi Pavlic, Ken Miller, Andy Stravers, Caitlin Andrews, Joe Tafoya, Jake Dizard, Katie Putnam, Clare Brock, Roberto Armijo, Gio Altamirano, Omar Awapara, Ahmed Siddiqi, Hadill Calderon, Iasmin Goes, Cathy Wu, Robert Shaffer, Maraam Dwidar, Elizabeth Rennick, Ayca Arkilic, Thomas Elliot, Kristie Kelly, Louise Liebskind, German Petersen, Julie Phillips, Luai Allarakia, Ryan Lloyd, Tommy Burt, Henry Pascoe, Josiah Marineau, Dan McCormack, Daniel Weitzel, Paula Muñoz, Nathalia Sandoval, Ina Taneva, Christina Frederick, Christina Noriega Bambrick, Chris Yarng, and Rachel Sternfeld. I also benefited immensely from the friends I made at conferences and math camp, especially Jami Nelson-Nuñez, Jessica Rich, Lindsay Mayka, Eduardo Moncada, Santiago Anria, Victoria Paniagua, Laila Wahedi, Paul DeBell, Brian Palmer-Rubin, Chris Schwarz, Max Eriksson, Gökhan Çiflikli, Andrew Brooks, Laura Gamboa, Eric Dunford, Chao-yo Cheng, Amanda Alvarez, Rebecca Cordell, Meneviş Cilisoğlu, Eoghan McGreevy-Stafford, Yuree Noh, Tara Buss, Chase Foster, Sarah Bouchat, Chelsea Estancona, Chrissy Ladam, Josh Lerner, and Jaira Harrington.

Thank you to my nonacademic support network for keeping things in perspective. Thanks to way too many friends to list, but especially Katherine Strandberg, Mari and Tiffany, Ana Kelson, Moni, Eva, Sam and Julho, Fabio, Britt, Marie and Jenna, and Belén. Thanks to everyone who let me pet their dog when I was stressed out. I owe a deep debt to the staff of too many cafés, but especially Shane, Jenn, and crew at Cherrywood, Paola and Ruth at Panther, Khatti and team at Flightpath, and Gilda and everyone at Magick. A big thank you to everyone from the bottom of my heart.

Thank you to everyone who gave me money and helped me publish the book. I was very fortunate to get a National Science Foundation Graduate Research Fellowship (2013163892) to embark on this project. This book is only possible because of that grant, which funded fieldwork, data collection, and a year of writing. Editors David Samuels and Ben Ansell and editor Aníbal Pérez Liñán published earlier article manuscripts. Portions of Chapter 2 were published as "Disobedient markets: Street vendors, enforcement, and state intervention in collective action." *Comparative Political Studies* 50.11 (2017): 1524–1555. I gratefully acknowledge Cambridge University Press for allowing me to publish this material in the book. Portions of Chapter 5 were published as "Bribery Cartels: Collusive Corruption in Bolivian Street Markets." *Latin American Research Review* 53.2 (2018). I gratefully acknowledge the Latin American Studies Association for allowing me to publish this material in the book.

The University of Miami and the University of Texas provided institutional homes for me and additional resources to finish the project. I thank the University of Miami College of Arts and Sciences for supporting a final round of fieldwork and the University of Miami Institute for the Advanced Study of the Americas for funding a book workshop. Raúl Madrid, Alisha Holland, David Rueda, Sallie Hughes, Merike Blofield, and Mike Touchton gave me invaluable feedback at and after the book workshop. I deeply appreciate invitations from Victoria Paniagua and the Kellogg Institute at the University of Notre Dame, Victor Menaldo and the Comparative Politics Workshop at the University of Washington, and José Antonio Hernández Company and the Political Economy Series at the Técnico de Monterrey for invitations to present and discuss my work. Samantha Kamath provided excellent research assistance and data-wrangling skills as I was rewriting the manuscript. I have immense gratitude for Dominic Byatt's editorial skills, Oxford University Press, and the useful feedback from three anonymous reviewers.

Thank you for making this possible.

Contents

List of Figures

List of Tables

1

Why Do Informal Workers Organize?

Every weekend in La Paz, Bolivia, Rosa works as a *champañera*, or champagne lady, selling champagne, photographs, and car decorations to newlyweds in a neighborhood park. Rosa is the founding director of the neighborhood's *champañeras*' union, which is one of hundreds of street vendor unions in La Paz. The position is unpaid, and the $10 to $50 that she makes as a *champañera* every weekend supplements the money that she makes scavenging recyclables at night. In São Paulo, Brazil, Renato sells cheap electronics from a cardboard box in Brazil's largest street market. Renato can make up to $100 on a good day, even though he spends a third of his time running from armed military police. Like Rosa, he works as a street vendor to scrape by on rent and support his daughter, but unlike Rosa, Renato does not belong to a street vendor organization and he dismisses work-based organizing as pointless. Both Rosa and Renato are young, poor street vendors in Latin American metropolises, but they participate in local politics and organizations in divergent ways.

Rosa and Renato are two of two billion informal workers around the world (ILO, 2018). Informal workers make up more than half of the global workforce (Baker and Velasco Guachalla, 2018, Holland, 2017, Vanek et al., 2014). An informal worker is anyone who holds a job and who does not pay taxes on taxable earnings, does not hold a license for their work when one is required, or is not part of a mandatory social security system. While many informal workers like Renato avoid organizing, others like Rosa join together with other workers (Agarwala, 2013, Grossman, 2020, WIEGO, 2016, pp.23–24, 197). Renana Jhabvala, a former chairperson of an international network of street vendor activists, states that "In every city in the world, there is always some organizing among street vendors" (Bhowmik, 2012, p. xvi). Survey data from around the world backs up Jhabvala's statement: the data in this book finds that informal workers organize in nearly every country for which data exists, but to varying degrees. In countries like the United States, a handful of informal workers like street vendors and domestic workers form small, scattered organizations, while in countries like Bolivia, informal workers like *champañeras*, fortune tellers, witches, clowns, gravestone cleaners, sex workers, and shoe shiners

Why Informal Workers Organize. Calla Hummel, Oxford University Press.
© Calla Hummel (2021). DOI: 10.1093/oso/9780192847812.003.0001

come together in powerful unions (Anria, 2018, Baker and Velasco Guachalla, 2018, Rosaldo, 2016). In countries as diverse as Bolivia, South Africa, South Korea, and India, national informal worker organizations represent millions of citizens (Agarwala, 2013, Lazar, 2007a, WIEGO, 2016).

For example, street vendors typically[1] hold jobs in the informal sector, where their pay is low, precarious, and variable, their work conditions are dangerous and stressful, and social security or health benefits are rare (King and Rueda, 2008, Rueda, 2007). While most do not belong to any work-based organization, a growing and politically active minority does (Agarwala, 2013, Grossman, 2020). In India and Bolivia, where street vendors formed national informal worker organizations, the organizations have negotiated with the government to largely regulate themselves (Hummel, 2017), receive money for public works (Tassi et al., 2015, p.92), and extend health benefits (Agarwala, 2013, pp.3–4). Why do informal workers organize? Why do some street vendors, like Rosa, start unions, while others, like Renato, avoid them?

I find that officials' actions can either encourage informal workers to organize or discourage their participation. Some officials offer informal workers cash and in-kind incentives to organize and participate in self-regulating groups that enforce local regulations. Sometimes, these incentives come as cash payments to informal workers: in La Paz, officials and street vendors report that some political parties and city administrations pay leaders to cooperate, while the El Alto city government signed a ten-year agreement to return half of all licensing fees to street vendor organizations. In India, the government issues debit cards to organized street vendors and other informal workers for healthcare expenses (Agarwala, 2013, pp.3–4). In many more cases, governments offer informal workers incentives that they can use to make more money, but only if the workers organize.

On the other hand, officials may ignore informal workers or respond to informal workers by cracking down on them with police raids (Resnick, 2019). Negative incentives come in many forms: officials may impose steep fines on workers who break one of hundreds of laws, police and inspectors may confiscate goods for sale or the tools that workers need to do their jobs, and politicians and bureaucrats may block, stonewall, or ignore informal workers' requests for meetings, explanations, or help. In places like the United States and Brazil, police have arrested, beaten, and even killed informal workers who were selling cigarettes, DVDs, or were otherwise trying to make

[1] Formal street vendors can exist, though they are rare. For example, owners of licensed food trucks or permanent artisan stalls at municipal markets that pay taxes and follow all local regulations could simultaneously be street vendors and formal businesses.

money in ways their governments deemed irregular. Increased policing takes resources away from informal workers and discourages them from organizing and participating in political processes, though it does not eradicate informal work.

In this book, I focus on cases of street vendors, their organizations, and their interactions with local politicians, bureaucrats, and police – I call all of these state agents "officials." Street vendors represent 4–15 percent of workers in major cities like Lima, Hanoi, and Johannesburg (Vanek et al., 2014, p.47) and form one of the main groups of informal workers in cities across the world (Cross, 1998, Grossman, 2020, WIEGO, 2016). Street vendors face many of the barriers to organizing that other informal workers like recyclers or mototaxi drivers face, but they have more autonomy and flexibility than informal domestic workers or laborers (Blofield, 2012, Rosaldo, 2016). The survey data in this book demonstrates that street vendor organizing does not appear to be dramatically different than that of people working in other informal jobs: in the Comparative Study of Electoral Systems data set that I analyze in Chapter 3, street vendors organize at rates similar to domestic workers and recyclers but less than agricultural laborers, for example. Among the many ways that officials can encourage or discourage informal workers' organizations and broader political participation, I primarily discuss street vending licenses as positive incentives in this book. In Bolivia, Brazil, and many other places, street vending licenses are resold on secondary markets for cash and can make an informal business more predictable, stable, and lucrative. Increased policing and especially confiscation by police are the primary negative incentives that I discuss in the cases.

However, government incentives for informal workers lead to another puzzle: Why do officials encourage people to organize, especially people who routinely violate public space, tax, and labor laws? For officials with career ambitions and governance goals, small budgets, and limited capacity, informal workers control an important resource: their compliance (Grossman et al., 2018, Rich, 2019). When officials need to clean up streets, improve traffic, or decrease pollution, they can turn to informal workers and their organizations to increase compliance with quality of life regulations (Goodfellow, 2015, Post et al., 2017). Faced with administrative constraints, officials in many places offer incentives to informal workers who organize. Officials then delegate enforcement roles to those organizations. Where successful, officials extract compliance and legibility from informal workers and markets. Revocable incentives like street vending licenses make informal workers and informal markets easier to control (Holland, 2017).

I argue that officials are more likely to encourage informal workers to organize under the following conditions: First, officials are more likely to intervene where informal workers' compliance affects officials' career advancement. Officials engage with informal workers, informal workplaces, and their organizations where workers' actions affect officials' careers. Otherwise, officials ignore informal workers where possible. Second, where the number and activities of informal workers exceed officials' enforcement capacity, officials are much more likely to encourage informal workers to organize. If possible, officials prefer to work with law enforcement to police informality, and doing so discourages organization. Third, informal workers are much more likely to start organizations where at least some informal workers have the know-how and resources to organize their colleagues. In places where informal workers know how to organize, they can capitalize on officials' attention and incentives. Where these conditions exist, incentives from officials promote organization, compliance, and civil society participation that would not otherwise exist. Leaders in informal markets use these incentives to make it worth their colleagues' time to join and participate in informal workers' organizations. Once informal workers organize, officials can bargain over legalization, regulation, and enforcement with a representative group. The group, in turn, enforces laws more thoroughly than officials could on their own.

In this book, street vendors and local officials in two municipalities in the greater La Paz metropolitan area of Bolivia and two districts in the greater São Paulo metropolitan area of Brazil illustrate how officials can incentivize compliance in informal markets and why this strategy encourages informal workers' organizations. The book presents twin puzzles – why do some informal workers organize and why do officials encourage potential lawbreakers to organize – and resolves both with a theory of strategic state intervention in collective action. The book marshals original interview, survey, administrative, and ethnographic data from bureaucratic offices and street markets to develop the theory. I ground the theory's assumptions in ethnographic data that I collected while working as a street vendor in La Paz and São Paulo. I then formalize the argument in a game theoretic model. I use machine learning techniques to estimate which survey respondents work informally and build a data set of over 39,000 informal workers across Latin America. I test the implications of the theory on the machine-generated data and on cross-national data from the Latin American Public Opinion Project, the Comparative Study of Electoral Systems project, and the Varieties of Democracy project. Regressions find significant associations between lower state capacity, higher personal resources, and organizing at work among informal workers. Case studies of unorganized and organized street vendors and the officials they interact with in the metropolitan areas of La Paz, Bolivia, and São Paulo, Brazil illustrate the model's equilibria. The case studies are supported by 162 interviews with street vendors and officials, ethnographic data from street markets and organizations, two original surveys, and an administrative data set of 31,906 street vending licenses. I conclude by suggesting that governments can increase compliance by delegating some enforcement to civil society groups.

This book is important because for decades, researchers have found that informal workers rarely organize or participate in civil society and political life, and that this lack of organization stunts political and economic development (Castells and Portes, 1989, Perry, 2007, Rueda, 2007). Scholars and policymakers often view informal workers as a hindrance to political and economic development. For example, Castells and Portes (1989) conclude that, "The more the informal economy develops, the more economy and society become relatively autonomous spheres of social action" (p.32), and argue that informal work is "disenfranchisement of the institutionalized power conquered by labor" (p.11). Scholars explain informal workers' purported low political participation with their uncertain legal status, high job turnover, low income and education, and high costs to organizing (King and Rueda, 2008, Naylor, 2004, Kurtz, 2004, p.265). The conventional wisdom holds that informal workers break laws, avoid taxes, produce less, and participate less in civil society than formal workers (King and Rueda, 2008, Schneider et al., 2010). This book challenges the conventional wisdom by demonstrating that informal workers organize and participate in civil society, and that officials incentivize their participation. The main contribution of this book is to formally demonstrate broad conditions under which informal workers organize and participate in political and associational life.

An emerging literature in political science asks how states engage with informal markets and how informality affects individuals' political participation (Baker and Velasco Guachalla, 2018, Bodea and LeBas, 2016, Feierherd, 2021, Grossman, 2020, Holland, 2017, Hummel, 2017, Auerbach et al., 2018, Thachil, 2020). This research builds on an established literature in sociology and explicitly considers officials' decisions about informal workers' lives and livelihoods. Auerbach and Thachil (2018) find that people living and working in informal settings value connections to the state and the ability to make claims on the government, and that they choose community brokers accordingly. Informal workers find themselves in positions similar to business owners in Schneider (2004)'s work: officials have immense power over the viability of an informal business or informal neighborhood and thus people cultivate ties to officials to protect their homes and jobs (Fernández-Kelly and Shefner, 2006, Goldstein, 2016, Hummel, 2018a). Holland's work finds that politicians strategically refrain from enforcing laws against informal work and housing when they need poor workers' votes and enforce where they do not (2016, 2017, 2018). Agarwala (2013) finds that informal workers organize into voting blocs and make claims on the state where pro-poor parties depend on their votes. I suggest that in many places, politicians and other officials take a much more active role in informal markets in pursuit of more than votes.

The book also contributes to the politics of enforcement (Holland, 2017, Amengual, 2013, Grossman, 2021, Post et al., 2017, Resnick, 2019, Weaver and Lerman, 2010). Enforcement affects informal workers more than other workers because informal workers commit minor infractions on a daily basis as part of their work. Informal workers who work in public, like street vendors, recyclers, and some sex workers, are more vulnerable to law enforcement and the criminal justice system than formal workers who regularly break laws. This is because informal workers' infractions are more visible to law enforcement than, say, infractions by formal bankers, and because many informal workers have low incomes, little savings, and low levels of education, which complicates successfully challenging tickets, harassment, or arrest. Similarly, informal workers who labor in private workplaces like homes and farms are vulnerable to exploitation by their often more formal employers for the same reasons and have little recourse to contest abuse (Blofield, 2012, Cornejo Villavicencio, 2020). When officials encourage people to organize and then delegate enforcement to them, officials increase participation within vulnerable communities. Where informal workers then interact with other workers instead of police, this strategy could decrease the number of people in criminal justice systems for minor infractions. Where governments can directly increase enforcement, like in Brazil and the U.S., street vendors and other informal workers like Renato are more likely to interact with law enforcement and the criminal justice system (Reiman and Leighton, 2015). Where governments delegate, like in Bolivia and India, informal workers like Rosa are more likely to create and participate in civil society organizations. These divergent paths matter for the workers caught up in them and their households (White, 2019). These trends also matter for society writ large because higher rates of civil society participation, particularly among poor citizens, improve democratic citizenship and well-being for everyone (Hunter and Sugiyama, 2014, Putnam et al., 1994, Touchton et al., 2017).

Political scientists working with informal workers and their communities focus on vote choice, clientelism, and voting bloc mobilization to explain state–society interactions because, as Holland (2017, p.4) states, "the poor have little to offer other than their votes." However, for officials with governance goals, career ambitions, and small budgets, informal workers control another important resource: their compliance (Grossman, 2020). When officials with little money or administrative support need to clean up streets, improve traffic, vaccinate a neighborhood, or decrease pollution, they can turn to informal workers and their organizations to increase compliance (Farthing and Kohl, 2010, Goodfellow, 2015, Post et al., 2017, Rich, 2019). The project pushes back against work that argues that informal workers organize in the absence of state actors or in reaction to police repression (Bodea and LeBas, 2016, Tassi et al., 2013, Thachil, 2020). The project contributes to work on the politics of enforcement and the growing literature on informal politics and governance (Auyero, 2001, Baker and Velasco Guachalla, 2018, Grossman, 2020, Holland, 2016, Hummel, 2017, Post et al., 2017, Weaver and Lerman, 2010), by arguing that informal workers are key to local governments' success outside of campaigns and elections.

This book demonstrates that officials' actions shape gray markets and determine who works informally and who works formally. Officials' decisions and actions also impact the conditions that informal workers labor in, how lucrative their work can be, and if they operate openly or if they work in fear and on the run. Officials can legalize or formalize work that they had previously outlawed, and the political bargaining processes outlined in this book lead to formalization. This process brings marginalized workers and communities into regulatory structures while giving workers reasons to participate in and support government projects. Legalization and formalization contribute to state building projects and strengthen civil society. Bruhn and McKenzie (2014), Soto (2000), and others find that most formalization policies have minimal effects and many governments know that large informal sectors are a persistent reality. Encouraging informal workers to organize and then delegating enforcement to those organizations is a strategy that works. Policymakers who are willing to work with informal businesses on development and civil society projects can formalize citizens through delegation strategies.

1.1 Informal Markets, Informal Workers, and Their Organizations

Across the Americas, 183 million people work in dozens of informal occupations (ILO, 2018). Research on the informal economy shows that informal workers exist in every country and that informal jobs make up most employment opportunities in many places (Vanek et al., 2014, WIEGO, 2016). Schneider, Buehn, and Montenegro (2010) estimate that 19% of the world's GDP comes from informal activity, ranging from national highs of 68% of GDP in Bolivia and Georgia to lows of 8% in the United States and Switzerland (pp.20–24). Informal workers typically work long hours to make approximately minimum wage, their jobs are often stressful and dangerous, and many also maintain a household (Bhowmik, 2012, pp.6–8, 20–21). As the data analysis in Chapter 3 demonstrates, informal workers organize in every country in the Americas, from a low of around 10% in Argentina, Chile, and Uruguay to a high of 30 to 40% in Haiti and Bolivia.[2]

Many different jobs meet the definition of informal work, which I define as any transaction of money, goods, or services in which the participants ignore relevant tax, reporting, or licensing requirements. Millions of people in retail, transportation, services, manufacturing, and agriculture work outside of tax, licensing, and social security structures. For example, producers and retailers have created open-air markets in every country in the region. Markets can be sprawling weekend markets where shoppers can find reasonably priced consumer goods sold at temporary stalls or the neat organic farmers' markets and artisans' exhibitions that serve niche consumer markets or specific holidays. Markets are typically colorful and loud, with sellers offering a variety of goods at prices lower than what a client would find in a formal storefront. Consumers can find bargains and haggle with vendors over prices, which are primarily paid in cash. Some market vendors have licenses, giving them some formalized relationship with the government, but even many licensed vendors do not pay taxes or enroll in social security. Many vendors employ people to help sell at a stall, haul goods to and from storage, or produce wares, and these employees are typically informal. Within these markets and in streets throughout a city or town, smaller sellers, who I term street vendors, sell similar goods that they carry in backpacks or on carts. Many market and street vendors purchase food, coffee, change, tape, and other things that they need throughout the work day from street vendors who specialize in servicing other vendors. Street vendors sell everything to the general public, from doll houses to dish towels, while juice and hotdog vendors work from carts around transportation hubs in nearly every country in the Americas, and photographers, locksmiths, and shoeshiners offer their services on busy streets the world over. Many of

[2] I suspect that rates of organization among informal workers are even lower in the United States, but the survey data from the U.S. does not ask the same organizational questions that are asked in the rest of the region.

these markets are highly organized and administered by a market or street association that most market vendors belong to. Organized vendors participate in these organizations to coordinate security and cleaning, and to resolve disputes.

From the United States to Paraguay, millions of people earn a living from public streets by offering informal transportation services or collecting recycling (Goodfellow, 2015). From gypsy cabs in Chicago to mototaxis in Rio, people use their own vehicles to offer quick rides for cash, often to people in the same neighborhood. In many places, motley fleets of old school buses and vans run public transportation lines throughout cities. These fleets often coordinate through transportation unions or driver organizations, where they set times, prices, and routes, and negotiate with the local government and other transportation unions. The driver may have some nominal claim to formality like a registered route or vehicle number, or may not, and drivers are rarely part of the government's business tax or social security structure. Drivers may employ people to collect fares, call out destinations to passerby, or maintain the vehicle. These employees receive their wages in cash and almost never register in the social security structure of their country.

Recyclers and salvagers work public streets as well, collecting aluminum, copper, and glass or salvagable appliances and furniture from the refuse of houses and businesses or directly combing public dumps for valuable material (Rosaldo, 2016, Gowan, 2010). Recyclers and salvagers often interact with officials and public employees. Recyclers partially work within the waste collection systems that city governments set up by selling materials at recycling centers or working in dumps (Medina, 2008). In some places, recyclers and salvagers organize and work with city officials on waste policy and implementation (Fergutz et al., 2011, Rosaldo, 2016, WIEGO, 2016). However, recyclers rarely participate in social security or tax structures.

In private homes around the Americas, people provide domestic services like childcare, cleaning, gardening, dog walking, and cooking (Blofield, 2012). People who work in domestic jobs typically have direct wage relationships with their wealthier employers, many of whom actively avoid paying into social security and tax structures for their employees. Some domestic workers work for many people, coming in to clean once a week or walk dogs once a day. Others work exclusively for one employer, live on their employer's property, and are essentially on call for any reason at all times (Hondagneu-Sotelo, 2001). Domestic workers' unions exist all over the world to provide resources, recourse for exploitation, and to lobby governments to improve labor protections (Blofield, 2012). Some of the most prolific and successful organizations operate in Bolivia, Brazil, and more recently and surprisingly, the United States (Harrington, 2015, WIEGO, 2016).

Formal and informal businesses from Argentina to Canada rely on groups of informal workers to quickly and cheaply produce goods. Farms in every country rely on informal laborers who are paid small amounts of cash to harvest and process everything from coca to strawberries. Seasonal, informal laborers follow different crops within and even across countries, often relying on a supply chain of informal housing, transportation, and medical care to make their work possible (Valenzuela Jr. et al., 2005). While their employers may register with national governments and pay business taxes on parts of their operations, they typically do not pay taxes or social security for all of the laborers who they hire. Similarly, small factories employ teams of workers to crank out large orders of T-shirts, baskets, candy, and many other products. While large factories often register and enroll their workers in tax and social security structures, smaller factories and workshops rarely do. At one end of this chain of production are people called piece workers who assemble goods such as shoes, cigarettes, or small electronics from parts and materials that a larger workshop provides. Piece workers collect raw materials from a supplier, assemble goods at home or other workplaces, and then return the assembled pieces by an agreed upon deadline and are paid per completed item (Agarwala, 2013). This work is largely informal. Few of these workers join unions or other work-based associations, but in some parts of India, Mexico, and Bolivia, piece workers, agricultural laborers, and contract factory workers organize to resist exploitation and set wages (Agarwala, 2013, Frundt, 2002).

People of all genders sell sexual goods and services in private homes and on streets all over the world. Sex for money supports millions of people and is a particularly important source of income for young people who formal employers do not want to hire (Moira, 2016). Sex workers protest and participate in political processes; in particular, many organize into unions and advocacy organizations that lobby local and national governments for laws that allow them to work with standard labor protections (Smith and Mac, 2018). In Bolivia, many sex workers belong to associations similar to other informal workers' associations, in Brazil, national sex workers' organizations have existed for decades, and in Nicaragua, the government delegates dispute resolution in some communities to members of a sex workers' union (Cabezas, 2019). Outside of a few highly regimented and exclusionary programs and New Zealand, which decriminalized sex work across the country, most sex workers labor outside of government-sanctioned markets (Smith and Mac, 2018).

Informal jobs typically pay less than many formal jobs and offer fewer benefits (ILO, 2018). Working-class people occupy most informal jobs, though some wealthier people opt for work off the books, and some people who work for themselves outside of social security and tax structures can make a lot of money. People of all genders work informally, though a higher share of working women and nonbinary people work outside of state structures than working men (WIEGO, 2016). Similarly, people of all ethnic identities work infomally, but ethnic and racial minorities are more likely to labor in informal jobs. People of all ages work informally, though many very young or old workers are overrepresented in informal labor. Anyone can be an informal worker and most working people have labored informally in housework, childcare, agriculture, or in an under-the-table job for a small business at some point in their careers. However, people from marginalized groups are more likely to work informally than those with more privilege in a society.

People enter informal jobs because they want flexibility, need immediate cash, or because they cannot find formal work (ILO, 2018). A person's circumstances influence this choice, as does the country that they live in and that country's economic conditions and labor market (Moira, 2016). During economic crises, more people enter informal work because they need cash immediately or because they cannot find formal work (Gerxhani, 2004). In lower income countries like Haiti and Bolivia, few formal jobs exist and many people cannot find formal work. In all countries, people may choose informal jobs because they prefer flexibility or because they are unqualified for the formal jobs that exist in their area. For example, working parents may choose informal work like piece work or street vending because they can work while watching their children, and people without high school diplomas struggle to find formal work in many countries.

Informal work can appear chaotic or unorganized. Informal work may appear to be outside of state control because it is outside of state structures by definition. This is rarely the reality of informal work. Informal workers minutely order, organize, and coordinate their work. Informal workers in markets, dumps, houses, workshops, and fields coordinate with each other and informal worker organizations. Registered unions of informal workers exist in nearly every city and sector, as activists, scholars, and surveys around the world document (Bhowmik, 2012, Blofield, 2012, WIEGO, 2016). For example, in one market that I worked in, unionized street vendors had apportioned space down to one tenth of a centimeter throughout the market. Furthermore, informal workers interact with governments and officials to varying degrees, even though they are outside of important state structures. Informal work varies in how organized an activity is, the proportion of workers that organize, or how much workers interact with officials. In this book, I examine this variation and demonstrate that interactions with officials influence how informal workers organize.

For example, workers within private houses and businesses interact with the occassional inspector at their job, and they interact with politicians, bureaucrats, or police as voters, residents, commuters, and protesters. Informal workers on public streets may interact with inspectors, police, city council members, and a variety of bureaucrats at their worksites. Where a public market, dump, or transportation line is partially coordinated with a city, informal workers may interact with city workers who do maintenance, surveying, or licensing. Informal workers also interact with officials as citizens. These interactions shape people's work lives and their political engagement.

1.2 The Argument

Why do informal workers organize? I find that interactions with officials influence why, how, and to what extent informal workers coordinate with each other. On one end of the spectrum, unlicensed street vendors, scavengers, or agricultural workers may coordinate loosely with the people who they work near to alert others when the police sweep through or to evade inspectors and other officials. On the other end, as I argue, officials can ask, direct, or even pay informal workers to organize representative groups to enforce regulations amongst themselves, negotiate with officials, or run markets, bus routes, and recycling systems. Where informal work is a persistent reality, many officials decide to organize and work with people in informal jobs.

I suggest that where many people work informally and officials do not have the money or personnel to police their activities, officials resort to unorthodox strategies. Officials are bureaucrats, law enforcement, or politicians with decision-making power over what people can legally do. Officials try to get informal workers to comply with regulations by encouraging people to form organizations. Officials can then delegate enforcement to groups that negotiate and work with them. To encourage organization, officials may offer informal workers access, meetings, policy input, licenses, identity cards, or even cash for cooperating with them.

I find that some local officials encourage informal workers to organize while other officials discourage organization. I also find that informal workers organize in many countries and organize more in places where government officials have few resources. I establish these findings with survey data from tens of thousands of informal workers in dozens of countries around the world. The book then follows people engaging or disengaging in local political processes within four intensive case studies in two countries. Activists start organizations in most cities and countries, but officials' intervention makes the difference between small, beleaguered organizations and massive, politically influential unions. I argue that officials encourage informal workers to organize where they need informal workers' compliance to complete projects and advance their careers but where the local government does not have the resources to police informal activity. I argue that officials are more likely to encourage informal workers to organize and then work with those organizations under the following conditions: First, where informal workers' compliance affects officials' career advancement. Second, where the number and activities of informal workers exceed officials' enforcement capacity. Third, where at least some informal workers have the know-how and resources to organize their colleagues. Where these conditions exist, incentives from officials promote organization, compliance, and civil society participation that would not otherwise exist. Leaders in informal markets use these incentives to make it worth their colleagues' time to join and participate in informal workers' organizations.

These incentives have far-reaching effects. Leaders in informal markets can use incentives to recruit people into organizations. The resulting organizations can make informal workers more manageable and legible for officials. For example, leaders in La Paz, Bolivia, and El Alto develop working relationships with officials and organize their members into groups, write up disputes and complaints in standarized letters and memoranda, and instruct members and new workers on how to interact with officials. Officials can offer or withdraw additional incentives in exchange for compliance, and people develop side hustles to capture rents from the incentives (Hummel, 2018a). Where officials offer incentives and leaders form large informal workers' organizations with them, the incentives directly increase civil society organization and participation among informal workers.

Conversely, where officials have the money and personnel to go out and police informal work, officials who face active informal sectors choose to increase inspectors and law enforcement. Increased enforcement discourages informal workers from organizing and participating in civil society by taking resources away from them through confiscation, fines, arrests, and assaults. These direct actions also reduce informal workers' resources and political participation through intimidation and increased stress and fear. Increased enforcement further discourages informal workers from organizing by signaling that officials are hostile and will not negotiate with them or their organizations.

Within every city and within each case in this book, some people participate in civil society and some do not. The book compares people *within* cases to establish the role of resources in individual participation decisions. On the other hand, officials' ability to enforce varies between the four local governments in the case studies in this book. I compare local governments *across* cases to establish the role of enforcement capacity. Extrapolating from the experience of street vendors and officials, I argue that governments can incentivize informal workers to participate in self-regulating organizations. Officials pursue this strategy where they need to increase compliance to do their jobs but where the number and activities of informal workers exceeds the government's capacity for direct enforcement. These incentives facilitate widespread collective action where informal workers know how to organize. Within these organizations, informal workers with some preexisting resources are more likely to participate than their most destitute colleagues.

The book makes a general argument about why and when officials intervene in collective action, and the conditions under which intervention helps people organize. The project uses street vendors, their organizations, and the city governments that they interact with as cases of state intervention in collective action. The argument should apply to all officials facing unorganized citizens. The theory should explain why informal workers organize or not in places with a civil society presence and a minimum level of administrative ability. The theory should explain officials' behavior when officials work within a government that has the capacity to collect taxes, implement budgets, and staff licensing offices. The theory does not apply to governments that could be considered failed states. Second, the theory explains why informal workers create and participate in civil society organizations, but it does not explain how civil society writ large develops. Given that some civil society groups exist and some people know how to organize a group, the theory explains why people start to participate and form new groups. Finally, the theory makes a general argument about when officials delegate enforcement and the conditions under which delegated enforcement promotes more participation in civil society.

1.2.1 Concepts

This book uses established concepts in social science, namely collective action, civil society, informal work, and state capacity. Collective action is the collaborative pursuit of common goals. Civil society is the broad category of people, groups, and organizations who articulate interests outside of government institutions. State capacity is the ability of a nation state and its agents to achieve its policy goals. Building on decades of collective action research, Ostrom (2007) and Olson (1965) offer theoretical frameworks for analyzing and explaining why people, including street vendors and other informal workers, start and join organizations. Their frameworks form the foundation of the book's theory of state intervention in collective action.

People with shared interests often fail to work together due to a set of common challenges known as collective action problems (Axelrod, 1984, Marwell and Oliver, 1993, Hardin, 1982). Olson (1965) demonstrated that individuals have incentives to free ride on others' efforts where possible. As a result, individuals often do not cooperate or work with others, even when they know that cooperation would improve collective outcomes. The logic behind Olson's result is that if people will benefit from a group effort regardless of their contribution, people do not contribute and will instead hope that someone else does the work for them. Overcoming this problem is particularly difficult for large, diffuse groups and, in most times and places, informal workers are a large, diffuse group.

After Olson, scholars tried to establish why people cooperate in some situations but not others (Axelrod, 1984, Hardin, 1982, Oliver, 1980, Schelling, 1978, Snidal, 1985). This work established that self-interested individuals with no central authority can still cooperate in many situations: for example, Hardin (1982) demonstrated that people with different preferences can coordinate mutually beneficial cooperation (pp.67–69). Axelrod (1984) and his collaborators demonstrated formally that individuals interacting indefinitely can establish stable expectations that facilitate cooperation (pp.11, 20–21). These findings have found widespread support in observational and experimental studies, most notably in a collaborative project between economists and anthropologists Joseph Henrich, Robert Boyd, Samuel Bowles, Colin Camerer, Ernst Fehr, and Herbert Gintis, who conducted ethnographic fieldwork and economic games in 15 remote communities around the world and found an even greater diversity of cooperative strategies than hypothesized (Henrich, 2004).

However, by looking at anarchic situations where cooperation is least likely, many scholars of collective action overlooked a key set of players in citizens' real-world decisions: governments and the officials who work within them. One exception is Marwell and Oliver (1993), who argue that government coercion is one of the main sources of collective action and that coercion is one kind of selective incentive, in that governments can force or threaten people into working together. Still, many governments induce collective action with noncoercive incentives.

Elinor Ostrom launched one of the most productive and applied research agendas on collective action by looking at when individuals, communities, and governments cooperate to preserve common pool resources (Ostrom, 1990).[3] Ostrom's work examined and compared collective action in the absence and then presence of a central state authority. Ostrom, like Henrich (2004), found a wide variety of cooperative strategies, as well as many examples of failed attempts (Ostrom, 2009, pp.14, 139, 180, 190).[4] Her later work developed broad frameworks for analyzing, understanding, and facilitating different types of collective action (Ostrom, 2007, 2009). Ostrom acknowledged the role of external authority and intervention in collective action, and criticized how policy interventions are designed, but did not elaborate a theory of state intervention (Ostrom, 1990, pp.22–24, 29, 40–41, 190).

I expand on Ostom's and Olson's canonical frameworks for analyzing diverse forms of collective action. I add an explicit governance-based logic that explains state intervention in citizens' collective action decisions. I develop the theory informally and formally and operationalize the concepts that I use with qualitative and quantitative data. My theory builds on Ostrom's work and adds the explicit logic that explains when officials have incentives to intervene in and facilitate collective action, and clear conditions under which officials free ride, intervene, or abstain.

Many people do solve the collective action problems they face and form neighborhood associations, church groups, book clubs, soccer leagues, activist circles, and many other groups that make up civil society. Civil society refers to the collection of organized groups that represent citizens' interests, from political interest groups to nonprofit sports organizations to neighborhood watch groups and storefront churches.

Resources and political context shape who participates in civil society (Cook, 2012, McAdam, 1982, Ostrom, 2007, Putnam, 2001). On an individual level, resources largely explain who organizes and participates and who does not: people with more education, income, free time, and social connections form and participate in civil organizations, while people with less tend to

[3] Ostrom won a Nobel Prize in Economics for this work, becoming the first, and of this writing, the only, political scientist to win a Nobel.

[4] Elinor Ostrom tackled questions about informality and informal workers' organizations in side projects, most notably Guha-Khasnobis et al. (2007), where she and collaborators discussed what makes for successful formalization policies.

work extra shifts and watch the kids (Hochstetler, 2012, Murillo, 2001, Brady et al., 1995).

On a national level, political context largely explains why some countries have more vibrant civil societies than others: governments that create a political context with opportunities for participation – for example, through voting, participatory budgeting, free public association, or broad consultation laws – see higher levels of participation (Flavin and Hartney, 2015, Mayka, 2019, Ostrom, 1990, Touchton et al., 2017). Conversely, as governments encourage less of this behavior or discourage participation with restrictive laws and outright repression, citizens participate less overall and factor this environment into their political decisions (Davenport, 2007, Ritter and Conrad, 2016, Levitsky and Way, 2010). This study formalizes political context to show the conditions under which officials incentivize collective action among informal workers. I demonstrate that political context is interactive (Goodwin, 2001, pp.24–25): informal workers help create the conditions under which they make collective action decisions.

Researchers disagree on why informal workers organize and participate in civil society. Many scholars simply assume that they do not organize (Naylor, 2004, Perry, 2007). These expectations follow the predictions of the larger collective action and civil society literatures, which find that people with fewer resources are less likely to participate in social movements, political parties, and unions than people with more (Ostrom, 2007, MacCarthy and Zald, 1973, Tarrow, 2011). However, existing studies document informal worker organizations all over the world (Agarwala, 2013, Fernández-Kelly and Shefner, 2006, Grossman, 2021).

Informal work and informal markets have existed for as long as governments have made a distinction between sanctioned and unsanctioned economic exchange. However, scholars have only named and studied the distinction between formal and informal markets for a few decades. Anthropologist Keith Hart coined the term "informal economy" in a 1973 paper (Hart, 1973, p.68), which contributed to the emergence of an interdisciplinary network of scholars studying unregistered economic exchanges. The first prominent studies on informal markets focused on the emergence or maintenance of these markets and their implications for international political economy.

Initial studies documented unorganized and politically atomized workers. For example, in one of the first sociological studies of informal markets, Castells and Portes (1989) and their collaborators argued that informal workers, because they were unorganized, threatened the gains made by formal unions in the last century (pp.11, 30, 32). In one of the most prominent economic studies, de Soto (1989) documented the complex incentive structures that informal workers face. He argued that changing those incentive structures could bring millions of poor workers into broad economic projects, but made no mention of informal workers' unions or organizations. Many later studies building on this work either assume that informal workers are categorically unorganized (Kurtz, 2004, p.265) and politically atomized (Perry, 2007, p.1), or empirically establish that many are unorganized (King and Rueda, 2008).

Activists and union organizers around the world know that informal workers organize and have been documenting these organizations for years (Bhowmik, 2012, WIEGO, 2016). Bhowmik (2012) and his collaborators as well as Fernández-Kelly and Shefner (2006) and their collaborators document startlingly wide variation in the level and types of organizations that street vendors participate in around the world. Bhowmik and his collaborators catalog street vendor organizations, their scale, and the problems that they face in dozens of countries, with representation from every region. Fernández-Kelly and Shefner (2006) and their collaborators explore informal workers and their organized engagement in local and national politics across Latin America. For women who work informally, the online WIEGO database keeps a user-updated record of informal workers' organizations all over the globe. The database suggests that, in most countries, at least some informal workers in sectors from street vending to manufacturing to sex work organize.[5]

Scholars outside of political science have tackled why and how informal workers around the world organize, and what explains the variation in their organizations. A number of studies responding to the first wave of research on informal markets document wide variation in the social and political participation of informal workers and offer explanations for this variance. Cross (1998) studied street vendor unions in Mexico City and their successful mobilization against the city government during Institutional Revolutionary Party (PRI) administrations. Cross argues that disagreement between state bureaucrats and politicians enabled street vendors' success at forming and maintaining politically active organizations (Cross, 1998, p.229). Additionally, Cross argued that the authoritarian structure of the Mexican state gave these organizations autonomy that they could exploit, but speculated that a transition to a multiparty state would not take that autonomy away (Cross, 1998,

[5] The database is very useful for establishing wide variation across countries and economic sectors. However, it is user-driven and an incomplete record of informal workers' organizations and therefore I do not use it in the quantitative analyses.

pp.6, 7, 230).[6] Similar to Cross, I argue that informal workers interact strategically with bureaucrats and politicians, and that in many times and places, officials have incentives to intervene in informal markets instead of ignoring them.

Agarwala's work on informal workers' organizations in India establishes useful foundations for this book's case studies (Agarwala, 2013). Along with Bhowmik (2012), Agarwala's work provides examples outside of Latin America that corroborate the dynamics that I document in Bolivia and Brazil. Agarwala (2013) argues that informal workers use their power as voters to demand policy change and that these demands succeed in political systems dominated by mass politics and where governments pursue economic liberalization. In many ways, this study corroborates Agarwala's research: workers' relationships to the government are key to their individual profits and organization. Furthermore, in Bolivia, informal workers have been successful at translating demands into policy in an age of mass politics (Anria, 2018). However, I find that informal workers have launched successful organizations even in places where the government actively rolls back economic liberalization, as is the case in Bolivia. Additionally, Agarwala acknowledges that many informal workers choose not to organize or join existing organizations (Agarwala, 2013, p.13), but does not seek to explain variation at an individual level.

In Bolivia, researchers have studied the country's massive informal workers' organizations. Working with street vendors in El Alto, anthropologist Lazar (2007a) examines how neighbors organize themselves into politically powerful groups like street vendor unions to make citizenship claims. My work corroborates Lazar's research on the internal dynamics of street vendor organizations and I use her research in my case study on El Alto. In La Paz, sociologist René Pereira Morató has published extensively on his work with street vendors, their organizations, and the city government (Pereira Morató et al., 2009, Pereira Morató, 2015). Pereira Morató's work charts the growth of street vending in the city and I use it to contextualize the argument in the case studies.

Anthropologists Tassi et al. (2013) work with street vendors across Bolivia and argue that the absence of the state gives businesspeople the space to build their own institutions that take on state-like roles in many places, including La Paz, El Alto, and Santa Cruz. However, the largest street vendor organizations are in the country's largest cities, which also house state bureaucracies. One of the main roles of the organizations in my and others' research (Agarwala,

[6] Cross (1998) and Elyachar (2005) are some of the only studies of informal workers' organizations under authoritarian regimes.

2013, Bhowmik, 2012, Lazar, 2007a) is to build and maintain relationships with local and national governments, which calls Tassi et al.'s state absence thesis into question. Working in Cochabamba, anthropologist Daniel Goldstein offers a more nuanced thesis of "organized disorder" and "disregulation" of intermittent and selective state engagement with informal markets and their organizations (Goldstein 2016, p.7). His research corroborates the dynamics that I observed in La Paz and El Alto. Goldstein asks a different research question than this project: why and how do the poorest informal workers survive? He argues that poor workers survive through the government's hands-off reproduction of informality. This book corroborates Goldstein's argument that local governments reproduce informality while suggesting that in parts of La Paz and El Alto, the reproduction may be more hands-on than hands-off.

Turning to the literature on state capacity, a government's ability to enforce laws is a central component of state capacity (Amengual, 2013, Besley and Persson, 2010, Soifer, 2012). Governments with more capacity may produce the same laws as governments with less (Amengual, 2013, p.527). Higher capacity governments interact more with civil society when officials implement laws because more capacity means more implementation. Therefore, defining state capacity as a government's ability to implement policy implies that governments with more capacity are more active in citizens' lives.

Research finds that more state capacity leads to better outcomes, like higher economic growth, more and higher quality services, and less violence (Besley and Persson, 2010, pp.1–2). Policymakers and researchers, however, disagree on how to build state capacity. Besley and Persson (2010) argue that governments build state capacity by investing in public infrastructure while Grindle (1997) and many others find that investments alone increase costs without necessarily increasing capacity. Amengual (2013) pushes for governments to make public investments while building partnerships with civil society (pp.528–529). To the contrary, Huntington (1968) cautions that an active civil society in weak institutional contexts leads to chaos, not capacity (p.4).

I examine the enforcement capacity of governments and the choices that officials make about how to use their limited resources. Holland (2016) asks why states selectively enforce laws and argues that politicians strategically choose which laws to enforce based on voting incentives. Holland (2017) establishes that these forbearance strategies amount to massive transfers or subsidies from the state to poor voters. In higher enforcement contexts like the United States, recent sociological research corroborates her argument by demonstrating that when governments aggressively enforce laws that primarily affect poor or informal workers, enforcement decimates household finances and violently disrupts daily life (Desmond, 2012, Goffman, 2015, White, 2019). Holland (2015) uses multiple types of evidence from Bogotá, Santiago, and Lima to establish that, similar to Agarwala's argument, pro-poor parties are more likely to forbear and elitist parties are more likely to enforce. I build on Holland's work by taking her dependent variable, enforcement, as one of my key independent variables. I also diverge from Holland on the concept of state capacity: Holland (2016) argues at length that state capacity and enforcement costs are separate explanations for enforcement outcomes; I suggest that state capacity shapes enforcement options. Finally, Holland's theory of forbearance and my theory of state intervention lead to different predictions for informal workers and markets: Holland predicts that high enforcement costs lead to forbearance which leads to continued informality, particularly under pro-poor parties, while I predict that high enforcement costs lead to delegated enforcement which leads to increased organization and the partial formalization of informal markets.

It is not clear how a government's capacity affects citizens' participation in civil society or politics. The conventional wisdom is that people living under higher capacity governments participate more because higher state capacity correlates with the political contexts and the individual resources that foster participation in civil society and politics (Putnam et al., 1994, Tarrow, 2011). However, another line of research finds that the weak reach of the state can encourage communities to organize themselves and build their own governance structures, public goods, and services (Bodea and LeBas, 2016, Grossman, 2021, Davies and Falleti, 2017, Tassi et al., 2013, Yashar, 2005). I subsume this research on self-help groups under grassroots activism and address it as an alternative explanation to state intervention in collective action.

1.2.2 Alternative Explanations

Existing research offers alternatives to the book's argument for why officials and informal workers interact and create organizations. One alternative explanation for why street vendors organize is that grassroots activists in the informal sector organize their colleagues without any intervention from officials and then demand state resources, leading to the large organizations and negotiations that I document in this book. I call this the grassroots activism explanation. Another explanation is that officials step in to encourage and work with these organizations because the organizations make it easier for officials to buy informal workers' votes or extract bribes from informal workers, which I will refer to as the clientelism explanation.

Grassroots activism and clientelism are present in the cases presented later in the book. Grassroots activism is an important force for informal workers. Many leaders embrace the narrative that they are rising up and fighting back against an absent, corrupt, or repressive government. Likewise, some officials are corrupt, incompetent, or repressive, and clientelist practices shape some officials' interactions with informal workers. Many street vendor leaders are accomplished activists and many officials deploy clientelist strategies. However, grassroots activism and clientelism alone do not drive or explain informal workers' organizations. Throughout the book, I will demonstrate what activism and clientelism do account for and evaluate whether the evidence supports these alternative explanations or not.

Grassroots activism could explain why any informal worker organizations exist and why people in places like Bolivia organize more than people in places like the United States. Bolivia has experienced massive cycles of mobilization from the 1952 revolution to the gas and water wars of the early 2000s and the broad social movements that propelled the *Movimiento al Socialismo* (MAS) to power (Anria, 2018, Davies and Falleti, 2017, Madrid, 2012). One alternative explanation is that prior forms of mass collective action create or enable abnormally large informal workers' organizations in places like Bolivia. However, South Korea, South Africa, and India all have national informal workers' organizations and very different histories of mass participation (Bhowmik, 2012, pp. 40, 232). Finally, while some individual vendors participated in the gas and water wars or campaigned for MAS, most did not, and very few mention past collective action as a factor in starting street vendor organizations. Instead, street vendors discuss the local government and potential costs and benefits of organizing.

Grassroots activists can and do start organizations to confront officials or fill in public goods and services where the state falls short (Grossman, 2021). Studies document extensive self-help groups among poor and informal workers, particularly in places where state capacity is low or absent (Bodea and LeBas, 2016, Nordstrom, 2004). Tassi et al. (2013) argue that informal workers in Bolivia organize to provide public goods and market structures in the absence of the state. The state may be absent in some areas, but street vendors and poor workers in this study report that they contend with officials every day. Street vendors report that they form and join organizations to negotiate with officials, as the ethnographic data in later chapters demonstrates. Existing research corroborates these reports, finding that many informal workers' careers depend on their relationships with officials (Cross, 1998, Fernández-Kelly and Shefner, 2006, Goldstein, 2016). Furthermore, if the civil society groups in this study were self-help or voluntaristic organizations, we would expect them to form in order to address specific problems where the government has less presence, like in the self-built neighborhoods of the La Paz and São Paulo metropolitan areas. Instead, the largest and most active organizations in the cases are in the downtown areas where the city government is most present. In peripheral neighborhoods, street vendors report forming or joining organizations to engage with the municipal government, and only after officials approach unorganized vendors.

Clientelism could explain why officials encourage informal worker organizations: organizations could facilitate vote buying (Auyero, 2001, Stokes, 2005). Researchers consistently find that bureaucrats and politicians extract votes from informal workers (Holland, 2015, Itikawa, 2006, Lazar, 2007a). These studies document clientelistic relationships between street vendors, organizations, and administrations, and develop a partisan logic to explain these relationships (Cross, 1998, Itikawa, 2010, Holland and Palmer-Rubin, 2015). Clientelism certainly exists in the cases' street vendor organizations: I observed appointed bureaucrats and elected officials making clientelistic appeals to organized and unorganized vendors. In particular, in La Paz, officials ask street vendor leaders to bring members to large campaign events to demonstrate the city government's popular support, corroborating what Muñoz (2018) observed in Peru. Additionally, interviewees elaborated on street vendors' roles in the partisan game between candidates, especially in local politics. I suggest that some governments directly intervene in collective action in order to increase compliance and regulate informal sectors. The strategy can exist alongside clientelistic practices and within a partisan logic, as it does in India and Bolivia (Agarwala, 2013, Lazar, 2007a). However, while partisanship and clientelism exist in street markets in La Paz, they do not appear to be a deciding factor in forming and maintaining organizations.

In private, street vendors scoffed at the parties that had made clientelist appeals and professed their vote choice for another party. Likewise, street vendors occassionally[7] received vests and scarves for participating in these demonstrations but not the larger incentives like licenses that help create organizations – and that street vendors ask for. Additionally, if clientelism were driving organizing dynamics, we should observe organizations starting around election season and official incentives following electoral cycles. Instead, organizations start outside of election season, and officials and street vendors

[7] Officials promise small incentives like shirts and food for attending a campaign event much more often than they deliver them.

sustain incentives and relationships across electoral cycles. Election season is a particularly maddening time to get anything done in Bolivian cities because officials focus on campaigns. Many officials do not show up to their regular jobs or do not complete routine processes and paperwork. Organizations centralize clientelistic appeals, but the unions do not and cannot monitor members' vote choices, suggesting that organizational incentives make for an ineffective vote-buying strategy (Muñoz, 2014, pp.79–80). Modes of clientelism may change with organization but do not appear to drive state intervention in collective action.

Officials intervene in the informal sector to encourage collective action, and they also engage in clientelistic and partisan strategies. Local and national governments across the Americas employ a bundle of strategies in their dealings with civil society. The process that I discuss in this project coexists with other strategies that include clientelism or follow an explicitly partisan logic. However, corrupt or clientelist incentives do not appear to be driving officials to encourage street vendors or other citizens to organize and regulate themselves.

1.3 Research Methods for Informal Markets

Informal work is difficult to study. Informal work happens outside of the state structures that collect data on workers and economic activity. Additionally, informal workers may not report semi-legal activity to survey enumerators and other field researchers because workers know that they are breaking laws and many fear punishment (Jensen et al., 2010, Olken and Pande, 2012). Researchers who study informality with interview and survey methods capture some self-reported informality. However, respondents rarely trust enumerators and likely under-report the extent of their informal activities (Olken, 2009, Jensen and Rahman, 2015). Researchers can overcome this barrier with careful qualitative work that builds trusting relationships between the researcher and informal workers. This choice has other trade-offs. Thorough qualitative work can draw a comprehensive picture of study participants' lives and work, but may or may not describe other informal workers' experiences. In this book, I address the trade-offs of different research methods for informal work by establishing broad trends with survey data and validating the trends with intensive ethnographic data.

I use data from the Latin American Public Opinion Project (LAPOP) and the Comparative Study of Electoral Systems (CSES) project to establish broad trends in informal work and organizing in Latin America and then around the world. I use these data because LAPOP enumerators ask thousands of people in 21 countries across the Americas comparable questions about themselves and their political participation every two years, creating the highest quality survey data set of the region. The regional data set contains 127,864 respondents, including 30,515 self-employed respondents from 2006 to 2012 and 15,783 informal respondents from 2006 and 2008. The CSES Module 4 and 5 data set contains 73,388 respondents across 42 countries from 2011 to 2018, including 7,081 respondents who reported that they were self-employed and worked in often informal jobs like street vending, domestic work, recycling, subsistence agriculture, and construction. The samples from each country are nationally representative and both projects ensure that enumerators solicit responses from rural areas as well as small towns and in multiple languages.

I run the existing LAPOP data on informal workers through a machine-learning algorithm to estimate who is an informal worker in later survey waves. In 2006 and 2008, LAPOP asked social security and employment questions that Baker and Velasco Guachalla (2018) used to identify informal workers. These workers come from all countries, ages, ethnicities, and genders, and work many types of jobs, including domestic work, agriculture, construction, and street vending. I use a random forests classifier, which is an algorithm from the machine learning family, to estimate a data set of informal workers. By estimating a larger data set of informal workers from existing but limited survey data, the random forests classifier addresses one challenge of data paucity in research on informal workers. I then use descriptive statistics to demonstrate that informal workers organize in every country in the Americas, but to varying degrees. Regression models demonstrate that state capacity and informal workers' resources help explain which informal workers organize.

In addition to the nationally representative surveys from LAPOP and CSES, I use original surveys of street vendors in La Paz and São Paulo in the case studies. The surveys provide broad, descriptive information about street vendors in each city. The surveys verify that the people I worked with and interviewed were typical of street vendors in La Paz and São Paulo. The survey data help me place research participants' experiences in the broader context of the street vending sectors in each city.

In the case study of the city of La Paz, I use administrative data on 31,904 street vending licenses from the municipality. The data set contains all active street vending licenses in the city as of 2019 as well as highly detailed information about the merchandise, stall, location, and work hours that the license permits. The data set also contains information about the street vendor association that the license is associated with and the 437 street vendor associations that have registered with the city. These quantitative analyses of off-the-shelf and original survey data suggest trends that I investigate further with qualitative data and analyses.

One of the main concerns with interviews or surveys of informal workers is that people hide or distort information. Ethnographic methods triangulate people's words with theirs and others' actions, and investigate discrepancies and changes over time (Jerolmack and Khan, 2014). Many ethnographic projects, including aspects of this one, revolve around the significance of documented discrepancies between words and actions (Lazar, 2007a, Lopez, 2007). Additionally, ethnography requires the researcher to build trusting relationships, which are particularly important for research on informal activities and other topics where research participants have good reasons to hide information (Auyero, 2001, Goffman, 2015). Through trust, triangulation, and time, ethnography overcomes several of the limitations that researchers of informal work encounter with survey and interview methods, namely misreporting, under-reporting, and finding participants. Additionally, ethnographic work can help inform other research strategies. For example, I identified key local officials through ethnographic work and interviewed them after the ethnographic phase of the project. I also developed my interview guide through ethnographic fieldwork. I developed the survey sampling frame and questions through ethnographic fieldwork and pre-tested the La Paz survey with a street vendor federation that I had developed a relationship with through ethnographic research. These features and advantages make ethnography particularly well-suited for studying micro-level informal activity (Contreras, 2012, Nordstrom, 2004).

I conducted fieldwork with one of La Paz's street vendor federations, several associations, the Markets Office, and the Municipal Guard in 2012, 2014–2015, 2018, and 2019. I observed meetings, engaged in conversations, interviewed street vendors and officials, patrolled with the Municipal Guard, and worked as a street vendor. I worked as a street vendor once a week in a prominent open-air market from March to May 2015 and helped out at the stalls of individual street vendors in other markets throughout the field research period. In addition to research in La Paz from 2014 to 2015 and in 2018 and 2019, I conducted interviews with officials and street vendors in El Alto, and engaged in participant observation in El Alto's markets, Markets Office, and during several parades and protests.

I began ethnographic fieldwork in La Paz by approaching the leadership of one federation and asking to observe meetings and work, as well as interview-consenting vendors. The leadership agreed on the grounds that I would give something back to the federation, and the *ampliado* – the meeting of the governing council of the federation, consisting of the elected leadership of the 142 affiliated street vendor associations – voted to let me observe.[8] I helped out around the office and in the markets where possible, primarily by running errands, watching stalls, and babysitting, and occasionally by translating or teaching English or computer skills. Most people in La Paz's markets are bilingual or trilingual, and I also learned conversational Aymara to improve my rapport with these vendors. I made contacts by meeting people at the federation and city offices, and when research participants introduced me to colleagues in the markets.

After I made acquaintances with a street vendor, I would ask if I could spend time with them at their market stall while they worked and if they agreed, I asked if I could help while I was there. Street vendors asked me to help with babysitting, making change, running errands, filling an order, cleaning, or watching the stall and attending to customers while they ran an errand. Street vendors periodically approached me with job offers.[9] After a few offers, I decided to work with one street vendor who I knew well and for several months I set up, worked, and packed up her stall the one morning a week that she did not work. In the evening, we went over which items I had sold and any issues that came up, and I gave her any money that I had made.[10] I also regularly assisted at the stalls of street vendors with whom I spent a lot of time, particularly the champagne ladies.

In Vila Velha, São Paulo, I conducted a mini-ethnography: I worked as an unlicensed street vendor for one to two days a week for four weeks in 2015. In 2015, I contacted a street vendor whom I had met in 2014 and who had offered to teach me how to sell as an unlicensed vendor, and he enthusiastically agreed to do so. I would meet him in the morning in Vila Velha and we would spend roughly U.S.$15 on half a dozen phone chargers and selfie sticks from his wholesaler contact on the street. We would buy a cardboard box and cheap cloth to make a mobile stall, and then sell on the sidewalk. The street vendor was part of a group of people who normally worked close to one another on the same block, and we would sell near them. I would sell until my partner decided

[8] This vote was taken after a debate between two leaders during the *ampliado* about whether or not I was an *espia yanqui* (Yankee spy), or an *hija del pueblo* (daughter of the people). The *ampliado* came to the consensus that I was a representative of the people of the United States, not American capitalist interests, and could continue working with them.

[9] For example, an older woman who was not part of the study approached me after observing me in the markets for several weeks with, "You know, I could really use a girl like you, you're blonde and you speak English and Aymara. Let me know if you want to work here in the mornings."

[10] I averaged about $10 in profit in a morning. I was not a very good street vendor.

to go home, typically after four to six hours of work. I had a notebook with me where I would mark down initial investment, costs, sales, and (frequent) police patrols, as well as notes. Military police frequently patrolled this market and when they started walking down the street, we would pack up in seconds and quickly walk or run away. While selling in a public space without a license is against São Paulo's municipal ordinances, it is less than a misdemeanor: people cannot be arrested, charged, or even directly fined for it. Police impound wares and street vendors can pay a fine to get them back. I gave all profits, typically U.S.$10–20, to my colleague. In the São Paulo cases, I rely heavily on interviews and use ethnographic field notes sparingly to contextualize unlicensed street vendors' working conditions.

Finally, I supplemented ethnographic fieldwork with 162 interviews in two municipalities in the La Paz department of Bolivia and two districts in the São Paulo metropolitan area in Brazil. I interviewed people representing a range of experiences and perspectives: organized and unorganized street vendors, street vendor leaders, rank and file street vendors, older people, younger people, city managers, lawyers, low-level officials and police. While I tried to interview a cross-section of the people that I observed working in and influencing the markets, I did not systematically sample interviewees. The interviews enabled me to discuss key themes in-depth. In order to do that, I targeted people who knew me and were therefore more likely to be forthcoming about potentially sensitive topics like conflicts within organizations, breaking municipal ordinances, and corruption. I pulled interview questions from the survey instruments, though I often inserted questions specific to the person I was interviewing. I gave people a list of interview questions beforehand if they requested one.

In the city of La Paz and in Vila Velha, São Paulo, I asked the street vendors with whom I had done ethnographic work if I could interview them in-depth towards the end of our fieldwork. In all four cases, I approached officials for interviews as well. In La Paz, Markets Office officials and Municipal Guard officials knew me and agreed to interviews after working with me. In El Alto and both São Paulo districts, I interviewed officials who had not previously worked with me. In central São Paulo, a collaborator and I supplemented the aforementioned survey of licensed street vendors with 30 interviews of unlicensed street vendors. During July 2015, I conducted additional interviews with street vendors in São Paulo. In June 2018, I conducted follow-up interviews with street vendors and interviewed São Paulo city officials in Vila Velha and Princesa Isabela. Interviews in the four cases ranged from ten minutes with very tight-lipped officials to three hours with street vendors who I knew well. A typical interview lasted 30–60 minutes. Interested readers can find additional information on interviews and sample questions in the appendix.

All quotes and anecdotes come from the ethnographic and interview data and have been anonymized, due to the semi-legal nature of participants' work. The person and location names I use are pseudonyms and some details like merchandise, position or rank, and location have been changed to ensure confidentiality. The exceptions to anonymization are elected officials who agreed to be interviewed on record and one national street vendor leader whom I did not interview and who frequently appears in the national press.[11]

1.4 Organization of the Book

This book demonstrates that informal workers and officials interact to co-produce organizations and compliance, similar to work by Amengual (2013), Nelson-Nuñez and Cartwright (2018), and Holland (2017). This study is not the first to suggest that officials can incentivize civil society to enforce laws or that states and societies co-produce governance (Post et al., 2017, Rich, 2019). Amengual and Fine (2017) use the cases of Córdoba and San Francisco to illustrate the benefits of collaborative enforcement work between local governments, unions, and NGOs. Rich (2013) documented federal officials granting money to activists to start new HIV/AIDS organizations in rural Brazil that could monitor local officials and help implement national HIV/AIDS programs. More surprisingly, Skarbek (2016) finds that some prisons delegate routine enforcement to prison gangs, which largely self-regulate.[12] Likewise, this study recognizes delegation as one strategy available to officials who are pursuing multiple goals and using multiple strategies simultaneously. This book contributes to existing research by demonstrating why and how this strategy works and suggesting conditions under which officials are more likely to strategically intervene in collective action. The book examines the application of this strategy in the informal sector and illuminates the unintended effects of delegation.

[11] The protocols follow guidelines from the University of Texas's and the University of Miami's Institutional Review Boards as well as guidelines from the National Science Foundation. Anonymized field notes and interview transcripts are available on request.

[12] Skarbek discusses the notorious San Pedro prison in La Paz, which has no guards inside and is run by prisoners' associations. Coincidentally, particularly combative street vendor leaders are routinely imprisoned there. While I was writing this manuscript, the former leader of the Confederation of Street Vendors of Bolivia was serving a sentence in San Pedro for ordering street vendor leaders to set fire to a government building in El Alto, which killed six city employees.

Chapter 1 has introduced and situated the puzzle of organized street vendors in the literatures on collective action, civil society, informal work, and state capacity. According to most scholars, informal workers do not organize, which makes the anecdote that this chapter opened with, about Rosa's champagne ladies' union and its affiliation with a national street vendor confederation, quite puzzling. The chapter has outlined an explanation for why informal workers organize and addressed prominent alternative explanations. Specifically, I find that officials encourage informal workers to organize self-regulating groups. I argue that this is most likely to happen where informal work strains the enforcement capacity of local officials, where officials have career and governance goals, and where some informal workers have the know-how to organize self-regulating groups.

Chapter 2 develops a theory of state intervention in collective action. I argue that as unorganized people increase enforcement costs, officials increasingly have an incentive to offer private benefits to people who organize self-regulating organizations. When officials intervene in this way, they reduce the barriers that kept people from organizing on their own. Officials can then bargain over regulation and enforcement with representatives instead of a mass of individuals. The theory builds on contributions from Olson (1965), Ostrom (1990), and Holland (2017). I then formalize the theory in a game theoretic model to show that officials and informal workers are strategically linked. I use the model to demonstrate the exact conditions under which we can expect organization as a result of intervention.

Chapter 3 introduces survey data from across the world and establishes broad trends in informal work and political participation. Descriptive statistics show that informal workers organize in nearly every country sampled and extensively organize in many. I estimate a data set of informal workers using survey data from the Latin American Public Opinion Project (LAPOP) and a machine learning algorithm. Regressions on the estimated data set, a data set of known informal workers, and a data set of self-employed workers suggest that informal workers are more likely to organize in low capacity countries. I then turn to survey data from the 42 countries around the world in the Comparative Study of Electoral Systems (CSES) database and find similar patterns between informal work, state capacity, and political participation. The quantitative analyses point to cases to examine in more depth. I selected two cities in the La Paz department of Bolivia, La Paz and El Alto, to see how informal workers interact with officials with lower enforcement capacity, and I selected two districts in São Paulo, Brazil, to understand how informal workers interact with officials with higher enforcement capacity.

Chapter 4 tells the history and structure of street vending in two municipalities in the La Paz department of Bolivia and two districts in São Paulo, Brazil. Chapter 4 grounds the game theoretic model's assumptions in observations from street markets in La Paz: I show that unorganized street vendors create negative externalities, that street vendors approach collective action decisions with a cost–benefit analysis, that officials offer private benefits to organized street vendors, especially leaders, and that once organized, street vendors self-regulate and bargain with officials.

Chapter 5 develops an ethnography of street vendors, their organizations, and the city officials who they interact with in the city of La Paz, Bolivia. The chapter is based on 14 months of ethnographic fieldwork in the city over four research trips in 2012, 2014 to 2015, 2018, and 2019. My fieldwork included interviews, participant observation at dozens of meetings between bureaucrats and organized vendors, ride-alongs with the municipal guard, a street vendor survey, working as a street vendor in a clothing market, and selling wedding services with a street vendor cooperative. I illustrate the theory's observable implications with ethnographic evidence from La Paz. I discuss how street vending has changed in the city and how officials have intervened in collective action decisions as the informal sector grew. I demonstrate that officials increased benefits to organized vendors as the costs of regulating markets increased. Additionally, the leaders that take advantage of these offers tend to have more resources than their colleagues, and as the offers increased, so did the level of organization among the city's street vendors. The chapter also discusses the many trade-offs that officials make in implementing different policies, and how officials manage the often combative organizations that they encourage.

Chapter 6 develops the theory in a comparative context, by adding case studies of organized and unorganized street vendors and the city governments that they interact with in El Alto, Bolivia, and two districts in São Paulo, Brazil. The chapter is based on original interview, survey, participant observation, and ethnographic data that I collected during a total of three months in each city over four research trips in 2012, 2014 to 2015, 2018, and 2019. As part of the project, I briefly sold selfie sticks as a street vendor in a central district of São Paulo in 2015. Comparing the city of La Paz to the neighboring city of El Alto holds many national-level features constant but varies city government enforcement capacity. Comparing two districts in São Paulo to each other and then La Paz and El Alto adds more variation on enforcement capacity. São Paulo – the large, modern metropolis of the region's richest country, with many employment opportunities, services, stable laws, and a history of labor organizing – should have more organized street vendors than La Paz, according to resource- or political context-based theories of collective action. Instead, only 2 percent of São Paulo's 100,000 vendors are organized, compared to 75 percent of La Paz's 60,000. I explain this difference with the interaction between individual resources, official incentives, and local government enforcement capacity.

Chapter 7 discusses the broader implications of the argument for the world's two billion informal workers. I advance the theoretical claim that when individuals break the law, they can paradoxically get help from officials to organize. I elaborate implications for effective formalization policies, using the mixed success example of a tax reform in Bolivia. The chapter concludes the book with implications for state intervention in civil society, as well as contentious politics, enforcement, and state building.

2

State Intervention in Collective Action

Natalia started working when she was eight years old, selling toys and candy to other children outside of a school in La Paz, Bolivia after her mother died. Decades later, she supports two daughters by working at the same stall in front of the school from 7 am to 7 pm every day. She does not take breaks because she fears being robbed. Natalia helped found a street vendors' association before she had children, and she has a license and relationships with officials from her role in that now-defunct association. She and the other vendors on her block are not formally affiliated with a street vendor union or association because forming or joining one would take too much time away from their work and families.

Natalia's story is common: street vendors around the world work long hours to make minimum wage, their jobs are hard, and many also have families to feed. Most do not have extra time or money to organize meetings or pay dues. If they have discretionary time or income, they choose to spend it on much-needed leisure or household needs. Street vendors and other informal workers can enumerate the potential benefits of organizing with their colleagues: co-ordinating cleaning, fair dispute resolution, or hiring a block security guard. Still, they would rather leave it to someone else to spend the time and money necessary to put a group together. Street vendors and other informal workers typically will not organize unless they can get an additional benefit for participating. Many informal workers face this common but intractable collective action problem.

A few blocks away from Natalia's toy stall, Elena also started working as a child, tending her mother's food stall while her mother ran errands or attended to union business. Elena's mother and her colleagues started a food vendors' union in the 1950s. They founded the union because La Paz city officials would meet with registered union members but not unorganized food vendors. Decades later, Elena serves as the elected leader of the same food vendors' union and represents three dozen women. As a union leader, she helps members maintain their annual vending licenses by shepherding paperwork through the city's Markets Office, staying current on policy and personnel

Why Informal Workers Organize Calla Hummel, Oxford University Press.
© Calla Hummel (2021). DOI: 10.1093/oso/9780192847812.003.002

changes in the Markets Office, and representing members to officials during conflicts. For Elena and the women she represents, street vending licenses make their businesses stable and profitable. They have formed and maintained an organization over decades to work with officials and keep their licenses.

In this chapter, I argue that officials take an active role in encouraging informal workers to organize when the activities of informal workers exceed local enforcement capacity. Once organized, officials encourage informal workers to regulate themselves. I present a theory in which the government's enforcement capacity, officials' career advancement, and informal workers' resources affect civil society organization and participation. I formalize the core of the theory in a game theoretic model. The chapter concludes with observable implications for the quantitative and qualitative data in the following chapters.

2.1 Collective Action

This project focuses on organizations. Collective action can lead to dozens of outcomes, and different studies take cooperation (Olson, 1965), protest (Kitschelt, 1986), cooperatives (Ostrom, 2015), public goods (Olken, 2010), or other phenomena as the outcome of interest. Organizing is one type of participation or collective action. This study examines organizations because they can be measured through qualitative and quantitative work, are durable, and can be tracked over time.

Street vendors stated in interviews that their professional organizations were their most important vehicle for collective action. Street vendors in Bolivia and Brazil made it clear that much of their political participation revolved around making demands to their local government through their organizations. While organizations like unions are forms of civil society participation, for many workers they facilitate collective and individual political participation like voting and protesting (Baker and Velasco Guachalla, 2018). By looking at organizations, I largely avoid the methodological pitfalls of other possible collective action outcomes, like systematic under-counting of small events or units, which bedevil research on protests (Earl et al., 2004, pp.67–68), or unclear conceptual boundaries, which is an enduring problem for social movement research (Della Porta and Diani, 2009, pp.5–8).

I define an organization as a registered group with bylaws. In the qualitative chapters, I focus on street vendor organizations, which I define as registered groups whose primary membership base consists of street vendors. In the quantitative data, I look at people who attended a professional association meeting. Professional associations are typically registered groups with bylaws that primarily represent people of the same profession. In both cases, the dependent variable is a clearly defined unit that I and other researchers can track and verify over time through interviews, official documents, and survey data. Table 2.1 sets out the definitions in this book.

Table 2.1 Concepts and definitions

Term	Definition
Informal work:	Any transaction of money, goods, or services in which the participants ignore relevant tax, reporting, *or* licensing requirements.
Informal worker:	A worker who does not pay taxes on taxable earnings, does not hold a license for her work when one is required, *or* is not part of a mandatory social security system. Falling into any one of these categories makes a worker informal for the purposes of this study.
Street vendor:	A person who sells any good outside and on public land at least once a week. Note that street vendors are not inherently informal but most are in practice (Bhowmik, 2012, Roever, 2005, de Soto, 1989).
Street vendor organization:	A registered group whose members are mostly street vendors from the same urban area and that states it represents street vendors in its bylaws.
Selective incentive:	A private benefit that people receive for participating in a collective endeavor (Hardin, 1982, Ostrom, 2007).
Negative externality:	A cost that an actor's actions create for an external actor.
Collective action problem:	Any issue that prevents people from working together when doing so is in their mutual interest (Olson, 1965).
Public good:	Anything that everyone can benefit from without reducing its value once it is provided; a good that is non-excludable and non-rivalrous (Ostrom, 1990, 2007).

Throughout the book, I alternate between discussing organizing specifically and participation writ large. I do this because organizations are particularly strong, enduring, and traceable forms of participation, and once formed, they must be sustained by other forms of participation. Additionally, informal workers participate in civil society and politics by attending protests, meeting with officials, improving their neighborhoods, serving on school boards, and engaging in many other forms of collective action that this project does not systematically track but that are important to discuss and acknowledge along with registered organizations.

2.2 Argument

Where people cannot find formal work that suits their needs, they will work informally. Acknowledging this reality, a common sentiment among street vendors and officials in Bolivia is, "We will always have informal work because we all have the right to bring bread home every day."[1] When policies or economic conditions make formal work harder to find, more people engage in informal work to make ends meet (Hart, 1973, Gerxhani, 2004, Bajada and Schneider, 2018). Extensive research by economists finds that countries with high poverty rates, stagnant economic growth, high taxes, and complicated labor regulations have large informal sectors (Gerxhani, 2004, Bajada and Schneider, 2018). Researchers also find that at the individual level, a preference for flexibility, personal legal complications, and scant qualifications push people towards informal work (Gerxhani, 2004, Rueda, 2007, de Soto, 1989). As a result, informal workers exist in every country, ranging from a small fraction of the economically active population in rich countries with clear regulations like the United States and Switzerland to the vast majority of workers in poor countries with notorious bureaucracies like Bolivia, Uganda, and India (ILO, 2018, Bajada and Schneider, 2018, Schneider et al., 2010).

A minority of these informal workers organize in most places, even without state intervention. Bhowmik (2012) and the WIEGO database of informal workers' organizations demonstrate that some informal workers organize in nearly every city around the world and many rural areas as well. However, in most places, a highly-motivated and relatively privileged minority of the informal sector participates in these organizations. These workers are grassroots activists. The members of these small organizations are other activists and career informal workers whose membership helps them professionalize and advance in their work.

For example, informal workers' organizations exist all over the United States but represent a minority of the country's informal workers: the National Domestic Workers' Alliance organizes thousands of domestic workers across the country and hundreds of street vendors organize in New York, Miami, Chicago, and Los Angeles, yet these groups represent a small fraction of the hundreds of thousands of domestic workers and street vendors in the United States. Their members are committed activists, career street vendors, and

[1] "Vamos a tener trabajo informal para siempre porque tenemos el derecho de llevar el pan de cada dia."

domestic workers who maintain their licenses and professional skills through these organizations. The National Domestic Workers' Alliance and the Street Vendor Project are dynamic, successful organizations, but without government incentives, they struggle to reach the majority of the informal workers in their sectors.

A majority of informal workers organize in only a few places. For example, in Bolivia, most informal workers appear to belong to an informal workers' organization. Most street vendors in Bolivia belong to an informal workers' union, as do most tailors, shoeshiners, sex workers, and many others. These organizations include committed activists, career street vendors, and people just starting out or supplementing their retirement income. Why do only a few informal workers organize in the U.S. while most informal workers in Bolivia join large unions?

I argue that governments' enforcement capacity, officials' career advancement, and informal workers' resources interact to encourage informal workers' organizations in some places and discourage organizing in others. As stated in Chapter 1, "official" refers to any politician, law enforcement officer, or bureaucrat with the ability to make decisions over informal workers' lives (Cohen and Gershgoren, 2016). I posit that officials are motivated by career advancement and that professional incentives shape how they engage with informal workers. Schneider (1993) finds this to be the case with bureaucrats and the businesses they regulate in Brazil, Mexico, Japan, the United States, and France; I expect this to hold with informal workers and businesses as well.

Officials typically want citizens to follow laws, pay taxes, and work formally. Most officials would prefer workers to be formal and many view informal workers as a headache that they would rather not deal with (Cuvi, 2016). Additionally, most officials prefer to work with other government employees – inspectors, regulators, and law enforcement – to enforce laws, rather than private citizens or potentially combative civil society leaders. Officials manage local informal sectors by increasing direct enforcement where and when they can. This strategy is common in places like the United States, France, and Brazil where local law enforcement plays a cat and mouse game with persistent informal workers. In these places, the threat of police action discourages many people from joining the informal sector and officials' hostile stance discourages existing informal sector workers from organizing.

However, officials cannot adequately enforce regulations where the informal sector exceeds the resources and capacity that local officials have for worksite inspections and law enforcement. Officials face governance dilemmas where informal activity exceeds enforcement capacity. Several factors contribute to this condition: the number and activities of informal workers, as well as theresources and capacity available to officials. When thousands of citizens engage in informal work, they strain the existing enforcement capacity of local police and inspectors. The activities that they engage in affect officials' enforcement abilities as well: thousands of citizens joining the informal sector by working in informal domestic work in private houses break labor and tax laws, posing challenges for labor and tax inspectors who cannot adequately inspect private homes and audit thousands of individual tax returns. Conversely, thousands of citizens joining in informal street vending break labor, tax, public space, traffic, and potentially importation and public health laws, creating new challenges for labor and tax inspectors, as well as public health offices, transit officials, and beat cops. What these workers choose to sell has additional implications for officials: under most legal systems, people selling books, soap, or flowers on the street break fewer laws and pose less of a challenge for local officials than people selling prepared food or counterfeit luxury items. If these same informal workers opt to sell more highly regulated and often more profitable commodities such as sex or drugs, they implicate more of the bureaucracy and further strain enforcement capacity. Thus, informal workers' activities, as well as sheer numbers, directly impact the enforcement strategies that officials choose.[2]

Officials have several choices where they cannot adequately enforce: they can ignore informal workers, they can engage in enforcement with the limited resources that they have, or they can work with people in the informal sector. Officials can also combine these options. All of these options have significant trade-offs. Ignoring or engaging in limited enforcement can create governance problems: formal businesses, homeowners, and other citizens complain about informal competitors, markets that block streets, or burgeoning redlight districts. Those constituents may organize or agitate against officials or their offices if officials ignore their complaints. Businesses and homeowners may push for underperforming officials to be fired or back a candidate proposing sweeping reforms in the next elections. Furthermore, many labor and safety regulations exist for good reason. Informal workshops, factories, mining, and logging activities can lead to environmental degredation (Andersson et al., 2006, Andersson, 2004, Orozco and Veiga, 2018). Ignoring

[2] People choose informal occupations based on what will be immediately profitable for them as individuals. I have yet to see or hear of informal workers intentionally and collectively choosing higher cost work to induce a cooperative response from officials, though this is a logical implication of the theory.

large numbers of people who are cutting corners and breaking safety regulations at informal construction sites or unregistered factories, for example, can lead to collapsed or burning buildings, while unregulated agriculture and food preparation can contribute to food-borne illnesses that cause much larger governance problems for officials.

Informal businesses are not the only offenders in these areas; largely formal businesses also cut corners, pollute the environment, and hurt or kill their workers, as successive oil spills, mining disasters, and factory fires show. Still, formal businesses often have more resources to upgrade to less harmful practices when pressured or to pay damages. Formal businesses may be easier for officials to audit or inspect because they routinely provide more information to governments than largely informal operations. To summarize, ignoring growing externalities from largely formal or informal businesses and workers is an option for overwhelmed and underresourced officials, but this tactic can complicate officials' attempts to govern.

Officials who care about their government careers face a series of decisions when working with people who work informally. Officials are typically busy people working with few resources and high expectations (Prendergast, 2007). To advance in their careers, most officials and especially bureaucrats need to complete the tasks assigned to them with the resources assigned to them, please their bosses, and avoid upsetting powerful people (Schneider, 1993). In other words, they need to do the day-to-day business of governing.

The first option for most officials is to ignore informal workers. Most officials already have more work than they can reasonably complete and do not want or need new problems, complaints, demands, or clients. Ignoring informal workers lets them avoid new problems, at least for some time. However, where informal workers and their problems block officials from completing projects, or where they upset powerful people, officials can no longer ignore informal workers and expect to advance in their careers.

Where possible, officials who cannot ignore informal workers will work with or hire more inspectors or police officers to increase enforcement. This tactic stays within the bounds of the state that officials are accustomed to, addresses the issue, and demonstrates to superiors and the public that the official and their colleagues are doing something. The enforcement approach is more appealing to officials where it creates a project or tasks through which they can demonstrate progress on governance goals to their superiors.

The wealthier São Paulo district governments under Mayors Gilberto Kassab and João Doria exemplified this approach: Gilberto Kassab introduced an agreement with the state military police through which district governments could directly hire off-duty military police to help with enforcement in the district. Many district governments hired officers to patrol and break up informal markets. District governments could also hire inspectors to investigate informal markets, construction, homes, and other potentially informal work sites. When informal workers blocked local projects or when powerful constituents complained, district governments hired as many police and inspectors as their resources allowed for. These actions broke up open-air markets in several neighborhoods of São Paulo, forced many street vendors and other informal workers out of their jobs, and discouraged some from joining organizations (Cuvi, 2016). The New York Police Department periodically employs a similar tactic, especially in New York's gentrifying neighborhoods.

I posit that increased enforcement, all else equal, discourages informal workers from organizing, takes resources away from informal workers, and deters people from entering the informal sector if they have other options. Several studies have argued or documented another outcome: informal workers or informal neighborhoods coming together to resist in the face of increased enforcement (Dosh, 2010, Grossman, 2021, Rosaldo, 2016, Thachil, 2020). The story of people rising up in the face of oppression is compelling. However, the cases and other studies demonstrate that when governments choose to increase enforcement against informal workers, they usually succeed in taking resources away from workers, arresting, beating, or even killing workers, and deterring organization (Goldstein, 2016, Hummel, 2018b, Pinheiro-Machado, 2011). I suspect that scholars are particularly interested in the few instances in which this does not happen, and as a result we may see more research on those instances relative to others, leading to selection bias in the literature.

In many cities around the world, hiring more officers or inspectors is not an option. In others, the number and activities of informal workers overwhelms the personnel that local government can hire. The activities of informal workers may continue to stall projects or upset powerful people, creating governance dilemmas and blocking local officials' career advancement.

Left with no easy options or quick fixes, officials may choose to work with people in the informal sector. In La Paz and parts of São Paulo, officials recalled trying to enforce regulations, police a district, or start a new infrastructure project in an area with many informal workers and few resources. Many described the futility of this approach: informal workers would disappear in one area only to return a few hours later or start work in another area. Officials, frustrated with the projects that they were supposed to be completing, then recalled approaching informal workers and proposing a new project, meeting with workers, or negotiating for collaboration and compliance. Officials in this position seek out existing or potential leaders in the informal sector. Officials encourage motivated, experienced, charismatic, or educated informal workers to organize their colleagues, and encourage existing groups to self-regulate, grow, and reorganize.

For example, one low-level official in La Paz recalled trying to build a new *teleférico* station[3] in a neighborhood with many street vendors. To start the project, the official's office needed to move street vendors who were working at the site, and then needed them to not protest, block, or sabotage the site. The official approached the street vendors, addressed them as a group, developed a relationship with them, and continued to talk and negotiate with them for over a year in order to keep construction on schedule. The official's office offered licenses around the area and input into the project in order to keep the street vendors from disrupting construction. The street vendors' compliance was a necessary component of delivering a large infrastructure project to the city. The official's career advancement, as well as his boss's and his boss's boss's, were riding on an on-time delivery of functioning infrastructure. In São Paulo, officials accomplished similar projects around the 2014 World Cup by paying for a massive influx of military police (Hummel, 2018b). In La Paz, this official and his office worked with street vendors to extract compliance.

Elected officials face slightly different incentives than appointed bureaucrats. To advance in their careers, elected officials need to win elections, as well as complete the governance projects that they proposed or promised, complete tasks assigned to them with the resources available, please their superiors, avoid or negotiate upsetting powerful people, and build a constituency. Revitalizing neighborhoods, cleaning up the streets, reducing crime, and building infrastructure are all common campaign promises and municipal projects across the ideological spectrum (Itikawa, 2010, Roever and Skinner, 2016). Informal workers like street vendors and recyclers often become targets or scapegoats in these projects (Cuvi, 2016, Resnick, 2019); they also have the potential to block or complicate these projects. Elected officials with more resources often hire more enforcement personnel and crackdown on informal workers during these projects, as happened in the revitalization projects of Mexico City or the World Cup preparations in South Africa and Brazil (Hummel, 2018b, Roever and Skinner, 2016).

[3] The mass transit system in La Paz includes a system of gondolas, called the *teleférico*, that carry passengers above the city in the same way that other cities' metros carry passengers underground.

Elected officials can strategically deploy a variety of tactics with informal workers. Instead of simply ignoring informal workers – which many do and many informal workers complain about – elected officials can develop forbearance strategies. Alisha Holland has extensively theorized forbearance and documented the strategy across Latin America (Holland, 2015, 2016, 2017). Elected officials who choose forbearance choose not to enforce against at least some informal workers in their constituencies. Selective non-enforcement can be an explicit or tacit agreement between informal sector representatives and elected officials, as is the case in Bogotá, Colombia, or it can be the unofficial and unilateral policy of a local official or office.

However, where elected officials need to complete governance projects in areas with many informal workers or particularly disruptive activities, forbearance may not be enough. Informal workers and their activities may block projects. Or informal workers may frustrate other powerful constituents. In these cases, officials may turn to active encouragement, intervention, and coordination with informal workers' organizations. These organizations may work with officials on projects and they may become new constituents, or allies in governance or electoral campaigns. Politicians care about re-election and electoral logic can enter into their engagement with informal workers (Agarwala, 2013, Holland, 2017). However, I suggest that governance, particularly compliance and the day-to-day logistics of managing long-term plans and projects, contribute as much or more than votes to relationships between informal workers and their governments.[4]

I suggest that governance shapes relationships between informal workers and officials more than votes because in most places the groups of informal workers that officials work with do not control enough votes to change election outcomes. Even in places where informal workers make up a majority of voters, informal workers have diverse political preferences, their organizations are not unified, and neither organizations nor politicians can monitor individual workers' vote choices (Baker and Velasco Guachalla, 2018, Muñoz, 2018). Conversely, they can make or break projects that change officials' career outcomes. Both officials and organizations can monitor who shows up to a protest or who complies with existing projects and laws. For example, the votes of the few hundred street vendors working around the *teleférico* site in La Paz has little effect on local electoral outcomes, but their compliance with or protest of the project affects officials' chances of promotion. Scaling up, the votes of

[4] These are not mutually exclusive activities. Officials may need to complete projects and demonstrate effective governance throughout their administrations in order to win their next election.

the more than 30,000 street vendors with licenses from the La Paz city government are still too few to change local election results, but protests from a few thousand of those street vendors paralyzed the work of the city government for months in 2016.

In places like Bolivia where informal workers make up the majority of voters, one would expect that the votes of informal workers could have huge impacts on election outcomes. In Bolivia, politicians expect this too and thus politicians from across the ideological spectrum court informal workers, make alliances with their organizations, and develop sector-specific policy. Local and national politicians elaborated that they must work with and incorprate informal workers in policies and campaigns. As a result, all Bolivian parties attract votes from informal workers, splitting this potential voting bloc. While a few thousand informal workers switching allegiances are unlikely to change local or national electoral outcomes with their votes, they can affect the viability of governance projects that change the outcomes of officials' careers by facilitating or blocking the project.

In countries like Bolivia, the bureaucracy and civil society are fertile training and recruiting grounds for political candidates (Anria, 2018, Schneider, 1993). Bureaucrats can use policy innovations, completed governance projects, and their relationships with informal workers to move into electoral politics. Alliances with informal workers' groups do not deliver huge numbers of votes, but they can signal to party recruiters that a bureaucrat or leader could mobilize civil society networks to campaign or govern.

Officials encourage informal workers to create and join self-regulating organizations because officials have professional incentives to regain some level of compliance from informal markets. Officials around the world build their careers on successfully completing projects like improving traffic, cleaning up streets, or improving waste collection and public health (Goodfellow, 2015, Grossman et al., 2018, Rosaldo, 2016). Governance projects like these require increasing the minute, everyday compliance of citizens with quality of life regulations. In places with many informal workers, these governance projects require increasing informal workers' compliance with a host of local regulations. Where officials cannot change behavior through increased enforcement, they can encourage organized groups and self-regulation. This strategy has the added benefit of making officials appear responsive to and engaged with constituents.

Where officials can advance their careers by organizing informal workers and collaborating with their representatives, I suggest that they will do exactly that. Similarly, where officials can advance their careers by working with law enforcement to crack down on informal work, I expect that they will choose that strategy.

Importantly, officials who are motivated by career advancement pursue policies for noble and ignoble reasons. For example, one former official in La Paz improved safety, traffic, and sanitation in multiple market districts. He encouraged many informal workers to form unions and dramatically improved compliance in several markets. He advanced his career as a result of his work and publicly stated laudable, noble goals and motivation. He also encouraged the unions he worked with to publicly campaign for the mayor's party if they wanted favorable treatment and accepted expensive gifts while making important decisions. These clientelist and corrupt practices also enriched him and advanced his career. The programmatic, corrupt, and clientelist strategies maintained informal workers' compliance by giving groups and individuals multiple ways to work with and influence officials.

Giving resources to potential civil society leaders raises other dilemmas for officials: people can use those resources to challenge the government (Bodea and LeBas, 2016, Nelson-Nuñez and Cartwright, 2018). For example, in 2005, the El Alto street vendor federation wrested a generous agreement from the struggling city government and then ran one of the federation's leaders as a mayoral candidate and defeated the incumbent. Informal workers can also engage in organized, strategic noncompliance to extract more incentives from officials (Grossman et al., 2018). For example, some associations in La Paz try to wrangle new licenses from the city government by giving new members unofficial permission to build new stalls and then engaging in destructive protests if the city removes the stalls. Or, leaders may embezzle resources instead of using them to develop organizations, and resources can spark unintended competition (Hummel, 2018a). Officials learn from these processes and their predecessors' mistakes. Officials manage these trade-offs by making incentives revocable (Holland, 2017), by playing leaders off each other, and by splitting up organizations before they get too powerful, as the case study of La Paz in the empirical section of the book elaborates further.

Many officials choose some combination of the choices laid out above. For example, in La Paz, Bolivia, officials work closely with street vendor associations and delegate routine enforcement roles to them. They focus their limited enforcement capabilities on repeat offenders whom the associations refer to them, and on people selling dangerous or illegal goods, like adulterated alcohol and stolen phones. They then ignore the smattering of vendors in peripheral neighborhoods until the number of street vendors is large enough to legally form an association, which requires 24 people, or the neighbors complain.

Informal workers, for their part, are happy to get incentives from the government. As Natalia and Elena's stories at the beginning of this chapter illustrate, informal workers know that they would benefit from pooling resources with their colleagues to share the costs of services and collective tasks. However, informal workers have many competing demands and would rather someone else put in the work. Where some informal workers know how to organize and officials step in with extra incentives, official incentives help informal workers overcome these barriers to collective action.

In most places and occupations, informal workers' ability to turn a profit depends on their relationships with officials (Bhowmik, 2012, Cross, 1998). Informal workers know this and regularly approach officials individually or in groups to ask for licenses, leniency, forbearance, policy input, and projects. When officials approach them to develop working relationships, or respond to their requests by asking them to organize, informal workers are generally wary but receptive.

Official incentives can help informal workers coordinate around collective solutions and compensate leaders for their work. For example, official incentives can include cash, extra licenses, or other bonuses to leaders that effectively pay leaders for their extra time and effort. This is a strategy that officials use in Bolivia, and it makes taking on a leadership role worthwhile for many people.

For example, Rosa and her colleagues in the *champañeras* union from Chapter 1 started out as a group of unorganized neighbors selling in their peripheral neighborhood. The municipal guard approached them one day and issued warnings for selling without a license, warning them that their wares would be confiscated if they continued to sell without licenses. The women went to the city's largest street vendor federation and the Markets Office to start the licensing process. They formed the *champañeras* union as part of the years-long process to acquire licenses. Rosa is a reluctant union leader because the position involves a lot of unpaid work. She took the position because she has more time, money, and experience than most of her colleagues, who are younger women with small children. As union leader, she received her license first, months and in some cases years before the others did.

To summarize, I argue that informal workers organize where some of them know how to mobilize their colleagues and form groups, where informal workers and their activities exceed officials' enforcement capacity, and where officials can advance their careers by extracting compliance from informal workers' organizations. Where informal workers do not know how to organize, organizations do not form. Where informal workers have know-how and the other conditions do not exist, a few informal workers form small organizations.

Where informal activities exceed capacity but their noncompliance does not affect officials' career advancement, officials simply ignore the informal sector. Where all three conditions exist, informal workers and officials interact to create large organizations.

2.3 Formal Model

This section builds a game theoretic model that formalizes the strategic interaction at the heart of the theory laid out above. The formal model demonstrates how interactions between an official and informal workers create levels of organization ranging from unorganized individuals to small groups to universal organizations. The model establishes clear conditions that lead to these different outcomes. The simplification of the model enables precise causal analysis, but the trade-off is that the model necessarily leaves out complexities that are important to collective action decisions and that the ethnographic account captures.

I model the theory mathematically to demonstrate that the argument that officials encourage informal workers to organize – particularly where informal workers break many laws and exceed local enforcement capacity – is counterintuitive but logically consistent. There are sound theoretical and empirical reasons to expect that informal workers would not organize: organizing requires money and time that informal workers typically do not have and informal workers typically do not organize in the OECD cities where many academics live and work, and where officials collect high-quality data.

It is counterintuitive that officials intervene to help, or even pay, people who are breaking laws. I use game theory to show when and why this dynamic develops. Additionally, I start with a canonical collective action model, an n-person public goods game, and show that the theory builds on existing work. The model that I create contains the equilibrium outcomes that Olson (1965) and Ostrom (1990) analyzed as well as the equilibrium outcomes that this book's theory expects. The modeling exercise makes it clear that we need only a few additional and realistic assumptions to have a situation in which an official pays people to organize. The assumptions we need are that another player (the official) exists and that the official has a payoff distinct from the informal workers but dependent on the public goods game.

The model also addresses the alternative explanation that informal workers organize in a few places like Bolivia because those places are culturally distinct in an idiosyncratic way that facilitates organization. While culture can certainly play a role in collective action that is not addressed here (Peredo Beltrán, 1992, Tilly, 1986), the model demonstrates that we do not have to model or include culture to explain situations in which informal workers organize. Modeling the theory in this way facilitates moving from the illustrative cases of street vendors in La Paz and São Paulo to a more general explanation of why informal workers organize in some places but not others.

In the model, I assume that all people are rational in that they have goals in any given decision, are aware of their goals, and make decisions in pursuit of those goals. Note that rationality in a game theoretic model is different from the colloquial meaning of rationality (Quackenbush, 2004). Here, rationality means that a person has stable preferences about their available choices for the duration of the game and does not sabotage them. In other words, people know what they want and choose accordingly. Relaxing the rationality assumption does not change the results as much as one might think: for example, modeling bounded rationality with an error term, in line with random utility models or stochastic discrete choice games (Fischer and Qaim, 2012, Signorino, 2003), produces high and low contribution equilibria similar to the existing model's results.[5]

I assume that informal workers want to maximize their profits as well as their benefit from public goods and official incentives. Benefits could be material or immaterial. For example, a material selective incentive like a license for a larger stall increases the amount of merchandise that a street vendor can sell. A material public good like market security decreases losses to theft. Benefits can also be immaterial, like symbolic representation in policy negotiations. In the empirical chapters, I show that street vendors primarily consider material benefits in their organizing decisions. The model can also accommodate workers with other considerations. Additionally, I assume that the official wants to minimize costs. This model's assumptions about actors, their costs, their options, and their interactions are listed in the notation table in Table 2.2 and illustrated in the game tree in Figure 2.1.

In the model, an official chooses whether or not to intervene in informal workers' decisions to cooperate. First, a group of informal workers plays a public goods game. In public goods games, players decide to contribute to a public good or not. This reflects the reality of many informal workers, who start working as unorganized individuals and then decide whether or not to form a group. In this model, every informal worker who decides to join an

[5] Motivated readers can add an error term and rework the proofs in the appendix to this chapter. Less motivated readers can imagine their favorite Greek symbol representing an error term tacked onto the equilibrium conditions.

Table 2.2 Game theoretic model notation

v_i	a given worker; informal worker *i*.
s	the official.
j_i	a given joiner; joiner *i*.
x	the official's offer, where $0 \leq x \leq 1$.
n	total number of workers.
k	the number of workers needed to provide the public good, where $0 < k \leq n$.
m	the number of workers who organize.
g	the public good, where $0 \leq g \leq 1$.
e	the official's cost of enforcement where $0 \leq e \leq 1$.
c_i	the cost of organizing to worker$_i$, where $c_i \sim U[0, 1]$.
c_{ji}	the cost of organizing to joiner$_i$, where $c_{ji} \sim U[0, 1]$.

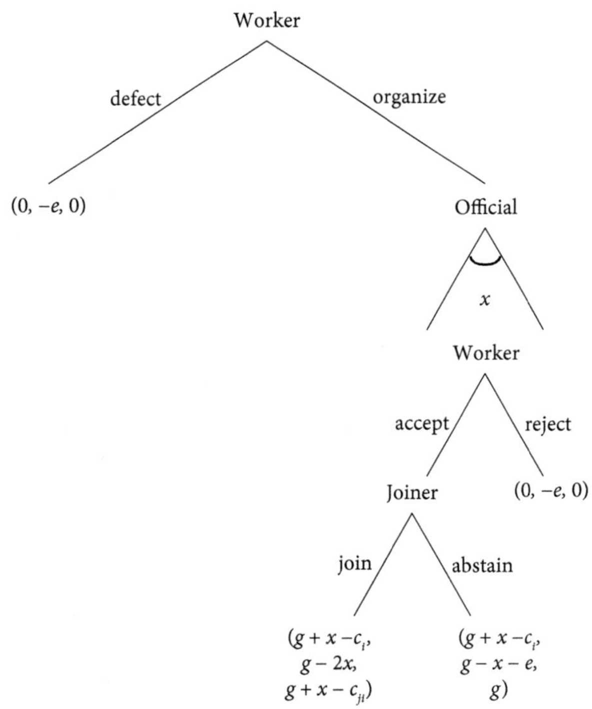

Fig. 2.1 Stylized representation of the game theoretic model where $n = 1$ and $j = 1$

organization pays a cost of time and money, and if enough informal workers contribute, they generate a public good. We denote enough informal workers as k informal workers. The public good could be compliance with local laws or the order, safety, and steady flow of traffic that a street vendor organization can bring to an open-air market. While citizens may value a public good differently – for example, street vendors in a market may value a clean and orderly market more than the neighbors who shop there, who in turn value it more than residents across the city – all citizens can potentially benefit from public goods of compliance or order.[6] Every informal worker who does not join the organization benefits from the public good but does not pay an organizing cost. These informal workers generate an enforcement cost – a type of negative externality – for the official. Organized informal workers then enter a bargaining stage where the official offers them a selective incentive. We can think of selective incentives as licenses, cash, or policy input. Once the official and the organized informal workers have reached an agreement, other informal workers, denoted as joiners, can join the organization. Joiners pay a cost to join and receive a selective incentive. In this game, the selective incentive is endogenous to the model.

The game has complete information, which means that informal workers can anticipate if they will receive a selective incentive when they make their organizing decisions, even though the official offers the incentive in the following stage. This feature is similar to observed bureaucratic behavior, in that officials often say that they will extend benefits to group members, but only deliver once an organization has formed. Each founding informal worker has an opportunity to accept or reject the offer. Once the organization is established, other informal workers can join. Joiners pay a simplified cost, receive the previously determined benefit, and do not bargain with the official. Table 2.2 summarizes the model notation and Figure 2.1 illustrates the structure of the game.

In the model, an official, n founding informal workers, and j joiners play a finite and complete information game. Subgame perfect equilibrium is the appropriate solution concept for finding the equilibria (all proofs in the chapter's appendix). The model demonstrates that the official offers an incentive that will encourage informal workers to organize as long as $x < e + \frac{g}{k}$; in other words, as long as the incentive is less than the public good and enforcement

[6] A more canonical example would be a park: any citizen can visit a public park and enjoy it as a public good. However, some people will value a given park much more than others. Many people will never go near the park, but that does not change the park's status as a public good. We can think of a clean and orderly public market in a similar way. The differences in valuation do not change the market's status as a public good.

savings that compliers generate. The informal workers' calculus depends on whether the actions of their colleagues are enough to provide the public good, and whether the official's incentive sufficiently offsets their personal organizing costs.

2.3.1 Equilibrium Stategies and Outcomes

The model has equilibrium strategies (stated formally in the appendix, with proofs) that account for organizational outcomes ranging from no organization to universal organization. These outcomes reflect the empirical record and existing collective action research. First, the model produces an equilibrium outcome in which no one contributes and no one organizes. This outcome is similar to Olson's (1965) work, where g is large, but the official does not intervene and informal workers do not organize. Second, the model leads to an equilibrium outcome that resembles Ostrom's work (1990, 2007): some informal workers will organize to capture a sufficiently large public good, even without state intervention. This project shows that officials can free ride on informal workers' efforts: the official benefits from the public good and reduced externalities without contributing.

This model's contribution is in the following three equilibrium outcomes: if the public good is lower than the kth worker's costs, the official offers an incentive that offsets the kth worker's costs. In this situation, the official would rather offset informal workers' organizing costs than be left with the negative externality that the workers generate if they stay unorganized. This leads to a low contribution outcome where some workers with costs lower than the incentive organize, and a high contribution outcome where k informal workers organize. In these scenarios, all joiners with costs lower than x join the new organization. Finally, if enforcement costs are higher than any other parameter, the official will offer an incentive that induces universal organization. Under this condition, the official saves money by paying everyone to organize. Left to their own devices, unorganized informal workers would generate large enforcement costs for the official and the official prevents this by paying for universal organization.

Relative costs explain variation in this model. To see this, fix the parameters at given values save one and then examine how an endogenous variable moves with changes in that parameter (proofs in the appendix). Here, we look at how the official's offer, an endogenous variable, changes with the public good, organizing costs, and enforcement costs. First, as the value of the public good increases, the official's offer increases. Both the official and the informal workers enjoy the public good, and as the public good increases, it gives resources to the official that they can then spend on incentives. We can also fix *g* and restate this result in terms of individual organizing costs: as the workers' costs increase, they require higher offers from the official to organize.

The official's enforcement costs have a different relationship with the offer. Where enforcement costs are less than the *k*th worker's organizing costs minus the value of the public good, the official offers nothing. Once enforcement costs pass that threshold, however, the official will make an offer up to the value of the enforcement costs that maximizes the number of organized informal workers. The intuition here is that where enforcement costs are high, it is cheaper for officials to induce organization than pay for enforcement. Relative costs explain variation in these outcomes: as enforcement costs decrease, the official makes smaller offers and informal workers form smaller organizations. As enforcement costs increase, all else equal, the official makes larger offers and consequently informal workers use them to form larger organizations, and more joiners are attracted to the new organization.

The model's results are robust to a range of changes: if costs are private instead of public, if the distribution of costs changes, if there is no *k* threshold, or there are more specific cost and benefit terms, the model produces similar equilibrium results (see appendix for robustness checks).[7]

The model requires simplifying assumptions and presents a simplified version of the theory that I elaborated in the first part of this chapter. The model explains organization with endogenous selective incentives; it does not directly model self-regulation. Self-regulation is an empirical fact in the ethnographic case study developed in the qualitative chapters: virtually all street vendor organizations in La Paz and El Alto that receive official incentives enforce at least some local ordinances. Additionally, public goods games are one way to model collective action decisions. A moral hazard or coordination game would model different aspects of the decision and produce different results.

The theory addresses the alternative explanations for informal workers' organizations that I discussed in Chapter 1: grassroots activism and clientelism. We need grassroots activists to start organizations. Grassroots activists supply the organizing know-how that makes any organization possible. Grassroots

[7] I thank Scott Wolford for suggesting game theoretic robustness checks, see Bell and Wolford (2015).

activists on their own create the first equilibrium outcome: in the absence of state intervention, some informal workers form small organizations.

To create the larger organizations in the other equilibrium outcomes, informal workers need incentives from the official. Likewise, the official in the model offers informal workers a private benefit in a transaction that could be construed as clientelist. In the equilibrium outcome where the official pays some informal workers but does not pay them enough to organize and produce a public good, we could interpret this transaction as clientelist. In the equilibrium outcomes where informal workers take the incentive and produce a public good, the informal workers and the official create a benefit that anyone can enjoy, which is a programmatic outcome, rather than a clientelist one. The model contains the alternative explanations and demonstrates that grassroots activism and clientelism account for some of the exchange and some of the informal workers' organizations that we observe. However, to explain the range of outcomes, we must understand how informal workers' noncompliance creates negative externalities for officials abnd how officials can address those externalities by working with informal workers programmatically.

To summarize without notation, the model presents a situation in which unorganized informal workers create costs for public officials but organized informal workers provide a public good. Knowing this, an official can pay to change the structure of the workers' decisions by offering organized informal workers an endogenously determined private benefit. The negative externality pushes the official to endogenously incentivize a k group – the group of people that must contribute in order to provide a public good – because collective action helps the official avoid the burden of negative externalities. The model shows the conditions under which officials will not intervene: when intervention costs more than the negative externality or where officials can free ride on the informal workers' efforts. It also shows that officials will intervene when paying informal workers to organize is cheaper than paying enforcement costs. Variation in relative costs explains variation in organizational outcomes: as informal workers' personal costs increase, they accept a smaller range of offers, decreasing the parameter values under which we observe organization. On the other hand, as enforcement costs increase, officials make larger offers and informal workers form larger organizations.

2.3.2 Observable Implications

The theory implies that we should observe the following patterns in the empirical chapters. The theory expects that the lower a government's enforcement capacity, the more its officials delegate to civil society, and that the more incentives officials offer, the more informal workers organize and participate in civil society. Conversely, where a government's enforcement capacity is high, its officials delegate fewer enforcement roles to civil society. In higher capacity cases, the theory expects that officials offer fewer incentives and directly enforce more, and that this discourages informal workers from organizing and participating in civil society. Thus, we should observe higher levels of organization and participation in lower capacity places than in higher capacity places. Second, official incentives encourage individuals to organize and participate in those organizations where they otherwise would not, leading individuals to use their pre-existing resources to take advantage of official incentives. Therefore, the theory expects that people with greater resources participate to receive state incentives more than people with fewer resources. Thus, we should observe informal workers with greater resources participating more than informal workers with less.

The equilibrium conditions imply that some officials offer incentives to civil society while others do not and that some informal workers participate because of those incentives while others do not. The theory generates predictions for officials and informal workers operating in different contexts. The theory does not expect organization where individuals have few resources, regardless of enforcement capacity. Where informal workers have some resources and enforcement capacity is low, the theory expects officials to encourage organization. The more resources informal workers have, the more organizing we should see. Conversely, as enforcement capacity increases, officials should offer fewer incentives. Where officials have considerable enforcement capacity and informal workers have few resources, we should expect to see no organizing activity. However, if informal workers' resources increase, we should expect to see small amounts of organizing without state intervention.

To summarize, I argue that informal workers are more likely to organize where officials benefit from negotiating with a representative group and where officials provide incentives that help informal workers overcome barriers to collective action. This process is interactive in that informal workers' noncompliance affects officials' enforcement costs. If informal workers collectively push enforcement costs high enough, they create the condition under which officials may find it more efficient to solve their collective action problem than to enforce.

3
Informal Work in Numbers

Why do informal workers organize? This book advances a theory of state intervention in collective action in which officials in some places offer incentives to informal workers who start and join organizations. Officials in other places crack down on informal workers with law enforcement, which discourages organization. This chapter analyzes quantitative data on informal workers. The Latin American Public Opinion Project (LAPOP) supplies survey data from 21 countries in Latin America and the Comparative Study of Electoral Systems (CSES) includes data from 42 democracies around the world. Importantly, the surveys demonstrate that informal workers organize unions and professional associations in nearly every country for which we have data. I then create a larger data set of informal workers across Latin America with a machine learning algorithm and compare that data set to the known survey data. Logistic and mixed effects regression analyses then demonstrate that individual resources and state capacity explain why informal workers organize around the world. Finally, I use the data and analyses in this chapter to select cases to examine in-depth in the following chapters.

3.1 Organizing by Numbers

The statistics in this chapter paint a broad picture of informal work across the world. The descriptive statistics in this section confirm some of the conventional wisdom about people who work informally: on average, informal workers tend to be poorer and less educated than their formal counterparts, in line with what existing research expects (ILO, 2018). Informal respondents in the LAPOP and CSES data sets exhibit a range of ages, education, and wealth levels – as Baker and Velasco Guachalla (2018) and others note, informal workers are a heterogeneous group with porous boundaries. However, departing from the expectations of existing research, many informal workers organize

Why Informal Workers Organize. Calla Hummel, Oxford University Press.
© Calla Hummel (2021). DOI: 10.1093/oso/9780192847812.003.0003

Table 3.1 Descriptive statistics for continuous variables in the LAPOP data set

	Min	Max	Mean	Standard deviation
Known informal workers				
Education (years)	0	18	8.32	4.43
Wealth index (LAPOP)	–3.99	2.96	–.40	1.77
Age	16	99	37.99	13.57
Likely informal workers				
Education (years)	0	18	8.39	4.25
Wealth index (LAPOP)	–3.99	2.96	–.37	1.70
Age	16	99	38.40	13.96
Self-employed workers				
Education (years)	0	18	8.34	4.36
Wealth index (LAPOP)	–3.99	2.96	–.20	1.75
Age	16	99	40.77	13.78
Likely formal workers				
Education (years)	0	18	11.71	3.98
Wealth index (LAPOP)	–3.99	2.96	1.05	1.16
Age	18	96	38.35	11.72

at work: across the LAPOP samples, 20% of informal workers belong to a professional association or a union.[1]

The CSES data show similar trends. People who are self-employed and work in often informal jobs like domestic work, subsistence agriculture, and street vending report significantly lower levels of education and wealth than their more formally employed compatriots.

The CSES data reflect patterns similar to those in the LAPOP data sets. Informal workers are more likely to live in rural areas and identify as men than formal workers. Informal workers in the CSES data set organize at work, but at lower rates than in the LAPOP data sets and at significantly lower rates than formal workers.

Tables 3.5 and 3.6 dispel the myth that informal workers do not organize. The descriptive statistics in Tables 3.5 and 3.6 establish that informal workers exist and organize in nearly every country for which we have data. In the LAPOP data sets, informal workers comprise a significant minority of the respondents in each country and organize as much as formal workers. We have

[1] In political science, we typically precede these numbers with a detailed discussion of where the data come from, how we constructed the variables, and why we made certain coding choices. I have relegated this discussion to the Quantitative Appendix.

Table 3.2 Binary variable proportions for LAPOP workers

Worker Type	Proportions	
Known informal workers		
Professional organization	21% Participants	79% Nonparticipants
Gender	67% Men	33% Women
Urban	59% Urban	41% Rural
Likely informal workers		
Professional organization	20% Participants	20% Nonparticipants
Gender	65% Men	35% Women
Urban	60% Urban	40% Rural
Self-employed workers		
Professional organization	21% Participants	79% Nonparticipants
Gender	67% Men	33% Women
Urban	61% Urban	39% Rural
Likely formal workers		
Professional organization	20% Participants	80% Nonparticipants
Gender	63% Men	37% Women
Urban	79% Urban	21% Rural

Table 3.3 Descriptive statistics for continuous variables in the CSES data set

	Min	Max	Mean	Standard deviation
Likely informal workers				
Education (categories)	0	9	3.59	1.77
Wealth categories (CSES)	1	5	2.54	1.32
Age	18	96	48.80	16.04
Likely formal workers				
Education (categories)	0	9	5.09	1.96
Wealth categories (CSES)	1	5	3.13	1.37
Age	18	96	48.64	15.79

fewer informal respondents in the CSES data set, but at least some informal workers organize in nearly every country. Looking at Tables 3.5 and 3.6, we can move from asking if informal workers organize to asking why some informal workers organize while others do not and why informal workers organize in some places more than others.

The cross-tabulations in Table 3.5 suggest an association between informal worker organizations and state capacity. The countries with more organized informal workers have governments with relatively low capacity. In Bolivia,

Table 3.4 Binary variable proportions for CSES workers

Worker Type	Proportions	
Likely informal workers		
Professional organization	10% Participants	90% Nonparticipants
Gender	60% Men	40% Women
Urban	60% Urban	40% Rural
Likely formal workers		
Professional organization	26% Participants	74% Nonparticipants
Gender	50% Men	50% Women
Urban	77% Urban	33% Rural

Table 3.5 Organized informal workers by country and measure, LAPOP

Country	Known informal workers, % organized	Likely informal workers, % organized	Self-employed workers, % organized
Argentina	15%	10%	11%
Bolivia	43%	34%	34%
Brazil	25%	15%	18%
Chile	16%	14%	16%
Colombia	16%	13%	16%
Costa Rica	13%	14%	16%
Dominican Republic	24%	22%	25%
Ecuador	23%	21%	23%
El Salvador	13%	14%	15%
Guatemala	14%	14%	15%
Haiti	30%	42%	43%
Honduras	19%	17%	20%
Jamaica	19%	20%	22%
Mexico	19%	19%	19%
Nicaragua	23%	20%	23%
Panama	15%	13%	13%
Paraguay	12%	14%	15%
Peru	32%	29%	31%
Uruguay	15%	13%	15%
Venezuela	13%	10%	10%

Table 3.6 Organized likely informal workers by country, CSES

Country	Informal workers, % organized	Country	Informal workers, % organized
Argentina	4%	New Zealand	12%
Australia	7%	Norway	16%
Austria	10%	Peru	5%
Bulgaria	4%	Philippines	7%
Canada	44%	Poland	1%
Czech Republic	9%	Portugal	3%
Finland	23%	Romania	1%
France	7%	Serbia	19%
Germany	12%	Slovakia	3%
Greece	30%	Slovenia	0%
Hong Kong	8%	South Africa	4%
Iceland	72%	South Korea	6%
Ireland	20%	Sweden	31%
Israel	13%	Switzerland	1%
Japan	22%	Thailand	18%
Kenya	2%	Turkey	17%
Latvia	12%	United States	5%
Mexico	10%		
Montenegro	6%		

Peru, Ecuador, the Dominican Republic, Nicaragua, and Haiti, more than 20 percent of informal workers belong to work-based organizations. Conversely, informal workers in higher capacity countries, like Chile, Uruguay, and Costa Rica, organize at rates below the regional average. Still, cross-tabulations do not account for the many factors that influence individuals' decisions to join organizations and there are many informal workers in low capacity countries, like Paraguay and Guatemala, who do not organize.

In the CSES data summarized in Table 3.6, informal workers organize in every country except Slovenia. Rates of organizing at work vary dramatically from 1 percent in Poland, Romania, and Switzerland to 72 percent in Iceland, again pointing to the question of why some informal workers organize while others do not.

State capacity may be part of the patterns in the CSES data set but its role is less clear. The countries with the lowest rates of organizing are all European countries with medium to high levels of state capacity. Lower capacity countries like Kenya and Peru have low to middling rates of organization. Likewise, countries with powerful labor movements, like France and Mexico, have middling rates of organization and countries with national informal workers' organizations, like South Africa and South Korea have below average rates of organizing among potentially informal respondents. Rates of organization do not clearly break along the lines of other important political variables, like democracy or ideology: the most organized informal workers are in highly democratic welfare states with, at the time of the survey, leftist administrations. Still, many leftist administrations in highly democratic welfare states do not have highly organized informal workers. More surprisingly, a number of authoritarian governments that hold limited elections, like Turkey, Thailand, and Hong Kong, have notable rates of organized informal workers.

One important caveat for the CSES data set is that it contains fewer workers than the LAPOP data sets: the coding scheme identified only 7,081 respondents as likely informal workers and only 6,324 across 36 countries also answered questions about organizing at work. As a result, each country has only a dozen to a few hundred likely informal respondents. Austria, Canada, Serbia, Slovenia, Portugal, and South Africa have fewer than 50 respondents each. Thailand has the most respondents at 544, while Canada and Serbia have the least at only 16 respondents. In contrast, countries in the LAPOP data set have a few hundred to a few thousand potentially informal respondents.

The CSES data set lends important leverage on one dimension: occupation. The CSES data has detailed occupational data which we can use to distinguish between different types of informal work. The first three chapters of this book discuss informal workers as one group and the later chapters use street vendors and their organizations as case studies. While we know that informal workers are a heterogeneous group, the book does not explicitly theorize how those differences influence organizing or how street vendors may or may not be systematically different from domestic workers, recyclers, or other informal workers. The occupational data in the CSES surveys enables us to compare different groups of likely informal workers. Table 3.7 shows the rates of organization across various categories.

Table 3.7 demonstrates that while most likely informal workerrs do not organize, a notable minority organizes across occupational categories. About 10 percent of likely informal workers organize, from a low of almost no one in piecework to 17 percent of subsistence agriculture workers. Most groups hover around 10 percent including the emblematic informal occupations of street vending, recycling, and domestic work. Roughly 8 percent of street vendors in the CSES data set organize, which puts them at a rate comparable to most other categories.

Table 3.7 Likely informal workers by occupation, CSES

Occupation	Informal workers, % organized	Informal workers, % unorganized
Subsistence agriculture	17%	83%
Domestic workers	9%	91%
Street vendors	8%	92%
Recyclers	9%	91%
Laborers	11%	89%
Piece workers	2%	98%
Informal transportation	7%	93%
Other self-employed services	10%	90%
Other self-employed agriculture	16%	84%
Other self-employed trades	8%	92%

3.2 Estimating Informality with Machine Learning

How do we identify informal workers in surveys and related data? I put the LAPOP data set through a machine learning algorithm to generate a data set of 39,572 likely informal workers from the 2006, 2008, 2010, and 2012 LAPOP survey waves.[2] The algorithm takes individual-level variables and country-level variables and predicts who works informally and who works formally, using Baker and Velasco Guachalla (2018)'s data as a reference. After training the algorithm on Baker and Velasco Guachalla (2018)'s identified informal workers, the algorithm predicts which respondents in later survey waves are likely informal workers. The algorithm issues a binary prediction for if a given respondent is informal or not, based on their nationality, demographics, and job, as well as a probability that a respondent is informal or not. This approach creates a data set of 39,572 likely informal workers across Latin America.

With a machine learning approach, researchers feed data into an algorithm that learns patterns to predict output (Breiman, 2001b, p.199). To generate the informal worker data set, I used a random forest classifier, which generates predictions from *n* decision trees.[3] Random forest is one technique in the field of machine learning methods (Breiman, 2001a, p.5). Machine learning methods

[2] I stopped at 2012 because LAPOP stopped asking the professional association question after 2012.

[3] Specifically, I used the off-the-shelf random forest classifier in R's caret package. Details in the replication code and caret documentation. See Muchlinski et al. (2016) for an excellent comparison of random forest and logistic regression in R using the caret and randomForest packages.

like random forest classifiers typically outperform OLS and logistic regression in making predictions (Muchlinski et al., 2016).

Random forest classifiers create decision trees to partition the data (Breiman, 2001a, p.5). As the stylized example in Figure 3.1 illustrates, decision trees partition data to classify observations, creating conditional relationships between the variables. Random forest classifiers are particularly useful for social scientists because, unlike several other machine learning methods, they can handle continuous and discrete variables, missing data, and unbalanced classes, and produce useful metrics like error rates and variable importance measures (Muchlinski et al., 2016, p.89).

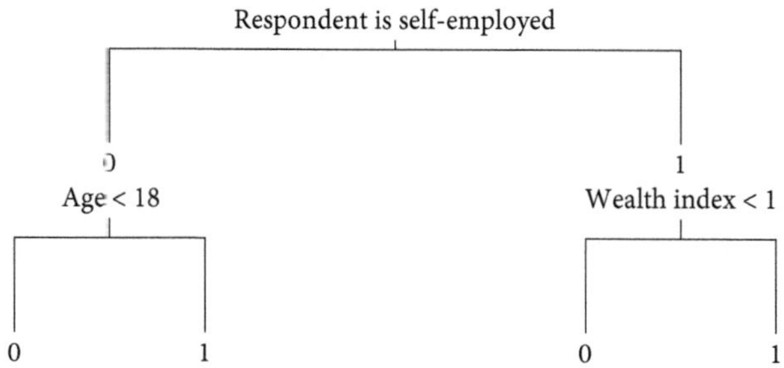

Fig. 3.1 Stylized example of a decision tree classifying informal workers and formal workers

Decision trees are analogous to flow charts: the highly stylized decision tree in Figure 3.1 illustrates how a decision tree partitions data into increasingly smaller groups in order to make a prediction. Each terminal node in the decision tree is a prediction. In this example, if a respondent is self-employed (Figure 3.1's first split, to the right) and the respondent is wealthy (Figure 3.1's second split to the left), the tree ends in 0, which means that it predicts that the respondent is not an informal worker. Conversely, if a respondent is self-employed and the respondent does not have much money, the tree ends in 1, in other words, the tree predicts that the respondent is an informal worker. Variables further up in the decision tree carry more weight because they contribute to more partitioning. For instance, job status partitions all observations in this example and is therefore more important to the model than age, which partitions many but not all observations. Again, Figure 3.1 is a highly stylized example; the decision trees that preliminary analyses grew for this project frequently had dozens of distinct conditional relationships between many variables.

Random forest techniques grow a large number of decision trees from randomly selected variables in a data set. The models in this project used 1,000 trees per model, which is the point at which additional complexity did not increase the precision of the analyses' results. A random forest classifier randomly samples variables at every node, making each decision tree different. The model learns by finding the optimal local split or value of the sampled variable at that node that most clearly separates all remaining informal workers from formal workers. After growing a forest of decision trees, the random forest technique bundles and averages decision tree predictions to generate results (Breiman, 2001b, p.205).

Selecting parameters like the number of trees to grow is an iterative process that relies more on guidelines than formulas (Muchlinski et al., 2016, p.94). To select parameters, I compared models with different threshold values for different parameters and selected the values that maximized precision without adding unnecessary computational complexity. For example, a model with 1,000 trees takes several more hours to run than a model with 100 trees, but the results are much more consistent across models. A model with 2,000 trees generates very slightly more precise results and adds considerably more computing time.

Random forest models generate several types of results. First, random forest models generate error matrices, which are categorized predictions. We evaluate the model's accuracy with error matrices. To develop a random forest model, the researcher splits a data set into a training data set and a test data set. In this case, I used the 2006 and 2008 LAPOP data sets with Baker and Velasco Guachalla (2018)'s informal worker operationalization and randomly sorted the responses into training and test data. The model learned which combinations of variable values belong to informal workers and which combinations belong to formal workers in the training data and built a predictive model from that information. The model then predicted which respondents in the test data set were informal and compared its predictions to the labeled data. The error matrix in Table 3.8 summarizes how well the model performs on test data.

The error matrix reports that of the 5,923 respondents in the test data, the random forest model built with the training data correctly predicted the

Table 3.8 Random forest model error matrix

Prediction	Formal	Informal	Error rate
Formal	3997	221	5%
Informal	348	1357	20%
Overall accuracy	90%		

informal status of 90 percent of respondents. The model correctly classified 95 percent of formal workers and people who are not employed and incorrectly classified 5 percent of them as informal. The algorithm correctly classified 80 percent of informal workers and incorrectly identified 20 percent as formal workers or others. Note that for the analyses in this chapter, the more important error rate is of formal workers misclassified as informal workers, which is relatively low at 5 percent. We should be concerned about people who are not informal workers and who are included in the informality data set. We can check this concern by comparing results with the data sets of known informal workers and self-employed people. We are less concerned about undercounting informal workers by misclassifying some as formal.

Typical informal workers in the data set include people like Respondent 53,929, a 42-year-old man in rural Peru who responded to the survey in 2008. He is self-employed, has two kids, attended some college, participates in a union and other organizations, and does not pay social security. The algorithm assigns him a 92 percent probability of being informal and labels him informal. Comparing against Baker and Velasco Guachalla (2018), he does not pay social security and is an informal worker. Respondent 5,981 is in a very different situation. She is a 25-year-old woman in urban Honduras who responded to the survey in 2006. She did not complete elementary school, has one child, has no household wealth, does not belong to any organizations, and works for a private employer. The algorithm assigns her an 89 percent probability of being an informal worker and classifies her as such. Comparing against Baker and Velasco Guachalla (2018), her employer does not pay social security and therefore she is an informal worker.

Conversely, the algorithm is less certain about some respondents and does misclassify some people. For example, Respondent 21,407 is a 59-year-old woman with no formal education and few assets who works in rural Chile and responded to the survey in 2006. She is a salaried worker in the private sector and the algorithm gives her a 51 percent chance of being an informal worker. She was misclassified: her employer pays social security and therefore she is a formal worker. In another example, Respondent 53,934 is a self-employed 42-year-old woman with a high school education in a large city in Peru. The algorithm assigns her a 90 percent probability of being an informal worker. However, she pays into the social security system and is a formal worker by our definition.

Given the difficulties of estimating the informal workforce (ILO, 2018, Bajada and Schneider, 2018), these are promising results. To estimate informal workers across the world, the ILO compiles household and work surveys from dozens of different countries and examines millions of responses. This is a labor intensive process and the underlying data are not comparable across countries and often not comparable across time. Similarly, Schneider and his collaborators gather a wide variety of indicators for their models. The models rely on countries and international organizations accurately and regularly reporting national-level development indicators. On the other hand, the random forest estimation method quickly produces a relatively accurate estimate with a handful of variables found in most public opinion surveys.

Post-estimation plots show which variables contribute most to the model's predictions. I examine different variables' contributions in the variable importance plot below. Figure 3.2 plots each variable's contribution to the random forest model. The measure on the x-axis is the mean decrease in GINI score for each variable. The GINI score measures predictive accuracy by assessing how the model worsens when a given variable is removed (for a more thorough discussion, see Muchlinski et al. 2016, pp. 97–98. Note that the GINI score is unrelated to the Gini index of inequality). Therefore, the higher a variable's decrease in GINI score, the more important it is to the model's accuracy.

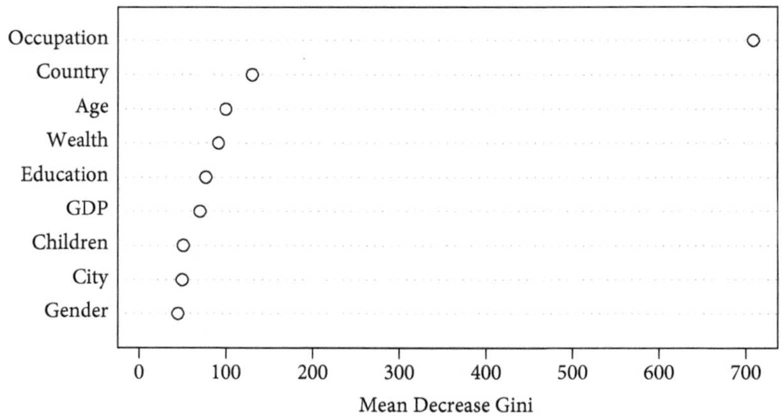

Fig. 3.2 Variable importance in the random forest model, ranked from highest to lowest predictive power, as measured by GINI score

The plot demonstrates that occupational category is far and away the most important predictor of informality. This is unsurprising, as occupational category is the main labor variable in the model. This tracks with existing research which finds that most self-employed workers and small businesses in the Americas are informal (Hussmanns, 2004, ILO, 2018). After occupational category, predictive power drops off significantly. A respondent's country adds to the model's predictive accuracy, which matches existing research demonstrating that some countries in the region, like Nicaragua and Guatemala, have much higher levels of informal work than others, like Uruguay. A self-employed worker is Nicaragua is almost definitely informal, while a self-employed worker in Uruguay may pay into the social security system and follow relevant tax laws. Age also contributes to the model, again reflecting existing research on the curvilinear relationship between age and informal work, where young workers and older workers are particularly likely to labor informally (ILO, 2018). The predictive accuracy of variables like gender, children, and wealth, fall below a GINI score of 100, meaning that these variables marginally contribute to the model's predictions.

The variable importance plot further demonstrates that researchers do not need a lot of data to predict if a person works informally or not. The variable importance plot and the error matrix suggests that researchers can accurately predict informality with individuals' employment status, country, and age. A sparse predictive model using only occupation, age, and country generates startlingly similar predictions: the overall accuracy rate is 89 percent instead of 90 percent and the informal worker error rate is 16 percent and the formal error rate is 9 percent.

With the predictive model, I can feed the algorithm subsequent waves of survey data on ocupational status, size of the respondent's city, age, children, gender, education, household wealth, country, and the country's GDP per capita for that year and generate predictions of informality for every respondent. I follow this process to generate a data set of likely informal workers across survey waves. For example, Respondent 56,658 is a self-employed 32-year-old man from a small town in Mexico who responded to the survey in 2010. The random forest algorithm assigns him a 93 percent probability of being an informal worker and labels him as an informal worker in the predicted data set. Conversely, Respondent 164,167 is a 35-year-old man who works for the government in a rural part of Argentina and responded to the survey in 2012. The algorithm assigns him an 84 percent probability of working formally and labels him a formal worker in the predicted data set.

The model generates predictions and classifications for 127,864 survey respondents across four survey waves. Of those respondents, the model classifies 39,572 of them as informal workers. For the following analyses, we use the data set of predicted informal workers. The analyses also compare these 39,572 likely informal workers to the 30,515 workers who reported themselves as self-employed to LAPOP enumerators and the 15,021 respondents from 2006 and 2008 that are informal per Baker and Velasco Guachalla (2018)'s operationalization of informality. The trends identified in the following sections are generally consistent across these three subgroups and the CSES data set of likely informal workers.

3.3 Regression Analyses

The book's theory posits that state-level and individual-level variables combine to shape informal workers' organizing decisions. Existing research suggests that other variables could shape these decisions as well. Regression analyses can evaluate the theory's proposed association between state capacity, resources, and informal worker organizations while holding important factors constant. Unlike the cross-tabulations in the first section of the chapter, regression models can estimate the effects of many variables at once, and account for the influence of other important factors.

3.3.1 Data sets and Variables

I compare results from four data sets in the regressions: the machine-generated data set of predicted informal workers from four LAPOP survey waves between 2006 and 2012, a data set of self-reported self-employed informal workers from the same four survey waves, a data set of informal workers that uses Baker and Velasco Guachalla (2018)'s operationalization of informality from LAPOP survey waves in 2006 and 2008, and a data set of people in typically informal jobs from election year surveys from CSES between 2011 and 2018.

The project's dependent variable is informal worker organization. I operationalize informal worker organization in this chapter as individual-level participation in a professional association or union. Professional association or union attendance is likely a conservative measure of informal worker organization: if an individual reports attending an association's meeting, that implies that the association exists and the individual participates in organizational activities. This is a high bar for collective action. Many people participate with their colleagues in other forms of collective action that do not require a registered organization or regular meetings. For example, in Brazil, many informal workers who I worked with who consider themselves organized would report themselves as self-employed but may not report attending a meeting in the last 12 months because meetings are infrequent and attendance is not required. Based on similar information from Bhowmik (2012), pp.210–211, on six Latin American cities, Roever (2005), pp.117–135, on Lima, and Itikawa (2006), pp.344–345, on São Paulo, I suspect that this association measure undercounts organized informal workers across the region.

The logistic models estimate the effects of state capacity, as proxied by a sparse index of governance variables from the Varieties of Democracy Project. I construct an index using data on life expectancy, GDP per capita, and government cybersecurity capacity, which I combine through a principal components analysis. Scholars identify several key dimensions of state capacity: revenue, administration, and coercion, and each variable proxies one of these dimensions (Hanson and Sigman, 2013, Hendrix, 2010, Soifer, 2015). The index includes GDP per capita because it is a common proxy of the revenue dimension of state capacity (Fearon and Laitin, 2003, Hendrix, 2010). Comparing 15 common operationalizations of state capacity, Hendrix (2010), p.274, recommends that researchers operationalize state capacity with measures of a state's revenue-generating capacity because they account for more variation across states than other measurement options. Life expectancy proxies a government's administrative capacity and its ability to increase well-being (Gerring et al., 2012). Life expectancy indirectly measures important public goods like public health systems and access to healthcare, food, and education. The cybersecurity capacity variable from V-Dem proxies a state's security, coercion or enforcement capacity. It is an expert-coded variable that attempts to directly measure state capacity on a specific dimension. Importantly, these three variables have nearly complete data across the countries and years in the survey data sets, while more direct measures of enforcement capacity, like police per capita or law enforcement spending, do not.

The models also estimate the effect of informal workers' resources, as proxied by education, on organizations. I operationalize individual resources with education because for individuals, education is one of several key personal resources that help people participate in politics (Fischer and Qaim, 2012, p.1258). On average, people with more education know more about the political system than people with less education. They also know more about how to participate in politics and civil society, and how to find useful information (Brady et al., 1995). Additionally, officials listen to constituents with higher levels of education more than constituents with lower levels of education (Hummel, 2016). This project uses education because people reliably report their education levels in surveys, unlike other important resources such as income or social networks. Furthermore, most people complete formal education before they enter the workforce. This means that education is a personal resource that is causally prior to civil society participation for many individuals, unlike income or social networks. Additionally, I can trace education across the case studies as well as the data sets. LAPOP's educational variable is a count that records the number of years a person spent in formal education, while CSES's educational variable groups people by years completed.

I include alternative measures for individual resources. In the CSES data set, most respondents answered an income range question, which is included in some models. In the LAPOP survey, most respondents answered questions about their household assets. Household assets are binary variables: did a respondent have a telephone, TV, or refrigerator or not, except in the case of vehicles, which is measured as a short ordinal scale. I compiled these questions into an index using a principal components analysis that demonstrated that the questions capture the same underlying factor: household wealth. Additionally, some models use age as a control. Age is a continuous variable starting at 16 in the LAPOP data set and 18 in the CSES data set. Other studies also use age as a measure for social capital (Fischer and Qaim, 2012, p.1258). Age is squared because of the nonlinear relationship between age and informal work: younger people and older people are more likely to work informally than middle-aged people (ILO, 2018).

The models include controls that the literature on civil society participation identifies as potential confounding variables. I include important demographic information, in particular, age, gender, and where a person lives. Gender is measured as a self-reported binary indicator for if the respondent identified themselves as a man or a woman to the survey administrator.[4] I include a binary control for whether a respondent lives in an urban or rural area, because workers in urban areas and rural areas have different social networks and infrastructure to use when organizing, and may have different employment and educational opportunities not captured by other variables. While an important literature exists on how individuals use ethnicity as a resource in collective action (Madrid, 2012, Varshney, 2001, Yashar, 2005), I do not include controls for ethnicity because CSES's and LAPOP's ethnicity

[4] Nonbinary people exist in every country, but given widespread discrimination, few surveys ask about gender identity and few nonbinary people identify themselves as such to survey enumerators.

questions change by country, the resulting dozens of categories have significant missing data, and the demographic categories are not cross-nationally comparable.

3.3.2 Regression Tables

I first use logistic regression models with fixed effects for countries and years and with standard errors clustered by country to estimate the effects of state capacity and education, as well as additional individual factors, on the likelihood that an informal worker attends professional association or union meetings. I use the logistic regression models for ease of estimation and interpretation. Additionally, the clustered standard errors adjust for the differences between respondents in different countries and the fixed effects for countries and years account for the shifts in political context between Mexico and Switzerland, or 2006 and 2008.

I then reanalyze the data with mixed effects logistic regressions. Mixed effects models can account for variables at the individual level, like gender and years of education, as well as variables at the country level, like state capacity or regime type. Mixed effects models nest respondents within larger groups (Snijders and Bosker, 1999). Mixed effects logistic regression models estimate effects for binary outcomes, like whether or not a person attended an association meeting. For this project, I build mixed effects logistic regression models that nest survey respondents within their countries of residence. However, mixed effects models do not generate stable estimates with low numbers of groups in the highest level, in this case country, and interpretation is more tenuous than with a fixed effects logistic regression.

Table 3.9 reports the results of fixed effects logistic regressions on the four data sets using only the variables of theoretical interest. These models report the effects of the independent variables of interest – the state capacity index and education – on professional association and union participation. The fixed effects for countries and years are suppressed. The first model analyzes the informal workers identified in 2006 and 2008, the second analyzes the machine generated data set, the third analyzes self-employed workers from LAPOP, and the fourth analyzes likely informal workers in the CSES data. One star signifies statistical significance at the .05 level or below.

The estimates in Table 3.9 reflect the theory's observable implications. The state capacity index is consistently negative and significant. The consistently

Table 3.9 Sparse logistic regressions modeling informal workers' participation in work-based organizations

	Known informal workers (LAPOP)	Predicted informal workers (LAPOP)	Self-employed workers (LAPOP)	Likely informal workers (CSES)
Education	.023*	.024*	.031*	.121*
	(.009)	(.005)	(.006)	(.039)
State capacity	–.485*	–.199*	–.184*	–1.032*
index	(.156)	(.043)	(.035)	(.492)
	N = 15,783	N = 39,572	N = 30,515	N = 6,189
	Countries = 20	Countries = 21	Countries = 21	Countries = 34
Year and country fixed effects suppressed.				

Standard errors in parentheses below coefficients. All tests are two-tailed.
*$p \leq .05$

negative and statistically significant estimates indicate that informal and self-employed workers in lower capacity states are more likely to participate in professional associations than their colleagues in higher capacity states. Individual-level resources also matter in these sparse models: the more educated a worker is, the more likely they are to participate. The effects are stable and significant across the four data sets of informal and self-employed workers. However, other factors could be driving these results. We turn to fixed effects models with more controls to evaluate this possibility in Table 3.10.

Table 3.10 reports the results of fixed effects logistic regressions on the four data sets. These models report the effects of education and a state capacity index as well as several demographic controls on professional association and union participation. The models examine the effects of gender, age, urbanicity, and household wealth on organizational participation. The first model analyzes the informal workers that Baker and Velasco Guachalla (2018) identified in 2006 and 2008, the second analyzes the machine generated data set, the third analyzes self-employed workers from LAPOP, and the fourth analyzes likely informal workers in the CSES data. One star connotes significance at the .05 level.

The results of these four fixed effects models with full controls support the theoretical expectation that informal workers with more resources organize more and that informal workers in lower capacity states organize more than

Table 3.10 Logistic regressions modeling informal workers' participation in work-based organizations

	Known informal workers (LAPOP)	Predicted informal workers (LAPOP)	Self-employed workers (LAPOP)	Likely informal workers (CSES)
Education	.055*	.056*	.059*	.086*
	(.009)	(.006)	(.008)	(.044)
State capacity	−.396*	−.219*	−.195*	−1.411*
index	(.175)	(.045)	(.038)	(.379)
Women	−.556*	−.459*	−.442*	−.188
	(.058)	(.073)	(.064)	(.118)
Urban	−.604*	−.604*	.612*	−.497*
	(.096)	(.082)	(.071)	(.240)
Household	.006	.003	.002	.094
wealth	(.021)	(.016)	(.018)	(.052)
Age	.060*	.061*	.050*	.094*
	(.010)	(.007)	(.008)	(028)
Age squared	.001*	.001*	.001*	.001*
	(.000)	(.000)	(.000)	(.000)
	N = 15,783	N = 39,572	N = 30,515	N = 4,776
	Countries = 20	Countries = 21	Countries = 21	Countries = 31
Year and country fixed effects suppressed.				

Standard errors in parentheses below coefficients. All tests are two-tailed.
*$p \leq .05$

informal workers in higher capacity contexts. The results further bolster the patterns established in the rest of the chapter: the negative and significant coefficients on the state capacity index suggest that informal and self-employed workers organize more in lower capacity countries, and the consistently positive and significant coefficients on education suggest that informal workers with more resources and social capital organize more than their less privileged colleagues. The control variables support what other scholars have noted about labor organizing: in most places, women organize less than men, older workers are more likely to organize than younger workers, and people in rural areas organize more than people in urban areas.

The regression coefficients in Tables 3.9 and 3.10 are log-odds, which are not directly interpretable. To understand the estimated effect of the predictors on participation, we exponentiate the coefficients, transforming them into odds ratios. Negative log-odds become odds ratios between 0 and 1 and positive log-odds become odds ratios above 1.

The positive log-odds coefficient of .055 for education in the known informal workers' data set from LAPOP becomes an odds ratio of 1.056. An odds ratio of 1.056 means that for every additional year of education, an informal worker in this data set is 6 percent more likely to have attended association or union meetings in the last year. Conversely, the negative coefficient on state capacity of –.396 becomes an odds ratio of .673. This means that for every additional point in the eight point index, an informal worker in a given country is 33 percent less likely to have attended association or union meetings in the past year. Similarly, women in this data set are 43 percent less likely on average to attend meetings than men, and urban informal workers are 45 percent less likely to have participated in meetings than informal workers in rural areas.

The magnitude of the results is relatively stable across the LAPOP data sets: every additional year of education boosts the likelihood of organizing about 6 percent. Every additional point on the state capacity index reduces the likelihood of organization from 18 percent in the self-employed data set to 33 percent in the known data set. Likewise women are 36 percent to 43 percent less likely to organize than men, while urban workers are 46 percent less likely to attend meetings than rural workers in all three data sets.

In the CSES data set, moving up an educational category increases the likelihood of having attended meetings by 9 percent while every additional point on the state capacity scale reduces the likelihood of organizing by 75 percent. Urban workers are 40 percent less likely than rural workers to organize and while women are less likely than men to attend meetings, the gap is small and not statistically significant in the CSES data set.

We can visualize the changing rates of organization by graphing how the predicted probabilities of attending association or union meetings change for different values of a given variable. The graphs in Figure 3.3 show the predicted probabilities for different values of education and state capacity in each data set, holding the other variables in the models in Table 3.10 at their means. The graphs in Figure 3.3 demonstrate that the relationships between organizing, state capacity, and resources are similar across the four data sets.

Figure 3.3 shows large and dramatic shifts in the probability that a given informal worker will organize at work. More education increases the likelihood of organizing at every level of state capacity. In the lowest capacity places, highly educated workers have over a 60 percent chance of organizing. Their

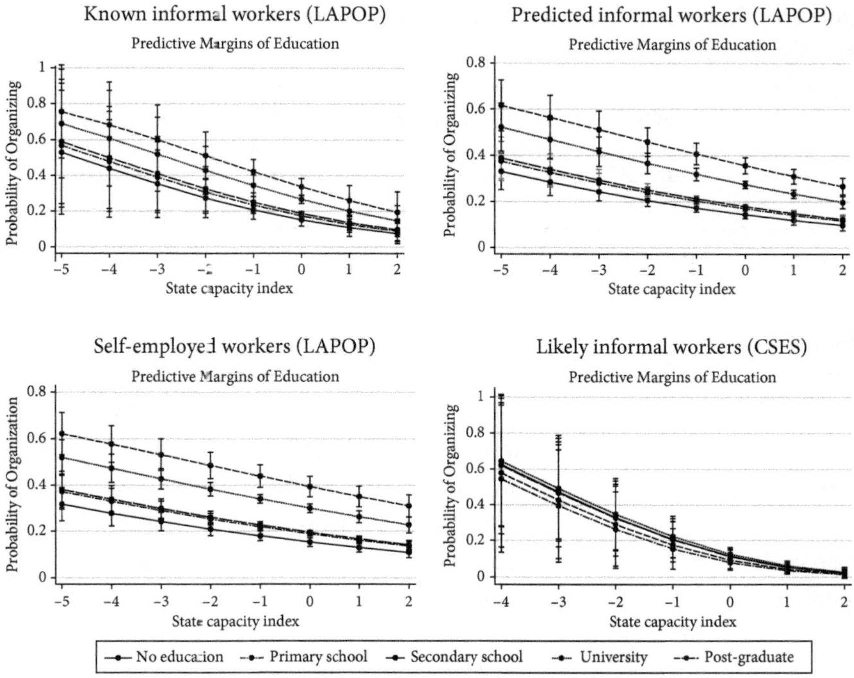

Fig. 3.3 Predicted probabilities for state capacity and education

colleagues who never attended school have a lower chance of organizing, ranging from 30–50 percent. As state capacity increases, the gap between the most educated and the least educated shrinks: in the highest capacity places in the LAPOP data sets, the most educated have a 30–40 percent chance of organizing while the least educated have about a 15–20 percent chance of organizing. In the LAPOP data sets, there is a big difference between attending university and not: at most levels of state capacity, people who attend some university have at least a 10-point lead over everyone else. This changes for the likely informal workers in the CSES data: all workers have around a 60 percent chance of organizing at low levels of state capacity and less than a 10 percent chance at high levels of state capacity. In the CSES data set, the advantages of education disappear at high levels of state capacity.

There are alternate ways to estimate the effects of individual-level and country-level factors on organizing decisions. In particular, mixed effects models account for effects at multiple levels: respondents or other units can be grouped at the city, state, or country level. The mixed effects logistic regressions that I build here group respondents by country. The drawback of the mixed effects approach is that it requires large numbers of units at each level

Table 3.11 Individual and country-level effects on informal workers' organizations

	LAPOP known informal workers	LAPOP likely informal workers	LAPOP self-employed workers	CSES likely informal workers
Education	.055*	.058*	.059*	.090*
	(.006)	(.004)	(.004)	(.035)
State capacity	−.160*	−.212*	−.198*	.237
index	(.072)	(.031)	(.039)	(.140)
Women	−.554*	−.458*	−.440*	−.196
	(.046)	(.029)	(.039)	(.108)
Urban	−.600*	−.601*	−.609*	−.459*
	(.045)	(.030)	(.034)	(.122)
Household	.005	.002	−.004	.096*
wealth	(.015)	(.010)	(.011)	(.042)
Age	.059*	.061*	.050*	.095*
	(.008)	(.005)	(.006)	(.022)
Age squared	−.001*	−.001*	−.001*	−.001*
	(.000)	(.000)	(.000)	(.000)
	N = 15,783	N = 39,572	N = 30,515	N = 4,802
	Countries = 20	Countries = 21	Countries = 21	Countries = 33
Year and country random effects suppressed.				

Standard errors in parentheses below coefficients. All tests are two-tailed.
* $p \leq .05$

to generate reliable estimates. While we have large numbers of survey respondents, we have only a handful of countries in each data set, which casts doubt on our estimates for state capacity and other country-level variables.

The mixed effects analyses estimate random effects for countries. The analyses feature random effects for countries because we should expect different countries to shape individuals' organizing decisions in different and even divergent ways (Putnam et al., 1994, p.182). People in a given country come to organizing with a shared repertoire of collective action, shared understandings about the political system, and face similar constraints (Tilly, 1986). Thus, we should expect people in a given country to organize in ways that resemble other people in their country.

Table 3.11 reports the results of mixed effects logistic regressions on the four data sets. These models report the effects of education and a state capacity index as well as several demographic controls on professional association and union participation. The models examine the effects of gender, age, urbanicity, and household wealth on organizational participation. The first model analyzes the informal workers that Baker and Velasco Guachalla (2018) identified in 2006 and 2008, the second analyzes the machine generated data set, the third analyzes self-employed workers from LAPOP, and the fourth analyzes likely informal workers in the CSES data. One star means significance at the .05 level.

The results of these four mixed effects models with full controls largely support the theoretical expectation that informal workers with more resources organize more than workers with less, as well as that informal workers in lower capacity states organize more than informal workers in higher capacity contexts. The results support the patterns established in the preceding tables: the negative and significant coefficients on the state capacity index suggest that informal and self-employed workers organize more in places with low capacity, and the consistently positive and significant coefficients on education suggest that informal workers with more resources and social capital organize more than their colleagues with less. The state capacity index is positive but insignificant in one model that has fewer individual observations. The control variables support what other scholars have noted across the region: women organize less than men and people in rural areas organize more than people in urban areas. The 20 to 30 countries in each data set limit the power of the analyses at the country level; the estimates and the standard errors may be unreliable. Still, the analyses follow the same general patterns as the fixed effects models.

We can also evaluate alternative explanations for why informal workers organize with these data. We know that political context affects the opportunities available to labor organizers all over the world (Ostrom, 1990, 2015). Democracy in particular shapes civil society in dozens of ways. Democracies typically have stronger civil society organizations than non-democracies because democratic governments allow and may encourage civil society organizations and political participation while most non-democratic regimes actively repress civil society (Cross, 1998, Elyachar, 2005, Touchton et al., 2017). Research on informality expects informal workers to organize more in democratic regimes (Agarwala, 2013). We can evaluate this contention with fixed effects logistic regressions on the four survey data sets and the polyarchy index from the Varieties of Democracy project.

Table 3.12 Democracy and informal workers' organizations

	LAPOP known informal workers	LAPOP likely informal workers	LAPOP self-employed workers	CSES likely informal workers
Education	.055*	.056*	.059*	.085*
	(.009)	(.006)	(.008)	(.044)
State capacity	−.333*	−.207*	−.189*	−1.631
index	(.153)	(.061)	(.048)	(.445)
Democracy	1.426	1.524	1.342	41.060
	(1.379)	(1.128)	(.944)	(52.833)
Women	−.555*	−.458*	−.441*	−.188
	(.058)	(.073)	(.064)	(.118)
Urban	−.670*	−.605*	−.613*	−.497*
	(.096)	(.081)	(.070)	(.240)
Household	.006	.003	−.020	.094
wealth	(.020)	(.016)	(.017)	(.052)
Age	.059*	.061*	.050*	.094*
	(.009)	(.007)	(.008)	(.028)
Age squared	−.001*	−.001*	−.001*	−.001*
	(.000)	(.000)	(.000)	(.000)
	N = 15,783	N = 39,572	N = 30,515	N = 4,776
	Countries = 20	Countries = 21	Countries = 21	Countries = 31
Year and country fixed effects suppressed.				

Standard errors in parentheses below coefficients. All tests are two-tailed.
*$p \leq .05$

Democracy has a positive but statistically insignificant effect on the probability that a given informal worker participated in an association or union in the last year in Table 3.12. Note that the table reports coefficients in log-odds, which are not directly interpretable. The state capacity index and education remain significant and in the expected directions when accounting for democracy. However, these analyses do not prove that democracy has no impact on informal workers' organizations: we have few observations and little variation in the democracy variable in this sample as all countries are nominally democratic. A larger sample of countries or years may yield different results.

Table 3.13 Political competition and informal workers' organizations

	LAPOP known informal workers	LAPOP likely informal workers	LAPOP self-employed workers	CSES likely informal workers
Education	.055*	.056*	.059*	.084
	(.009)	(.006)	(.007)	(.044)
State capacity	−.394*	−.219*	−.195*	25.214*
index	(.175)	(.031)	(.037)	(1.055)
Party	.184	−.175	−.041	28.264*
Competition	(1.053)	(.853)	(.765)	(.995)
Women	−.556*	−.459*	−.442*	−.188
	(.058)	(.073)	(.063)	(.118)
Urban	−.604*	−.604*	−.612*	−.497*
	(.096)	(.082)	(.071)	(.241)
Household	.006	.003	−.002	.094*
wealth	(.021)	(.016)	(.018)	(.028)
Age	.061*	.061*	.050*	.095*
	(.010)	(.007)	(.008)	(.028)
Age squared	−.001*	−.001*	−.001*	−.001*
	(.000)	(.000)	(.000)	(.000)
	N = 15,783	N = 39,572	N = 30,515	N = 4,776
	Countries = 20	Countries = 21	Countries = 21	Countries = 31
Year and country fixed effects suppressed.				

Standard errors in parentheses below coefficients. All tests are two-tailed.
*$p \leq .05$

Democracy has many dimensions. A number of researchers attribute part of the positive effects of democracy on well-being to political competition (Coppedge et al., 2011, Berliner and Erlich, 2015, Gerring et al., 2012). Research on informality expects that parties court informal workers more aggressively in places with many informal workers and more political competition (Agarwala, 2013, Holland, 2017). The Varieties of Democracy project has a party competition variable that we can include in the fixed effects analyses to evaluate if overall political competition affects the probability of participating in an informal workers' organization.

Table 3.13 reports log-odds coefficients for political competition, variables of theoretical interest, and controls on the probability of a given informal worker attending an organizational meeting. Political competition is not statistically significant in most models and the direction of the effects jumps around between data sets. At least with this measure, inter-party competition does not appear to have a notable effect on informal worker organization.

Another alternative explanation is that officials encourage informal workers' organizations because the organizations help officials buy votes or support. We can evaluate this possibility with the Varieties of Democracy data on the prevalence of vote buying in a country during election years. We include this variable in the models and see how it affects the association between education, state capacity, and informal worker organizations. Table 3.14 evaluates this explanation with fixed effects models of the four survey data sets.

Vote buying is statistically significant in two models, but changes signs. Keep in mind that the table reports coefficients in log-odds, which are not directly interpretable. For known informal workers in the LAPOP data set, vote buying in election years decreases the probability of attending meetings the previous year, while the opposite is true for likely informal workers in the CSES data set. While education and state capacity remain significant and in the expected directions for most models, state capacity promotes organization in one model and education is insignificant in another. Note that these analyses include fewer respondents than the other analyses because Varieties of Democracy collects vote buying data for election years only. Thus, the relationships may change because the sample is different. These results suggest that vote buying and clientelism may play a role in informal workers' organizing decisions, but the results are not robust or consistent.

The introductory chapter discussed the possibility that grassroots activists create and drive informal workers' organizations and then engage officials. We can evaluate this possibility with data on civil society participation. The Varieties of Democracy data set has a comprehensive index of civil society strength and participation that tracks the types of civil society organizations in a given country, their membership, and their influence in the political system. We can use this index to proxy the larger context of activism in a country and evaluate if more civil society activism explains higher levels of informal worker activism.

The analyses in Table 3.15 show that civil society breadth and influence is an important predictor of informal workers' organizing activity. The civil society index is positive and significant in every model and the effect, reported in log-odds, is relatively large. The results demonstrate that individual resources

Table 3.14 Vote buying and informal workers' organizations

	LAPOP known informal workers	LAPOP likely informal workers	LAPOP self-employed workers	CSES likely informal workers
Education	.053*	.059*	.059*	.057
	(.009)	(.009)	(.007)	(.042)
State capacity	1.119*	−.450*	−.436*	−5.33*
index	(.064)	(.023)	(.037)	(.133)
Vote buying	−6.032*	−.180	−.170	.509*
	(.233)	(.160)	(.175)	(.066)
Women	−.613*	−.557*	−.544*	−.160
	(.119)	(.112)	(.098)	(.122)
Urban	−.438*	−.556*	−.626*	−.553*
	(.097)	(.114)	(.108)	(.122)
Household	.009	.010	−.002	.082
wealth	(.026)	(.018)	(.020)	(.054)
Age	.054*	.058*	.051*	.105*
	(.001)	(.009)	(.008)	(.031)
Age squared	−.001*	−.001*	−.001*	−.001*
	(.000)	(.000)	(.000)	(.000)
	N = 5,979	N = 11,531	N = 9,182	N = 4,434
	Countries = 11	Countries = 14	Countries = 14	Countries = 27
Year and country fixed effects suppressed.				

Standard errors in parentheses below coefficients. All tests are two-tailed.
*$p \leq .05$

and state capacity remain important and largely statistically significant predictors of informal workers' organizations, even when accounting for the broader civil society environment. While these factors help explain informal workers' organizations, they do not reduce the explanatory power of state capacity or individual resources. These factors, along with gender, family, and location, contribute to a comprehensive picture of why some informal workers organize more than others.

The descriptive statistics and regression analyses on the data sets of informal and self-employed workers establish broad, cross-national patterns in line with the theory. The patterns are consistent across data sets and statistical models: informal workers appear to organize more often in lower capacity contexts and when they have more resources. Still, the cross-national analyses on survey data raise additional questions about why we see these patterns and how informal workers make organizing decisions.

3.4 Case Selection

Case studies of how officials, informal workers, and their organizations interact and develop over time can address more detailed questions about exactly how and why informal workers organize. Interviews, participant observation, and documents offer more detailed answers than the numeric survey data that this

Table 3.15 Civil society and informal workers' organizations

	LAPOP known informal workers	LAPOP likely informal workers	LAPOP self-employed workers	CSES likely informal workers
Education	.055*	.056*	.058*	.085
	(.009)	(.006)	(.008)	(.044)
State capacity index	−.236	−.209*	−.184*	−2.855*
	(.191)	(.045)	(.035)	(.583)
Civil society	2.366*	2.102*	2.213*	20.738*
	(1.184)	(1.007)	(1.005)	(8.162)
Women	−.556*	−.459*	−.442*	−.188
	(.058)	(.073)	(.063)	(.118)
Urban	−.605*	−.603*	−.612*	−.497*
	(.096)	(.082)	(.071)	(.240)
Household wealth	.006	.003	−.002	.094
	(.020)	(.016)	(.018)	(.052)
Age	.060*	.061*	.050*	.094*
	(.001)	(.007)	(.008)	(.028)
Age squared	−.001*	−.001*	−.001*	−.001*
	(.000)	(.000)	(.000)	(.000)
	N = 15,783	N = 39,572	N = 30,515	N = 4,776
	Countries = 20	Countries = 21	Countries = 21	Countries = 31
Year and country fixed effects suppressed.				

Standard errors in parentheses below coefficients. All tests are two-tailed.
*$p \leq .05$

Table 3.16 Informal workers' organizations in Bolivia

	LAPOP known informal workers	LAPOP likely informal workers	LAPOP self-employed workers
Education	.034*	.038*	.028*
	(.016)	(.008)	(.010)
State capacity		−.922*	−.903*
index		(.133)	(.152)
Women	−.309*	−.198*	−.258*
	(.128)	(.069)	(.079)
Urban	−1.014*	−.653*	−.686*
	(.146)	(.077)	(.087)
Household	.006	.034	.052
wealth	(.049)	(.027)	(.031)
Age	.115*	.085*	.083*
	(.026)	(.014)	(.016)
Age squared	−.001*	−.001*	−.001*
	(.000)	(.000)	(.000)
	N = 1,215	N = 4,377	N = 3,285

Standard errors in parentheses below coefficients. All tests are two-tailed.
*$p \leq .05$

chapter analyzes. The survey data can help us make principled choices about which cases to examine in depth.

Pathway cases illustrate a broader theory and illuminate the causal process (Gerring, 2017). Logistic regression analyses demonstrate that Bolivia and Brazil function as pathway cases for the theory. In the single country analyses in Tables 3.16 and 3.17, the variables of interest, education, and state capacity are significant and in the expected directions: higher levels of education and lower scores on the capacity index are associated with more organizational participation in Bolivia and Brazil.

Bolivia supplies more informal workers to the LAPOP data sets than any other country and frequently tops global rankings of informality (Bajada and Schneider, 2018). Bolivia has some of the lowest GDP per capita numbers in the Americas and a notoriously low-capacity state. Levels of education, as well as social and material capital, have been improving across Bolivia, and Bolivian

Table 3.17 Informal workers' organizations in Brazil

	LAPOP known informal workers	LAPOP likely informal Workers	LAPOP self-employed workers
Education	.125*	.109*	.110*
	(.034)	(.021)	(.025)
State capacity		−2.008*	−1.716*
index		(.361)	(.436)
Women	−.754*	−.198*	−.773*
	(.261)	(.150)	(.1859)
Urban	−1.984*	−1.509*	−1.892*
	(.291)	(.165)	(.201)
Household	−.082	−.130*	−.110
wealth	(.102)	(.061)	(.070)
Age	.116*	.065*	.079*
	(.050)	(.030)	(.039)
Age squared	−.001	−.001	−.001
	(.001)	(.001)	(.001)
	N = 483	N = 1,844	N = 1,166

Standard errors in parentheses below coefficients. All tests are two-tailed.
$^{*}p \leq .05$

respondents in the data set exhibit a range of resources.[5] Bolivia is an important case to understand and an exemplary pathway case for this theory. Note that in Tables 3.16 and 3.17, state capacity is omitted in the known worker data set because there was only one year of survey data collected in both countries and thus one value for state capacity.

Bolivian informal workers illustrate the argument across individuals and for officials working with low levels of state capacity. However, we need another case to investigate the argument in higher capacity contexts. Brazil introduces more variation in state capacity and illustrates the argument for informal workers working in higher capacity areas. The theory predicts low levels of organization among Brazil's informal workers because the Brazilian state is comparatively strong and invests heavily in direct enforcement. Additionally,

[5] Pathway cases illustrate theories, but they do not test them. While some political scientists caution against selecting on the dependent variable when testing theories, other methodologists note that selecting on the independent and dependent variables is appropriate for theory development in pathway cases.

Pamplona (2013) finds that informal workers in Brazil have low levels of education compared to other working Brazilians. Brazilian informal workers organize below the median level of organization for the region. As the largest country in the region, Brazil is a useful and important pathway case to analyze. Logistic regressions in Table 3.17 report estimates for the variables of interest.

The analyses in Tables 3.16 and 3.17 point to a consistent pattern across the region and within the cases of Bolivia and Brazil. Interviews and participant observation with informal workers and officials in Bolivia and Brazil can demonstrate why these patterns emerge. Additionally, careful qualitative work can adjudicate between possible alternative explanations for the patterns in the quantitative data.

The qualitative cases focus on cities within these two countries because the officials that informal workers interact with are primarily city-level officials. In most places, national officials shape the economic and labor market policies that push people into or out of the informal sector (Gerxhani, 2004). Once in the informal sector, city officials have immense amounts of discretion over the licensing, regulation, and enforcement policies that informal workers contend with (Bhowmik, 2012). These decisions can encourage informal workers to organize or discourage them from collective action. As decentralization and municipal reforms spread around the world, city officials in Bolivia, Brazil and many other places have the political and financial power to change informal workers' lives (Post, 2018). In places like La Paz and El Alto, Bolivia, officials make and implement policy that enriches some informal workers while impoverishing others. In places like São Paulo and Rio de Janeiro, Brazil, or Miami and New York City in the United States, city officials make and enforce policies that preserve some workers' livelihoods while ending the lives of others. These power dynamics make city-level officials and city-level policy the appropriate level of analysis for the qualitative case studies.

To conclude the chapter, I argue that officials and informal workers interact to encourage civil society participation in some places but not others. I suggest that where governments do not have the capacity to enforce regulations, officials offer incentives to workers to form and join civil society organizations that regulate daily life. Informal workers who have the education and other resources to harness these incentives may then opt to participate and negotiate collectively with the state. In support of the theory, this chapter presents regression analyses on survey data from self-employed and informal workers across the world. The data demonstrate that informal workers organize in nearly every country for which we have data.

The regression analyses in this chapter suggest that more education and a lower capacity government encourage informal and self-employed workers to participate in work-based organizations. In the following chapters, ethnographic case studies of officials, street vendors, and their organizatons in the La Paz, Bolivia and the São Paulo, Brazil metropolitan areas illustrate how the theory applies to people's lives and livelihoods.

4

Street Markets in La Paz and São Paulo

This chapter establishes the political, economic, and social incentive structures that officials and street vendors contend with in the La Paz and São Paulo metropolitan areas. It develops and demonstrates the array of positive and negative incentives that officials and street vendors use to shape organizations. It matches the broad expectations from the models in Chapters 2 and 3 to finer grained ethnographic, interview, and survey data from the cases. The chapter discusses the history and structure of markets and street vendor unions in greater La Paz and São Paulo. The cases compare central La Paz to the poorer neighboring city of El Alto and downtown São Paulo to a peripheral district. Officials and vendors in the four cases operate under different local governments. I rely on original interviews with officials and street vendor leaders as well as published oral histories and secondary literature to construct a history of these organizations. I then use ethnographic data from La Paz to demonstrate that the modeling choices and assumptions in Chapter 2 are grounded in street vendors' experiences. In sum, this chapter suggests how officials' interventions vary over time, creating a history of highly structured organizations around La Paz and fleeting organizations around São Paulo.

4.1 A History of Market Organizations in La Paz

In La Paz, Bolivia, the crowded western market district begins at the Witches' Market off Sarganaga Street, extends through the Black Market on Graneros Street and the Tumusla Street clothing market and peters out after the produce, flower, skull, and tattoo vendors in the streets around the cemetery. Around 60,000 people – 5 percent of the capital's population – work as street vendors and 31,906 of these hold vending licenses from the city's Markets Office (Paz, 2015). Of La Paz's street vendors, a staggering 75 percent belong to a street vendor organization. Street vendors are part of the approximately 80 percent of working-age people in Bolivia who hold informal jobs (Bolivia, 2013). Shamans, photographers, tattoo artists, shoeshine boys, and bakers all work as

Why Informal Workers Organize. Calla Hummel, Oxford University Press.
© Calla Hummel (2021). DOI: 10.1093/oso/9780192847812.003.0004

street vendors in La Paz and the hundreds of associations they belong to are just as varied: there is a wisemen's union and several champagne ladies' associations, as well as the more common micro-retailers' unions and bread vendors' associations. Each association belongs to one of several citywide federations, which are affiliated with the Bolivian Labor Central or the Confederation of Street Vendors of Bolivia.

Many people in La Paz make a decades-long career out of street vending, while others rotate in and out of the occupation to fill gaps in employment and make ends meet. Established vendors sell high profit margin products like clothes and beauty products at licensed stalls, which can be permanent kiosks, called *anaqueles*, carts, or tents and platforms, called *tarimas*, that are reassembled every day. Less established vendors walk continuously while selling anything from gum to plants to coat hangers from small boxes or sacks. Most vendors make roughly minimum wage, but a significant minority make a middle class living – for example, 34 percent of the street vendors who I surveyed in La Paz were homeowners – and a few have become wealthy (Tassi et al., 2013).

In 1972, 70 street vendor leaders from the La Paz department[1] founded the *Confederación Sindical de Trabajadores Gremiales, Artesanos, Comerciantes Minoristas y Vivanderos de Bolivia* or the National Confederation of Street Vendors, Small Retailers, Artisans, and Food Sellers of Bolivia (from here on referred to as the National Confederation of Street Vendors or the Confederation). The Confederation is an autonomous organization by and for street vendors that brings street vendor issues to the national government (Rojas, 1992, p.122). The Confederation likely represents between 200,000 and 300,000 street vendors around the country, which would make it one of the largest street vendor organizations in the world and potentially the largest proportional to national population. Over the decades, the Confederation's power has waxed and waned. While it has occasionally allied with specific administrations (Rojas, 1992, pp.118–123), it remains a largely grassroots labor organization.

The Confederation's membership rolls boomed after the passage of Decree 21060 in 1985 (Pereira Morató, 2008, p.1). The law was the centerpiece of a package of economic and political reforms, supported by international organizations and Bolivia's creditors, that was designed to stop runaway inflation and prevent worse economic crises in the future (Kohl and Farthing, 2006, p.73). In a massive blow to labor and formal employment, the law closed many

[1] In Bolivia, a department is a subnational administrative designation similar to a U.S. state.

of Bolivia's state-run mines and dismissed thousands of unionized government workers (Anria, 2018). The reforms did stop inflation and Bolivia has not experienced as profound an economic crisis since, but the solution cost the country's poor and middle class their savings and their jobs. Tens of thousands of people turned to street vending because it was an occupation that any person could try and that could bring cash into a household every day (Pereira Morató, 2008, p.2). Pereira Morató (2008, p.1) uses municipal records and interviews to estimate that in 1951, La Paz had 369 street vendors. In the 1980s, that number had ballooned to 18,217. The rate of the sector's growth started to steady in the 2000s after reaching nearly 40,000 in 2003 (Pereira Morató, 2008, p.1). The number of street vendors continues to grow and the city government estimated in 2018 that over 60,000 people worked regularly as street vendors.

On the plains above La Paz sits El Alto, a growing, indigenous, self-built city (Arbona and Kohl, 2004, Lazar, 2007a, Tassi et al., 2015). Ringed by Andean peaks, El Alto sprawls across the flat, windswept *altiplano* while La Paz sits in a protected and considerably warmer river canyon below. For much of La Paz's colonial history, the city government prohibited the indigenous population from living in the city center (Kohl and Farthing, 2006, p.41). Families settled on the precarious slopes of the canyon, creeping upward toward the canyon rim. Immigration from other parts of the *altiplano* and expanding water services built communities on the plateau in the 1900s (Arbona and Kohl, 2004, p.258). As internal migration increased in the second half of the twentieth century, El Alto transformed into a booming satellite community and separated administratively from La Paz in 1985 (Arbona and Kohl, 2004, p.262).

Long considered a *ciudad dormitorio* or bedroom community, El Alto became a social, political, and economic powerhouse in the 1990s and 2000s (Arbona and Kohl, 2004, p.258, 261). Most of the La Paz metropolitan area's industry and manufacturing started in or moved to El Alto to take advantage of the city's cheaper land and labor (Tassi et al., 2013, pp.5, 15, 226). Activists quickly learned that the city's placement between the capital, the international airport, and major highways made it possible to shut down the capital city with a couple hundred people and a few barricades (Dangl, 2007, pp.139–140). Its neighborhood associations and unions, particularly the Federation of Street Vendors of El Alto, played a major role in the 2003 gas war that barricaded the capital, toppled the government, and is widely credited to have brought Evo Morales, the country's first indigenous president, to power (Anria, 2018, Farthing and Kohl, 2014, Madrid, 2012).

The National Confederation of Street Vendors has its headquarters in El Alto, in a historic building above the offices of the *Central Obrero Regional*, or the El Alto Regional Labor Central, and the *Federación de Juntas Vecinales*, the Federation of Neighborhood Associations. Together, these three organizations represent most of the city's residents and El Alto's social and political power on the local and national stage (Lazar, 2007a, pp.12, 53–56).

The Confederation has negotiated and worked with the city government since its founding. The relationship between the Confederation and the city alternates between amicable and openly hostile. After a particularly bitter end to one city administration (Lazar, 2007a, p.115), the *Movimiento al Socialismo* (MAS) party ran street vendor leader Edgar Patana as its candidate for mayor. Patana is a former Regional Labor Center director and Confederation leader who sold books in the large 16 de Julio market in downtown El Alto. At the height of the Confederation's local and national power, Patana won two elections and served as mayor from 2006 until 2015.

4.2 A History of Street Vending in São Paulo

Across the continent sits São Paulo, the largest city in the southern hemisphere. Twelve million people live within the city limits and another two dozen neighboring municipalities bring the metropolitan area's population to 22 million. The city sprawls out over central São Paulo state, in southeastern Brazil. Street markets grew with the city over the decades, providing newcomers and professional street vendors with cash incomes. In 1953, Decree 2201 designated disabled street vendors and older street vendors as demographic categories that the city should give preference to in licensing (Itikawa, 2010, p.250). Pressures started to increase in the street markets and on the city council in the 1970s, as sustained urban migration pushed the city's vendors to a 40,000-person workforce competing for one of 1350 licenses (Itikawa, 2010, p.250). Increased pressures and rising unemployment led to a change in street vending policy in 1991, which recognized street vendors as workers with rights to city services and set out criteria for obtaining a license, maintaining preferences for disabled and older workers (Pamplona, 2013, p.230). While the law is still in force, later administrations have maintained some rights for licensed vendors while restricting licenses and increasing police activity targeting unlicensed street vendors.

São Paulo has hundreds of market areas and over 100,000 street vendors (Pamplona, 2013). The most concentrated and important street markets sit in the historic city center, though most districts have their own unofficial market center and nearly every neighborhood has a roving, once-a-week produce and household goods street market, known as a *feira*. In the central São Paulo district of Vila Velha, thousands of street vendors work from pre-dawn until well after midnight. They sell consumer goods from around the world, counterfeits, food, and artisan crafts. Two markets see the most activity and supply the rest of the country with cheap consumer commodities, especially clothes: a street market at the center of Vila Velha and an adjacent wholesale market. After a years-long battle with the city government, in which the government prevailed, the wholesale market now sits in a hangar a mile away from Vila Velha.

Four blocks make up most of Vila Velha's main street market. The area is full of warehouses, wholesale stores, and informal malls filled with stalls selling counterfeits. The stores are largely owned by businesspeople from successive waves of immigration from Asia, the Middle East, Europe, and other parts of Latin America. On the street, primarily Brazilian street vendors lead the zone's small retail businesses.

Two hours away by bus and train, the working-class district of Princesa Isabela sits on the city's eastern edge. Under the city government's decentralized district system, Princesa Isabela operates under its own local government, which has regulatory, licensing, and enforcement authority over markets and street vendors. Like many far-flung working class districts, Princesa Isabela has a municipal market building in the center of the district and an open air street market by the bus and train stations. Commuters pass through these commercial areas on their way to and from work in other parts of São Paulo.

Other parts of the district have open air neighborhood markets and mobile street vendors. The district government estimates that at least 800 people work primarily as street vendors in the district and many more work occassionally or part time in the markets. Around 200 are licensed by the city and another 300 are licensed by the district. The district regulates street commerce and enforces the hundreds of relevant laws around street vending.

4.3 Who Are Street Vendors?

Who are the people who work as street vendors in these cities? The average[2] street vendor who we surveyed in São Paulo worked as a career street vendor, held a license for a clothing stall, is middle-aged, did not finish high school and did not belong to a street vendor organization. The unlicensed vendors

[2] This composite holds continuous variables at their means and uses the most common category for categorical variables.

who we interviewed were younger, rotated between formal and informal work, and none belonged to a street vendor organization. About 50 percent of street vendors in São Paulo identified as women and 50 percent identified as men. The demographics between street vendors in central Vila Velha and peripheral Princesa Isabela were similar.

The average street vendor who we surveyed in La Paz held a license for a food stall, belonged to a street vendor association but did not identify with a political party, and had worked as a vendor for 23 years. Demographically, she was a 45-year-old woman of indigenous descent who completed eight years of school[3] and who owns a television, refrigerator, and cell phone but does not have a vehicle or regular internet access. Women comprise 80 percent of street vendors in La Paz, though as vending has become more profitable, more men have joined and are overrepresented in leadership (Hummel, 2016). Figure 4.1 summarizes descriptive statistics from the street vendor survey.

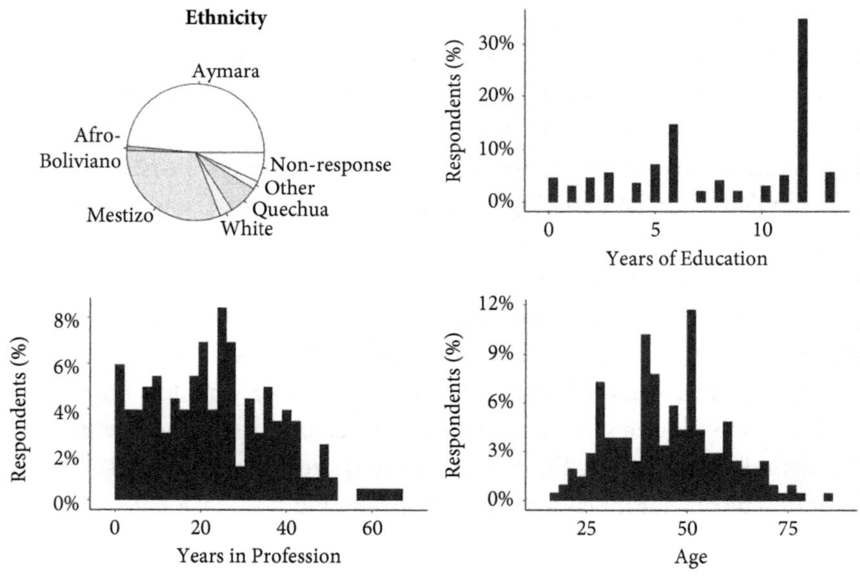

Fig. 4.1 Descriptive statistics from La Paz's street vending sector

In other words, the average vendor in La Paz is a career street vendor who makes enough to get by and has some social capital. Most street vendors in La Paz appear to fit this profile. However, the survey data contain a wide range of

[3] The average is eight, but the distribution is skewed. Thirty percent completed high school, which is the highest bar in Figure 4.1's education histogram. The second highest bar is at the end of primary school.

demographics and experiences. Some vendors work for subsintence-level profits and are one bad week away from financial ruin, though most street vendors enjoy more stability. On the other hand, some make a comfortable living, have bought plots of land, and built houses. Similarly, while street vendors on average are much older than most of Bolivia's economically active population, many street vendors started working as children and many seniors return to street vending after they have officially retired. Interviews with street vendor in El Alto suggested that the average street vendor in El Alto was similar to the average street vendor in La Paz. However, nearly all street vendors in El Alto belong to a street vendor organization and hold a license.

4.3.1 The Structure of Street Vendor Organizations

In El Alto and La Paz, all street vendor organizations that I came into contact with followed a remarkably similar structure and use nearly identical operational procedures. The organizations that Tassi et al. (2013, chapter 4), Lazar (2007, chapter 6), and Goldstein (2016, prologue) worked with in Santa Cruz, El Alto, and Cochabamba followed very similar organizational structures as well. These structures reflect union practices across Bolivia as well as practices common in Bolivian labor history (Anria, 2018, Dibbits et al., 1986, Peredo Beltrán, 1992). While there are many similarities between organizations, the extent to which leaders and members follow each group's rules and uphold democratic principles varies widely.

In contrast, the street vendor organizations in central and peripheral São Paulo rarely had clear bylaws and followed the preferences and directives of specific leaders. They had little structure and did not have regular meetings. None of the street vendor organizations that I came into contact with in São Paulo worked on clear democratic principles.[4] Luciana Itikawa's extensive work (2006, 2010) with street vendors in São Paulo documents few organizations and characterizes them as personalistic and fleeting (2010, pp.342–345).

Princesa Isabela has a history of street vendor organizations stretching back to the 1970s. The organizations have engaged with the district and city governments several times and sometimes won policy concessions or reversals. However, the organizations largely depend on the informal leadership of a

[4] The possible exception was a group set up by an NGO that tried to teach democratic decision-making to street vendor leaders, but this group was not an organization by and for street vendors as the other organizations were.

few charismatic men, who may pass on the organization to designated successors. The organizations do not meet regularly and do not have an established or dues-paying membership base. While the Princesa Isabela organizations are less predatory and more efficacious than some organizations in central São Paulo, they are not institutionalized to the same degree as Bolivian street vendor organizations.

Street vendor unions in Bolivia are highly organized and politically sophisticated groups. Interviews, interactions, and participant observation at official and unofficial meetings established a typical trajectory and structure for street vendor unions in La Paz and El Alto. Once a group of unaffiliated street vendors decides to found a new union, they buy a *libro de actas*, or book of acts, and write a founding statement. All founding members sign the statement, which may also be signed by a federation or confederation leader. Under Bolivian law, a group needs 24 members to register as a union. Many but not all organizations try to round up 24 founding members to meet this requirement. Most street vendor organizations eventually register as unions because official unions receive *personería jurídica*, legal personhood, and this extra document from the Labor Ministry facilitates some bureaucratic processes and gives leaders more standing with officials.

Once the group has a founding document, the members elect a *secretaría general* or general director as leader. The group typically elects additional officers as well. Practically all groups have a *secretaría de hacienda*, or treasurer, and a *secretaría de actas*, or record keeper, who records all of the group's activity and is in charge of documents. The treasurer or record keeper can act as a vice president of the group, or the union can elect a *secretaría de relaciones* or public relations director, who may also corral members or act as a second-in-command representative to officials. Larger groups may have a *secretaría de organización* or organizational director, whose job is to call meetings and make sure members attend. Groups commonly also elect a press secretary, a health secretary, who collects donations from members if another member gets sick, a sports secretary, who organizes social events for the group, and a standard bearer, who carries the group's pennant in parades. Organizations can also have appointed or elected *fiscales*. *Fiscales* are former leaders who form a semi-independent oversight committee to investigate allegations of corruption or abuse. Finally, the group may designate spokespeople and alternate representatives to attend bureaucratic or federation meetings. These one to 20-odd elected positions constitute the group's *directorio*, or elected leadership committee, which must be present to make demands to the government, represent the group to larger groups, and make decisions with members.

Groups then decide on their bylaws. Established unions or larger city or state federations often suggest a standard collection of bylaws. These bylaws include but are not limited to: the terms of all elected leaders (typically two years), how leaders call elections, how many members must be present for quorum, how frequently the membership meets, dues and how often dues are paid, the procedure for admitting new members (typically a membership-wide vote), what behavioral and business rules members agree to abide by, how to resolve disputes between members (typically a hearing in front of the full elected leadership committee), and a graduated schedule of sanctions for members who break the rules.

Once street vendors form an association or union, they can admit new members. Each group has their own process written into the bylaws. In a typical process, a prospective member approaches the elected leadership committee with a letter of intent. If accepted, the prospective member then presents their case to the full membership in a meeting. The membership then votes on their candidacy. If approved, the new member pays a joining fee, which can range from a few hundred *bolivianos* to a few thousand dollars. Some groups actively recruit new people, while others are highly restrictive. For example, Elena's food vendors' union from Chapter 2 capped the number of members decades ago and will only add a new affiliate if an older member retires or dies. In other words, street vendor unions in La Paz are selective and highly structured groups that actively and extensively screen their members.

Sanctions for breaking the rules are standardized. If a member catches another member breaking a rule, she is supposed to report the offending member to the leadership committee. The leadership committee then calls the member to a meeting where she can present her case. Making a case can involve photographic evidence, witness testimonies, testimony of hardship, or a heated argument. If the leadership committee decides that a member has broken a rule, they can levy a fine or bar the member from selling for a number of days. Many bylaws let vendors choose between paying a fine or not selling. While fines vary widely in amount – and the leadership committee may levy fines proportional to individual members' income or offense – suspensions are more standardized: for a first offense, a street vendor cannot sell for five days. For a second offense, they cannot sell for 15 days. For a third offense, they may be expelled from the union and the union leadership may make a formal request for the Markets Office to revoke the offending street vendor's license.

In practice, different groups vary widely in how closely they follow their bylaws. Likewise, some groups are extremely democratic, while others exist as a club or cash cow for a long-term leader.[5] On the democratic side, some groups do not formally elect leaders but instead rotate leadership, and all members are required to serve for two-year terms when it is their turn. For example, the small *champañeras* – champagne sellers – union consists of 12 affiliated champagne sellers and photographers and functions more as a cooperative with jointly held property than a union. Technically, all members vote on leaders and decisions, but the group typically reaches a consensus before making a decision. On the other hand, another union that I worked with had been headed by the same person for over 30 years who had a reputation for intimidation, particularly through arson. She was reelected every time she called an election, which was sometimes every two years, as stipulated in the bylaws, and sometimes not. As members left the union, she often appropriated their stalls for herself or her family. Across La Paz and El Alto, plenty of other groups exhibit an impressive level of deliberative democracy, like the *champañeras*, or a discouraging level of corruption, like the arsonist's association, and plenty more fall somewhere in between.

4.3.2 The La Paz Markets Office and Municipal Guard

The La Paz city government runs the administrative capital of Bolivia on a tight budget of $322 million dollars a year, according to the public budget the city released for 2017. The mayor's office oversees a professionalized city bureaucracy that delivers a wide variety of goods and services to the population of roughly one million. The bureaucracy includes several offices that are important to street vendors' businesses and organizations, including the Municipal Guard and the Markets Office.

Juan del Granado's centrist *Movimiento Sin Miedo* (MSM) party and its allies have controlled the city government since 2001 and significantly reformed the city bureaucracy. Del Granado won the 2000 mayoral race on a reformist platform, and the administration lived up to many of its original campaign promises. The party changed its name to Sol.bo after losing its national registration[6] for Juan del Granado's abysmal performance in the 2014 presidential elections. Del Granado passed the city administration to Luis Revilla in 2010, who was elected mayor in 2015. Revilla did not run in the 2021 mayoral race

[5] Grossman (2020) has found similar variation in Nigerian street vendor associations.

[6] Under Bolivian law, parties must get at least 5 percent of the national vote to maintain their registration. Juan del Granado received around 3 percent of the vote in the 2014 presidential election. Local parties like MSM that perform well in municipal elections but not national ones typically rename themselves, maintain their structure and personnel, and resubmit their paperwork.

and handed the administration to mayor Iván Arias. The administration reduced corruption by firing scores of employees, reorganizing existing offices, and creating new ones (Zúñiga and Heywood, 2015).

For example, prior to 2001, municipal law enforcement was notorious for taking small bribes from street vendors. The Markets Office did not exist. Street vendors in previous administrations made appeals directly to the mayor. In 2001, del Granado disbanded the city police and recreated the office by founding the Municipal Guard. New personnel were hired on renewable contracts that were much easier to terminate in the event of complaints. Del Granado also created the Markets Office to organize markets and engage with the city's street vendors.

The Markets Office employs over 70 full-time bureaucrats, who work in crumbling offices above a neighborhood market. The Markets Office operating budget was $200,000 dollars in 2017 and it largely pays for itself with licensing fees, according to its personnel. The director of the Markets Office holds considerable power over the city's 31,906 licensed street vendors and the 30,000-odd unlicensed street vendors. The director of the Markets Office oversees two divisions within the office, the Markets Division and the Street Commerce Division. The Markets Division administers the city's 87 physical market buildings and the thousands of market vendors who work within them. The larger and more contentious Street Commerce Division oversees the 31,906 licensed street vendors, their organizations, and the many unlicensed street vendors who petition the division for permits. The Markets Office employs a technical group of lawyers, architects, and engineers to assist the inspectors and officials in both divisions. The technocrats do their best to implement city policy to the letter, while the directorship of the office is a political appointment charged with building, maintaining, and controlling civil society support for the city government and its projects.

In contrast, the Municipal Guard employs around 150 guards who work out of offices and barracks within a new market building in the center of the city. Commanders from the national police, which is a division of the military and under the control of the Department of Defense, oversee the Municipal Guard. Police commanders regularly rotate in and out of the Municipal Guard leadership, spending a couple of months to a couple of years in rotation.[7] The guards themselves are hired on renewable short-term contracts after passing a competitive public entrance exam and a month of training. Guards stay for

[7] The national police are notoriously corrupt and the least trusted government institution in Bolivia. The rotations are designed to limit corruption.

years and receive raises with seniority, but they can be and are fired for citizen complaints or for violating any of the terms of their contracts. The guards are organized into a Transportation Division, a Government Installations Division, and a Street Commerce Division. The Street Commerce Division is the largest, with about 100 people, and is split into a foot patrol group that patrols a regular beat through busy market areas, a motorcycle patrol group that covers the entire city, and an operations group, which goes as a large group to remove repeat offenders.

The La Paz city government administers the country's main urban center on a shoestring budget. The city organizes and manages a large street vending sector through two offices: the bureaucratic Markets Office and the enforcement-focused Municipal Guard. Despite two offices dedicated to street vending, the 70 Markets Office officials and the 100 municipal guards assigned to street commerce cannot monitor and sanction over 60,000 street vendors across the city. These offices work with street vendor organizations to manage informal commerce in the city and make the city governable.

El Alto's city government structure is similar to La Paz, but with fewer personnel, a smaller budget, and haphazard infrastructure. For decades, El Alto voters have supported candidates who promise reform, representation, and better city infrastructure, but no administration has successfully delivered on its campaign promises. The city is expanding at a breakneck pace and the local government struggles to keep up. The city has added offices and administrators to cover more issues and neighborhoods, but largely delegates to powerful and highly organized civil society groups.

As the city government has grown, new offices have sprung up in unmarked, rented buildings across El Alto. The old Markets Office had perhaps six employees in 2012 and sat on the third floor of an office building in downtown El Alto, sharing space with the sports department and a public health office. In 2015, the office had a few more employees sharing the same space, but few showed up to work. By 2018, the new city government had moved the Markets Office to another, larger space in a different unmarked building in downtown El Alto. In 2019, the office moved yet again, into its own space on the edge of downtown. Employees showed up to work but the office was still unmarked and difficult to navigate. City employees appeared more adept at turning citizens away than providing help or accurate information. In interviews several years apart, city employees did not know the answers to questions about street vending regulations and recommended that I ask the Federation of Street Vendors of El Alto for that information. The El Alto city government also employs a civil force of Municipal Guards. However, the El Alto Municipal Guard focuses on traffic more than markets.

4.3.3 São Paulo's Enforcement Apparatus

Across the continent, successive São Paulo administrations have intervened in street vending with a heavy hand. A powerful mayoral office leads the São Paulo city government and the mayor's position is a storied springboard into national politics. Brazil's booming business capital alternates between right- and left-of-center administrations with ambitious plans for the metropolis. Some administrations have followed through with their plans and campaign promises. When these promises include calls to clean up the city, street vendors often suffer.

Under the mayor, the city government is divided into district governments. The district governments have been reorganized several times in the last few decades during local power struggles. During fieldwork in 2012, the district governments under Gilberto Kassab were sub-mayors. Kassab's sub-mayors were largely retired military and police captains who ran their districts with considerable autonomy. Successive administrations have replaced Kassab's captains with their own bureaucratic and political appointees and renamed the district government office. Despite the name changes, the district structure with autonomy over street vending decisions remains.

Three branches of local government enforce street market regulations in São Paulo: the Metropolitan Police, the district government inspectors, and the military police. The unarmed Metropolitan Police patrol the city and have limited jurisdiction over street vendors and commerce in São Paulo, similar to the Municipal Guard in La Paz and El Alto. The Metropolitan Police enforce the civil code and quality of life regulations, especially with regards to traffic. They sweep through busy streets and stop unlicensed street vendors, especially those blocking or obstructing traffic. They cannot, however, confiscate wares from street vendors. Only the district inspectors can confiscate and thus the Metropolitan Police typically bring an inspector on planned sweeps or are forced to wait, sometimes for hours, for an inspector to reach them.

The district offices issue, maintain, and revoke licenses for all street vendors in their district. Inspectors are housed within the district offices and answer to their local sub-mayor. Inspectors enforce hundreds of codes for all kinds of businesses within their district, including street vendors, artisans, and other micro-retailers. At least one inspector in each district is responsible for meeting with street vendors and managing street vendor issues and licenses. Thus, the central Vila Velha and peripheral Princesa Isabela district governments have autonomous control over street vendors in their areas.

In 2009, Mayor Gilberto Kassab introduced an agreement with the military police, where sub-mayors could request off-duty military police to patrol their districts on overtime pay (Cuvi, 2016). The agreement started in Vila Velha to police street vendors and then expanded to other areas of the city. Leftist Mayor Fernando Haddad maintained the agreement when he came to power. In 2018, conservative Mayor João Doria renewed the agreement, ensuring that military police patrol street markets in São Paulo. District governments contract military police for this purpose.

The powerful São Paulo government dedicates resources to police street vending. São Paulo manages 100,000 street vendors through two law enforcement branches and teams of local inspectors. The city government then delegates decisions and enforcement to district governments, which have considerable autonomy and variation in their choices. The La Paz city government organizes and manages a large street vending sector through strategic delegation. In contrast, El Alto negotiates and delegates to a highly organized street vendor sector that officials struggle to manage.

4.4 Grounding the Model's Assumptions in Ethnographic Data

The model in Chapter 2 makes several assumptions about informal workers and their interactions with officials. These assumptions simplify the mathematical model and are grounded in the experience of street vendors and officials, which I demonstrate in this section with data from La Paz. In particular, the model assumes that officials and street vendors are rational and engage in cost–benefit decision-making. The model assumes that informal workers make organizing decisions by considering the costs and benefits of each action and choosing the action that gives them the most benefit. Discussions with street vendors and field notes from markets and bureaucratic offices show that many vendors do approach organizing in a highly rational, cost–benefit fashion.

The model assumes that unorganized vendors create negative externalities, or additional enforcement costs, for the government. Interviews and participant observation with the Municipal Guard, the city council, and the Markets

Office demonstrate that unorganized vendors create larger enforcement costs than organized vendors.

The structure of the model assumes that the government intervenes in street vendors' decisions about organization and participation. The model assumes that officials approach vendors with offers that have concrete value to the vendors. In this section, quotes from vendors and officials demonstrate that officials offer cash, licenses, and policy input on a regular basis. Finally, the model assumes that once formed, organizations self-regulate. Ethnographic evidence from the Municipal Guard, officials, vendors, and field notes show that street vendor organizations regulate their members much more thoroughly than government employees could.

4.4.1 Licenses as Organizing Incentives

Organizing requires time, money, and skills that few street vendors have in surplus. As a result, street vendors will only organize with their colleagues when they expect significant benefits. If street vendors are not reasonably certain that they can get significant private benefits from officials by organizing, few choose to.

Natalia is a former vendor leader who currently works as an *independiente*, or licensed but unaffiliated vendor. While most licensed vendors belong to a street vendor organization, a small number do not. Natalia explained her decision to remain an unorganized vendor in cost–benefit terms.

> We are 15 here and we have discussed it, I could organize the 15. Don Jaime (the federation leader) told me that we can start with this. But when you are a leader it absorbs you. You don't have time to work or to spend with your family.

Natalia went on to explain that she does not need an association any more because she has a license that she received through a now defunct union.[8] In contrast, when vendors expect that they can get significant private benefits out of organizing, they do. In most cases, the biggest benefits come from the city government. One of the most compelling incentives for street vendors is

[8] The Markets Office issues licenses to individuals who belong to a union. If that union disbands, members with licenses keep them. Most choose to join another organization but some, like Natalia, become *independientes*. While it is legally possible for an individual to be licensed without going through an organization, it is very rare. I do not know of a single person who obtained a license without an organization in La Paz or El Alto.

a license. Another street vendor leader, Amelia, points to these benefits when explaining why she founded a union.

> First, I wanted to help my colleagues. Second, I wanted more stalls ... I've had a lot of stalls. I fought with the other founders, but I got four stalls in front (of her original stall) and three stalls in back. I have had others. First, I organized (a market street) and then the next street. Some stalls I sold, others I gave to my daughters.

In explaining her actions, Amelia pays brief lip service to altruism: she wanted to help. She then talks at length about the licensed stalls she has accumulated as a vendor leader. These stalls are worth $10,000 to $80,000 each in the market where she works. While Amelia does not explicitly mention the city government, only Markets Office officials can issue licenses. Officials facilitate a gray market in vending licenses by legalizing dubious name changes on existing licenses and issuing additional licenses to vendor leaders as payment for cooperation.[9] When officials offer incentives to individual street vendors for becoming leaders, they create opportunities for leadership as well as rent-seeking. Natalia recounted,

> In past administrations, the city paid a monthly stipend to vendor leaders. All of us wanted to be the leader; who wouldn't want to earn a stipend on top of what you can get from the members? There were many fights between street vendors.

City council member Pedro Susz, the former director of governance for the city government, confirmed in an interview that previous administrations paid civil society leaders for cooperation. He states that the payments achieved short-term cooperation but quickly mired administrations in financial oligations and rising demands from civil society. He documents a shift from financial incentives to deeper working relationships with civil society groups, including street vendor unions. These working relationships facilitated years-long negotiation processes over club amd public goods that civil society groups requested and that the city government delivered through infrastructure projects such as moving open-air markets to new covered market buildings.

[9] Both vendors and officials openly discussed this gray market and the tens of thousands of dollars that licenses sell for. Vendors openly discuss buying and selling licenses and allege that officials charge for name changes. Officials openly discuss offering licenses in exchange for cooperation, but deny taking money for name changes.

In these examples, officials offer valuable incentives to street vendors who organize, and the biggest incentives go to street vendor leaders. Officials strategically offer material incentives like valuable market licenses and even cash. In some instances – like Susz's market building projects and the licensing structure discussed in the following chapter – officials offer organized street vendors policy input on the regulations and projects that the vendors care about most. Street vendors use these offers to evaluate their organizing options through cost–benefit calculations. In some cases, like licenses and input, it is the vendors' actions that make some incentives so valuable. To the city government, licenses cost paper and time; it is the vendor organizations that enforce the rules printed on the licenses and make them valuable.

The theoretical model assumes that the actors within it are rational: they have clear goals and they make choices in pursuit of those goals. This section demonstrates that street vendors are small business owners working to turn a profit and manage their households. Street vendors start or join organizations when doing so helps their business, and they decide not to participate when organizing would take time and resources without delivering a clear benefit. Officials want to advance in their careers and manage the city. They offer incentives like licenses and cash to street vendors in pursuit of those goals. Street vendors then incorporate those offers into their organizing decisions.

Amelia's and Natalia's experiences demonstrate typical organizing sequences in La Paz and El Alto, which are captured by the model: vendors start working as unorganized individuals, typically in an area with few or no street vendor organizations. For example, Amelia works in a hectic market square in central La Paz. The city has grown around the square and when she founded her first union in the 1980s, "Plaza Mamani used to be empty, not full like it is now. There were just a few of us, women who were selling some food." When the city finds unlicensed vendors, it intervenes punitively by issuing citations or confiscating wares. Officials or vendor leaders with access to officials tell the unorganized vendors that they can only get a license by starting a new union or joining an existing one. Some vendors organize, typically those with more resources, while others try their luck avoiding local authorities. Once organized, vendors receive licenses and can negotiate with the government over other problems or benefits in the future. The game theoretic model in Chapter 2 simplifies the steps, but captures the basic process: an unorganized group has a range of costs and concerns, members of the group decide to organize or not, a government or official makes an offer conditional on organization, and given the vendors' decisions, the government delivers on its offer.

4.4.2 Enforcement Costs, Negative Externalities, and Governance

The La Paz city government employs 150 municipal guards to police commerce, including street vending. This is a small number relative to the city's 60,000 licensed and unlicensed street vendors. The guards split their personnel between routine patrols and operations. On routine patrols, guards walk around busy areas in pairs and spot-check licenses, inspect merchandise, and sanction unlicensed vendors. During operations, commanders send squads in trucks to remove repeat violators. Operations are costly for the city government and for individual guards: during operations, the city pays several squads of guards to deal with a small number of violators, and street vendors occasionally attack municipal guards during operations.

For example, Elisa is a guard who patrols markets in the afternoons and is frequently on-call for larger operations at irregular times. Like other guards, she makes a salary slightly above minimum wage and is not paid extra for late night or hazardous operations. She explains the different types of operations she participates in.

> When the operation is one stall, we can go during the day. But if we have to remove several, we have to go at night when (the vendors) aren't there. This happens when, for example, there are people who have permission to sell for one fair day and they stay for a week. Then, we go at night to remove them. In big operations, we are 50, up to 100 guards ... Every time, there are more vendors, more illegals. Now we are receiving complaints that there are a lot of illegal vendors around Eguino at night. So we have to go at 11 pm.

On a ride-along, Elisa's colleague Jhonny talked at length about his least favorite parts of his job. He described the fights that occasionally break out between city guards and vendors.

> Sometimes they start fights, there have been guards that were hit or had their faces cut trying to confiscate. This can be a problem when we're in markets, especially around meat. A lot of times we check for expired or uninspected meat, and if we find it we confiscate it, but the women have large knives and sometimes try to cut the guard.

Eduardo, a guard who had been with the force for nearly a decade, confirmed Jhonny's experience. Eduardo added that for him, the unorganized vendors in peripheral neighborhoods caused the most problems.

> Here in the center of the city, people know the rules. They know what they should be doing, and they usually make some attempt to do it. But in the periphery, it's really difficult, people are very rebellious. You come once and give a warning (to confiscate), and they say, "Fine, take it!" You come a second time and give a warning and it's the same thing. Then you come a third time to confiscate[10] and people get very upset, they yell for others, a crowd forms, and then it's two against 20 and you can't do anything and have to get out of there.

The guards speak to how vendors create sizable negative externalities for the city government by breaking laws repeatedly. Negative externalities contribute to enforcement costs. As discussed in Chapter 2, officials can ignore these negative externalities or try to control them, both of which come with associated costs. If officials attempt to control negative externalities, they must cover the enforcement costs of doing so. These costs quickly spiral if vendors break laws en masse or if the number of noncompliant vendors increases. While organized vendors do clash with the Municipal Guard, unorganized vendors create the most problems and the highest costs. These quotes suggest that if street vendors in La Paz were not as organized, the city government would have to spend more resources monitoring and enforcing basic public health and urban space regulations. In short, these quotes demonstrate that unorganized street vendors do generate negative externalities for officials.

In La Paz's established neighborhoods, street vendor associations internally regulate existing vendors and the city refuses to issue new licenses. This arrangement is mutually beneficial: a stable, regulated street vending sector limits competition and uncertainty, which benefits existing vendors, and keeps the city's enforcement costs low. In new neighborhoods without organizations, unorganized vendors set up shop and the process repeats itself.

For example, the champagne ladies started selling as unorganized individuals in a peripheral neighborhood of La Paz, as discussed in Chapter 2. When they received citations from the Municipal Guard, the champagne ladies had to form a union and affiliate with a federation before even meeting with the Markets Office director. The option to create a new organization and receive

[10] Per city ordinances, street vendors get two warnings for selling without a license or in excess of their license. The third time, the guards confiscate. In reality, people typically get more than two warnings because guards on foot patrol try not to confiscate. Foot patrol guards often ask guards on operation teams to confiscate instead. The first confiscation lasts 15 days and then vendors can claim their wares from the guards' warehouse. The second lasts 30 days and any subsequent confiscations are permanent. There are no fines and no legal charges or ramifictions.

licenses was available to them because they operate in a peripheral neighborhood without an established street vending presence. Ricardo, a photographer in the champagne ladies' association, explains the process he and his colleagues went through.

> Our licenses came this year. For this, we joined the champagne ladies, because (officials) do not want to give licenses to individuals, but an association helps ... The first month, people from the city came by asking for our licenses. You know, the day we submitted our paperwork they disappeared, they haven't come back to bother us.

Ricardo states the common knowledge: The city will not license individuals, but it will license union members. Ricardo then explained that photographers typically work in private buildings where they do not need vending licenses. The photographers only joined the union to get licenses and would not have joined if the city had not insisted. Once the union could demonstrate that they had begun the process of registering an organization – which is not a requirement for legally vending – the Municipal Guard stopped issuing warnings.

The Municipal Guard corroborated the champagne ladies' experience. One commander explained that telling new street vendors to affiliate with a group and meet with the Markets Office is part of the guards' protocol.

> First, we make them affiliate. When there are illegals in the street, we send them to affiliate with a union. Then, we send them to the Markets Office for documentation.

In these ways, officials intervene in informal markets and encourage street vendors to organize. Intervention encourages organizations that would not otherwise exist, like the champagne ladies' association. It also helps officials with few resources implement governance projects. In an interview, city council member Cecília Chacón outlined a proposed change in the municipal street vendor licensing policy and then stated, "What the city government really wants is to order and plan the development of the city." A former Markets Office director echoed this sentiment: "We continue to believe that licensing policy is an important factor in bringing order to the city."

Another official, Samuel, has worked directly with street vendor leaders for years in multiple positions in the Markets Office. He explained how he intervenes in street vendors' collective decision-making by rewarding compliant leaders. In his position, Samuel intervenes with positive outcomes for otherwise endless bureaucratic processes and with access to the bureaucracy.

> I have met with the associations so that they work with us, and there we establish another mechanism of negotiation. Working with us means that we will positively resolve the majority of the administrative processes that the leaders initiate. Why? Because that empowers the leaders with regards to their membership base.

Samuel explains that a major part of his job is to get street vendor leaders to work with the city government and cooperate with city projects using a range of incentives. The examples that he discussed included relocating stalls during infrastructure projects, resolving congestion around a busy market, and preventing unauthorized vendors from selling at new installations. The incentives that Samuel offers can be used for material gain, like extra stalls that leaders can use themselves or allocate to their members, or longer selling hours. Leaders can also use these incentives to cement their reputation as effective leaders, for example, by resolving a member's years-long request to upgrade their stall from a temporary stall to a semi-permanent stall.

Samuel can also incentivize compliant behavior by granting leaders meetings or text message responses to show their members that they have connections inside the Markets Office. In return, Samuel asks leaders for cooperation with infrastructure projects and compliance with municipal regulations. He explains, "We are 80 people against a universe of 60,000 street vendors, if not more ... We enter into negotiations to make these changes." In other words, La Paz's street vendors exceed the city's enforcement capacity and officials extract compliance from street markets by working closely with organized vendors.

The city tacitly bolsters the organizations' authority by making it exceedingly difficult for unorganized vendors to access the bureaucracy. On paper, any individual can petition the Markets Office and its officials. In practice, only cooperative and organized vendors receive meetings and favorable responses. For example, while former Markets Office Director Nicolás Medeiro regularly scheduled with some leaders and kept others at arm's length, he simply did not meet with unknown or unorganized street vendors. Former Director Ángel Gomez adopted a similar strategy: he posted his cellphone number around the office to give the appearance of transparency and accessibility, but only ever answered calls and texts from established union leaders.

As street vendors explained and I witnessed dozens of times, the office's official scheduling process serves to screen out the unorganized: individuals submit a notarized petition and letter into a citywide system, take the receipt to the Markets Office, follow up in person a week later to receive a meeting date and additional letter, and return to be rescheduled or told to wait for hours until they leave, at which point the process is dropped and must be restarted. As Auyero (2012) finds in the welfare bureaucracy in Buenos Aires, the waiting and bureaucrats' arbitrary discretion over poor people's lives grinds them down and encourages individuals to give up. Officials in La Paz take a slightly less cynical approach than officials in Buenos Aires by granting access to groups. Faced with maddening futility if they try to petition officials as individuals, the city pushes street vendors to organize if they want access.

Officials in the La Paz city government have governance goals and ambition, few material resources, and a lot of informal workers in the streets. Officials in the city government encourage street vendors to organize by intervening with an array of positive incentives, like licenses and policy input, and negative incentives, like bureaucratic intransience and selective enforcement. City officials then work closely with organized street vendors to regain compliance from informal workers and markets.

4.4.3 Self-Regulation

Street vendor organizations in La Paz have clear statutes and organizational hierarchies that help them resolve disputes. Most associations' statutes and written agreements with the city include a clause stipulating that vendors will follow all relevant municipal and organizational rules and cooperate with their colleagues, or face expulsion from the organization and revocation of any license. Street vendors frequently invoke these clauses. Isabel, a unionized clothing vendor, explains how agreements work between the city and the associations that operate in the market she works in.

> The associations sign an agreement with the city government that they will follow the city's regulations. In effect, this means that the association enforces most things. The city government just enforces a few things in the licenses: time and place and having one. But if the city government finds something wrong, they'll just write a letter to the association saying "Your affiliates are doing this and you need to stop it."

Municipal guards and their commanders explained that street vendor organizations actively collaborate with them in enforcing these rules. Guardswoman Elisa explains, "It's the street vendors themselves, the leaders, who call us. When we arrive, they are waiting to help us, and they facilitate our work." This statement was echoed by half a dozen other guards on separate ride-alongs in 2015 and 2018.

In additional interviews over multiple years and changes in leadership, municipal guards and their commanders volunteered that street vendor organizations actively collaborate with them. This dynamic was summarized by Municipal Guard commander Major Rodríguez (emphasis added),

> Frequently, the street vendors themselves make reports, about someone who is selling outside of their hours, or new illegal vendors, or people selling outside of their space ... *The street vendors regulate each other*. Since it hurts them to have more street vendors, and they know when a new person shows up, they are the ones that regulate.

Additionally, street vendors actively seek out the Municipal Guard. For example, when I started working with the Municipal Guard, I was worried that the street vendors who I work with would be angry that I was working with law enforcement. I told the street vendors who I worked with about what I was doing to avoid misunderstandings. To my surprise, street vendors reacted nonchalantly and confirmed their coordination with the Municipal Guard. When I told one rank-and-file vendor that I was going on ride-alongs, she responded, "(The Municipal Guard) do good work. We have called them to remove the (unlicensed) people that sell here because they compete with us."

The commanders of the Municipal Guard have established regular meetings with street vendor leaders, where vendors and law enforcement coordinate their efforts. Major González, one of the officers charged with managing the Municipal Guard, explained that, "They come here to coordinate. Every 15 days we have a meeting with the leader of the sector." These coordinating meetings have continued over years and across new leadership in both the Municipal Guard and the federations.

I saw firsthand how thoroughly organized street vendors regulate each other while working in a street market. I worked at a licensed stall in a large clothing market, where over 6,000 people work in self-policed shifts from 5 a.m. to midnight. The licensed vendor who I worked for began enlarging her stall by tenths of a centimeter every week. The Municipal Guard walks past her stall every morning, but did not notice these minute violations. Instead, colleagues reported her to her association's leadership, which conducted a surprise inspection. Fifteen leaders crowded around her stall, declared her in violation of her license, gave her a time and date to appear before the full elected board to determine a punishment, and threatened to report her to the city if she did not comply. She complied, attended the association's hearing, and was barred from selling for 15 days. When we discussed the punishment, she told me that even if leadership reported her, the city would probably tell the association to sanction her themselves. She complied because her association can prevent her from working by directing members to destroy her merchandise or stop her from setting up her stall, not because she feared the Municipal Guard. In extreme cases, the association leadership presents testimonies that a member does not follow regulations and asks the Markets Office to revoke their license.

In this example and others, street vendors carefully monitor each other, use their own institutions to enforce city ordinances, and only call the city if their own adjudication fails. While the city supplies incentives that encourage this behavior, the organizations' management and regulation of the markets make incentives like licenses and market stalls valuable to vendors. In doing so, the organizations enforce local laws more thoroughly than the city government.

This chapter discusses the history of street vending in the La Paz and São Paulo metropolitan areas, as well as the development of La Paz's active street market organizations. The chapter elaborates on the organizations' strong structural foundations and complex institutions. Ethnographic data from the Municipal Guard and street markets establish that the modeling choices in Chapter 2 are grounded in the reality of La Paz's street vendors.

Street market organizations in La Paz are not small voluntary groups begging for members. Instead, the organizations' bylaws and recruitment policies thoroughly screen potential new members and demonstrate that street vendor unions are selective organizations. Data from ride-alongs with the La Paz Municipal Guard and interviews with police commanders and Markets Office officials demonstrate that street vendors create considerable enforcement costs for the city, that the city actively works with street vendor organizations, and that once organized, street vendors largely regulate themselves. When 5 percent of the city sells on the street, it is prohibitively expensive for the city government to effectively police them. In La Paz, law enforcement relies heavily on organized street vendors to reduce enforcement costs. Outside of the Municipal Guard's spot-checking patrols, street vendors are the primary monitors and sanctioners of other street vendors. Both guards and street vendors make it clear that the organizations self-regulate, internally enforce local ordinances as well as their own rules, and coordinate with the city.

5

Managing Contentious Collective Action

Mavel Machicado was born into a street vending family in La Paz. She was eight years old when she started working at her mother's stall. As she grew older, Mavel saw that the clearest path for street vendor career advancement was through the university and the union ranks. Unlike older market women, she finished high school and started a law degree. She ran for the position of standard bearer in her street market union and won. Soon after, she ran for head of the union and won her election again. By age 25, she led the old and powerful Alto Huyustus union and owned a lucrative stall in the Huyustus street market. When the city government stoked internal conflicts to break La Paz's one street federation into competing federations, she seized on the opportunity and started her own federation. Mavel built the federation by courting unions in the center of the city that were disgruntled with the power struggles of the old federation. By 2015, she represented 70 associations with tens of thousands of affiliated street vendors.

As federation leader, Mavel Machicado developed daily working relationships with the city government and Markets Office officials. While fruitful, these relationships are also contentious: leaders demand frequent favors in exchange for compliance and threaten noncompliance for leverage, which Mavel is notoriously quick to do. Noncompliance can be anything from not enforcing space and merchandise regulations within the associations to closing the city's produce markets and surrounding city hall for weeks on end, which halts work throughout the city. Bolivians call these tactics *medidas de presión* or pressure tactics. Officials do not hesitate to play leaders off each other in order to manage these demands.

The party in control of the national government, the *Movimiento al Socialismo*, MAS, recruited Mavel as a candidate for La Paz city council, running against the city government's candidate. Mavel won, and since 2015 has represented street vendors on the La Paz city council. She has used her union and council positions, as well as her ability to call mass demonstrations, to propose new programs and halt others. Mavel's work as a federation leader and as a city council member demonstrates how important informal workers' organizations

Why Informal Workers Organize. Calla Hummel, Oxford University Press.
© Calla Hummel (2021). DOI: 10.1093/oso/9780192847812.003.0005

are to officials' work, career advancement, and governance projects in places like La Paz, where informal work exceeds local enforcement capacity. Her path to city council illustrates the complexity of officials' relationships with informal workers' organizations and the blurred lines between them.

The game theoretic model in Chapter 2 generates results in the form of equilibrium outcomes and comparative statics about officials' behavior and informal workers' organizations. If this model is useful for explaining why informal workers organize, then we should observe specific patterns in officials' work with street vendors in La Paz. In particular, we should observe officials making increasingly large offers to informal workers as negative externalities increase. We should also observe more informal workers organizing as these offers increase. Second, we should observe informal workers with more resources taking advantage of officials' offers.

These observable implications are different from what we would observe if grassroots activism or clientelism were the sole drivers of street vendor organizations. If grassroots activism was the main cause of these organizations, we would observe activists starting organizations and then approaching officials. We would also observe an upswing in organizing along with other activist projects. We would not observe officials directing street vendors to start organizations. If clientelism were driving these organizations, we would observe officials offering incentives to organize and turn out voters, and we would observe organizations following the electoral cycle. The evidence in this chapter and the previous chapter shows that grassroots activists are important leaders in street vendor organizations and that officials do make clientelist appeals to street vendor organizations. However, officials direct street vendors to start organizations as their costs increase, and these appeals do not follow electoral cycles.

This chapter presents original survey data and ethnographic work[1] with officials and street vendors, as well as an administrative data set of the 31,906 street vending licenses that the city has issued. The chapter demonstrates that the patterns in the data are consistent with the theory developed in Chapter 2. The chapter outlines the effects and implications of state intervention in informal market organizations in La Paz and illustrates the trade-offs of this strategy for the officials who choose it.

[1] Chapter 1 discusses methodological choices.

5.1 Increasing Costs, Increasing Offers, and Increasing Levels of Organization

The first street vendor organizations were small groups that came and went, starting in the late 1800s (Lehm et al., 1988, Dibbits et al., 1986). These became active in the city's labor movement, at turns cooperating with or clashing with the government over public space and labor laws. After the 1952 revolution, the new, revolutionary regime founded the Bolivian Labor Central and pressured street vendors to affiliate with it (Rojas, 1992, pp.118–120). In response to local politicians, many of the several hundred street vendors in the city formed small unions in the 1950s and 1960s (Pereira Morató, 2008, p.1). Elena's union, which her mother founded in 1965, was one of these:

> (My mother's union) was organized because of the problems they were having with the city administration. (The city) said they needed licenses, so the women formed a union.

In the long history of La Paz's street vending unions, we see no organizations until the 1880s and then, from the 1880s until the 1950s, a few grassroots activists founding small organizations that wax and wane with their leaders and the leaders' interactions with officials. This pattern is consistent with the model's first and second equilibrium outcomes at different times: no organization in the absence of state intervention, despite common interests, and at other times some organization by particularly motivated individuals in the absence of state intervention. We see more vendors forming and joining organizations after a revolutionary regime intervenes in the 1950s, consistent with the third class of equilibrium outcomes, but their organizations are still small. This changed in the 1980s.

During the hyperinflation and resulting economic crisis of the 1980s, over 18,000 unemployed Bolivians in the capital turned to street vending to survive (Pereira Morató, 2008, p.2). This dramatic increase in street vendors also increased the city's enforcement costs materially and politically: the city needed more personnel to enforce public space laws but did not have the revenue to hire them, and evicted street vendors could not find alternative employment amidst rampant unemployment. New unions formed in response to the city government's carrot-and-stick approach to street vendors. The city issued licenses to organized vendors who worked with the government and evicted those who remained unorganized, as Amelia experienced in the late 1980s.

> One day, the municipal guard[2] came to remove us. We asked ourselves, what will we do, what will we do? I had a friend who worked for the mayor and she said, why don't you form an association? ... We got the people, we went to the federation to affiliate, then we went to the city to ask for help ... Dr. MacLean (mayor from 1987 to 1991) said, "Help the party and I will help you." So we went to the party, we helped, and Dr. MacLean followed through. After a year, we all received licenses.

In Amelia's story, we see evidence of forbearance – the city selectively enforces in order to extract political support (Holland, 2016, p.232) – and clientelism, but also something more. The mayor did not just ask for votes, he instructed street vendors to organize and then distributed a large, concrete individual benefit to those who did. As enforcement costs from street vending increased and the city became increasingly chaotic, the mayor and his administration actively pursued a strategy of selective enforcement against unorganized and unconnected vendors while also increasing legal benefits for people who formed organizations. This sequence of events is in line with the theoretical model's observable implications. As officials' offers to organized vendors increased, the vendors' levels of organization increased as well, with more and more unions forming and affiliating with umbrella organizations at the local and national level.

In 2001, Mayor Juan del Granado's *Movimiento Sin Miedo* administration entered city hall. Del Granado thoroughly restructured the city government and renegotiated the written and verbal agreements that previous administrations had made with important civil society groups, including street vendors, transportation workers, and neighborhood associations. The city approached the street vendor organizations and asked for proposals for a new licensing system. The city and the street vendors then bargained over the new licensing system: the *pago único municipal*, or the one municipal payment system. The proposed system replaced and arbitrary and patchwork system of fees and bribes with a single licensing fee. The new system gave semi-permanent licenses and other incentives to organized street vendors.

[2] At the time, the city police force was called the *policía urbana* or the urban police. The city reorganized the force into the municipal guard in 2001. However, street vendors often refer to them as the same organization, or use the slang term *frutillitas*, little strawberries, which comes from the red uniforms that the guards have not worn for over a decade.

After rounds of public protest and closed-door negotiations, the city and the street vendors agreed to the new licensing system in 2003. All vendors who could demonstrate *sentaje* payments – an arbitrarily collected daily street vending tax – since 1994 could apply for a license. Street vendors would maintain their licenses by following city vending ordinances and paying a small annual fee. The fee depends on the stall and is usually about U.S.D.$10, rarely more than a day's profits. Officials and street vendor leaders claim the *pago único* as a victory that institutionalized organized street vending. Jorge, a former Markets Office official, describes the importance of and changes wrought by the licensing program:

> This unified, clear tax was a victory. This creates institutional relationships, an institutional relationship between the city and the federations ... The street vendors achieved recognition from the government, and since then it has been much more stable, people don't have to worry about what will happen tomorrow. The conflicts are no longer about stalls, they are about rules and schedules.

In this quote, Jorge explains that the *pago único municipal* is mutually beneficial for vendor organizations, the city government, and many vendors because it strengthens street vendor organizations and reduces conflict with the city. The *pago único municipal* gives street vendors an important benefit – semi-permanent licenses – in exchange for a small fee. Importantly, it is the street vendor organizations that facilitate those licenses and channel this benefit from the government to individual members. As a city council member explained, "First, (the associations) are our principal interlocutors." This creates stable and long-term relationships between the organizations and the city government. These established, mutually beneficial working relationships then reduce conflict between the city and informal workers. The relationships also encourage new vendors to form or join organizations that follow the city's laws in order to eventually receive licenses and other benefits.

Street vendor leaders also claim that the *pago único municipal* brought important and positive changes to street vending. They claim the program as their achievement, as federation leader Don Jaime declared many times in meetings and rallies. For example, before a street vendor assembly in 2014, he declared "The *pago único municipal* was our victory. It was the federation, we worked hard for it for many years, it was our struggle."

Officials echo this language. Former Markets Office director William Hernandez states, "The ordinance was written by the street vendors ... it has been a victory on the part of the street vending sector to have that municipal ordinance." The *pago único municipal* was a resounding victory for the organizations because it codified street vendor policy input: officials requested their proposals for reorganizing street vending and then negotiated a new policy based on the proposals that street vendor leaders made.

Organized street vendors have continued to work closely with the the city and have continued to propose, debate, and negotiate street vendor policy with city officials. In some cases, officials actively seek policy input from street vendors and their organizations. For example, Hernandez discussed the role of street vendor input in a later licensing project that he oversaw, "In the municipal ordinance (on licensing), they actively participated. Many of the articles were proposed by them." Thus, the policy role that the city established with organized street vendors through the *pago único municipal* continues through other policy projects that affect street vending.

In the fall of 2014, street vendors mobilized protests against a city council proposal to make restrictive changes to the *pago único*. Among the protest chants, printed and distributed to marchers on slips of paper, was "Long live the *pago único municipal*!" Protesters also chanted for the long life of the federation and for the death of opposing city council members. The death threats are not idle: street vendors in El Alto burned down a government building during a protest in 2016, killing six officials. William Hernandez reported receiving over 130 death threats while he was the Markets Office director and multiple current and former officials recalled street vendors showing up en masse at the Markets Office with gasoline, molotov cocktails, and razors.

The protest I attended in 2014, which ended in a meeting with the city council, is one of many instances in which street vendor organizations, once organized, engage with the government to bargain over policy and enforcement. It is also a sign that while the vendor organizations work with the government and enforce local laws, they remain autonomous and engage in contentious political negotiations with officials. Street vendors' compliance is necessary for city projects, and for officials' work, career advancement, and livelihoods. Officials and street vendor leaders negotiate incentives like licenses and policy input in exchange for street vendors' compliance.

Why did the city negotiate a partial legalization of street vendors in the early 2000s? In the 1990s and 2000s, thousands of new, largely unorganized vendors were joining a sector that was growing, but at decreasing rates. Thus, new vendors drove up the city's enforcement costs, but not as drastically as they had in the 1980s. However, negotiations over a new licensing system occurred under a centrist city government after citywide vendor protests and during nationwide mobilizations that forced the resignation of presidents (Kohl and Farthing, 2006). The city government faced moderate increases in material enforcement costs from increasing numbers of vendors but potentially high political costs from continued protest. Conversely, officials stood to gain significant benefits from an institutionalized and cooperative street vending sector: they would save money by shifting more enforcement and monitoring responsibilities to the federations and benefit from their political support. In fact, del Granado's administration did maintain control of city hall, while centrist and conservative parties across the country lost to the MAS party over the following decade (Anria, 2018, Madrid, 2012). Officials also successfully shifted monitoring and enforcement to street vendor organizations. Therefore, following the expectations of the model, growing enforcement costs over time led to increasing offers from officials to organized vendors, which in turn boosted the levels of organization among street vendors.

The city government conducted a street vendor census in 2012 and used the information to create a database of licenses. After the census and in consultation with street vendor organizations, the city stopped officially issuing new licenses. This decision, while controversial, protects existing license holders by making their licenses more valuable and controlling competition. Officials claim that the number of licensed street vendors has stayed at 31,906 since. This bends the truth: officials still issue temporary, street fair, and event licenses and transfer existing licenses, and these changes do not show up in the database. Restricting the number of licenses does not mean that officials stopped offering organizing incentives to street vendors, it means that the way those incentives are tracked and reported changed.

The city shared licensing data with me in 2019 after five years of requests. The data set lists 31,906 licenses in effect across the city as of October 2019. These stalls are mapped in Figure 5.1. Every neighborhood has street vendors, but some have thousands while others have a handful. The data set contains location, stall materials, dimensions, schedule, merchandise, and organizational affiliation for each license. The data set shows important trends in licensing across the city.

Nearly all licenses are affiliated with an organization: 30,213 of the licenses or 95 percent report membership in one of 437 associations or unions that are also registered in the data set. Only 1,693 licenses report that they are not members in a street vendor association or union. These numbers suggest that one of the only routes to a street vending license is through an organization that is registered with the city government. This strongly suggests that the city encourages informal workers to join and work with the city through larger organizations.

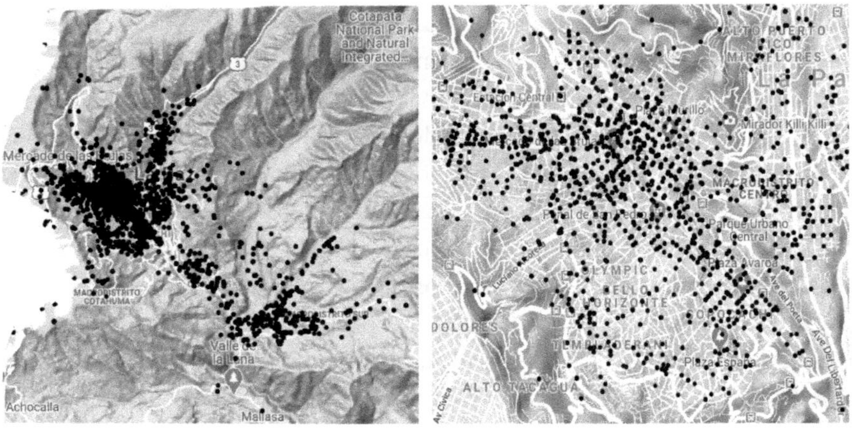

Stalls in La Paz

Stalls in central La Paz

Fig. 5.1 Maps of La Paz stall locations

The stall locations in the licenses cluster around the city center, as the maps in Figure 5.1 demonstrate.[3] In logistic regressions on the license data (reported in the Fieldwork Appendix), licenses in the central district are more likely to be associated with a street vendor organization than licenses in other districts. The geographic distribution of the licenses further supports the theory's implications while addressing some alternative explanations: the vast majority of licenses in La Paz are in the center of the city, close to government buildings and in full view of officials. This clashes with the theory that informal work and organizations occur primarily in the absence of the state (Tassi et al., 2015, 2013). Instead, the cluster of licenses suggests accumulated negotiations between street vendors and officials.

The licenses in the data set appear to cluster by market areas and thoroughfares more than by neighborhood income level or vote share: stalls are clustered in neighborhoods around the western market districts such as Max Paredes, San Pedro, and Cotahuma, with moderate concentrations of stalls along the main streets in neighborhoods like Sopocachi, Obrajes, Miraflores, and Calacoto. Some medium- and high-income neighborhoods close to main roads like San Pedro, Sopocachi, and Calacoto have many street vending stalls, while

[3] Each dot is a stall location. The stalls are coded by cross-streets, thus, these are not exact locations. In busy areas, many stalls share the same cross-street and those dots are stacked on top of each other; the concentration of stalls in central La Paz is denser than the map on the right suggests.

others further away from main roads like Alto Obrajes, Achumani, and Irpavi have few stalls. Likewise, some lower income neighborhoods with major thoroughfares like Cotahuma and Villa Fatima have many licensed stalls while other low-income neighborhoods, like Pasankeri, Pampahasi, and Chacaltaya have few. The wealthier southern neighborhoods with and without street vending stalls tend to vote for centrist parties led by the elite. The lower income neighborhoods swing to the left, especially the populist left, with and without large concentrations of street vendors.

Street vending licenses in La Paz are extremely specific. There are hundreds of merchandise categories. Licensed street vendors in La Paz sell everything from baby clothes to calculators to coca leaves. About half of the merchandise categories are types of food or clothes. However, only 431 simply say "clothes" and 1156 list "foods." Most vendors are licensed to sell more specific products: 6 people hold licenses for cotton candy, 12 can sell grilled cow hearts, 228 are potato vendors, and 231 are licensed for coffee and tea. In the clothes category, 15 people sell only gloves, 7 people sell ties, 212 people are underwear vendors, and 101 sell backpacks. Licenses with broader or higher margin merchandise categories are more valuable than licenses with narrower or lower margin categories.

In addition to location and merchandise, every license lists the stall material and dimensions, down to the centimeter, and the days and hours during which the license is valid. If a person changes their stall, merchandise, or hours without permission, the city or the association can revoke that license.

The licenses and the 437 associations and unions are heterogeneous. The largest association in the data set has 1664 licenses and is a clothing vendors' union in a prominent market district. It is one of the oldest and most powerful associations in La Paz and belongs to Councilwoman Machicado's federation. Councilwoman Machicado's association is the second largest in the database, with 930 licenses. The average number of licenses in an association in the data set is 69, suggesting that many of the 437 associations are large and well established groups.

The numbers in the data set and ethnographic data from street vendors suggest that most associations have both licensed and unlicensed members. Street vendors regularly reported that they and others joined organizations in order to eventually receive licenses, or that their association included many unlicensed vendors. Many people that I talked to agreed that the largest union in the data set has well over 2000 members, more than the 1664 license holders in the data set. Another prominent association that city officials estimated has thousands of members has only 199 official licenses in the data set, suggesting that most members are unlicensed or have other types of licenses.

The data set is systematically incomplete. The data set does not include temporary or special event licenses, which the city continues to issue and which, while revocable, are hardly temporary. Thousands of additional vendors and dozens of additional organizations hold licenses for fairs and events. Some are recognized holiday markets and temporary events: for example, the Alasitas and Christmas markets support thousands of vendors in at least half a dozen associations for the months of December and January. On the other hand, some special event licenses stipulate that the event reoccurs in the same place every Wednesday or Sunday and in effect operate like a permanent license, but do not appear in the city's statistical reports. The city offers special event licenses to newly organized vendors in new or sparsely populated areas.

The data set reveals important patterns in street vending across La Paz, like location and associational membership. However, the systematic omissions from the data set put limits on what the licensing data can tell us about why some street vendors organize while others do not. In addition to omitting unlicensed street vendors and licensed special event vendors, the data set does not include demographic information about license-holders. A survey I conducted in 2015 with 207 licensed and unlicensed street vendors across La Paz sheds light on street vendor demographic and social characteristics.

Why do some street vendors organize while others in the same city do not? In an original survey of street vendors in La Paz, 75 percent belonged to a street vendor organization and 25 percent did not. This suggests that licensed street vendors are much more organized than street vendors as a whole, as 95 percent of licenses in the city's database are associated with a street vendor organization. In line with the theoretical model's observable implications, the 25 percent of surveyed vendors who do not belong to a street vendor organization tend to be slightly younger, newer to street vending, and have fewer assets than organized street vendors, though none of these differences are statistically significant in logistic regression analyses (see Fieldwork Appendix). Descriptively, 89 percent of organized vendors hold licenses but only 46 percent of unorganized vendors do, and this difference is statistically significant (see logistic regressions models in the Fieldwork Appendix).

Logistic regressions on the La Paz survey data (reported in the Fieldwork Appendix) examine these differences between organized and unorganized vendors by looking at the predictors of organizational membership (see section 1.3 of Chapter 1 and the Fieldwork Appendix for the survey's sampling strategy, protocol, and survey instrument). The analyses find that licenses, the selective incentive that officials give for organization, strongly and significantly predict whether or not a street vendor is organized. Other demographic variables do not have statistically significant effects. Controlling for other factors, street vendors with a license are 11 times more likely to be organized than street vendors without a license.

Per the theory and the ethnographic evidence, licensing is endogenous to organization. The survey and the license database are snapshots and cannot tell us if street vendors get licenses because they organize, or if street vendors organize because they are licensed. Ethnographic evidence can help disentangle this possible endogeneity.

Compare Amelia, a longstanding union leader, and Natalia, an unorganized licensed vendor: on one hand, both are women of indigenous descent who started working as children and have decades of experience in the sector. Both have licenses, an important factor that this informal comparison holds constant. However, Amelia has 38 years of union experience, much of it as a leader. Additionally, Amelia has more time and resources than Natalia: at 56, Amelia has adult children and more material assets than Natalia, who at 40 supports two children in a rented house. Descriptively, Amelia and Natalia illustrate the theoretical model's implication that vendors with lower organizing costs use that advantage to organize more.

In line with research that finds that people with more resources participate more than people with less (Brady et al., 1995, Ostrom, 2007, Meinzen-Dick et al., 2002), the survey and interviews found that street vendor leaders tend to be better off relative to other street vendors. Additionally, rank-and-file street vendors actively promote leaders with a college education, as in Councilwoman Machicado's story at the beginning of the chapter. Similarly, the head of La Paz's main street vendor federation has a social science degree from a French university and his second in command has an architectural degree from Bolivia's main university. These leaders have spent decades as street vendors, but they are much more educated than most of their colleagues: we found that only 6 percent of survey respondents reported attending university.

Interviews with officials supported the propositions that street vendors with more resources organize more and that education is a particlarly important resource. For example, former Markets Office Director William Hernandez lamented that in general, street vendors do not have high levels of formal education. He then went on to explain that levels of education separate followers and leaders, "In the city of La Paz, there is an abysmal gap in education. That difference exists between street vendors, between those who become leaders and those that don't, there is a strong difference."

Additionally, only relatively well-off street vendors tend to accept leadership positions because they have enough income to redirect their time to the organization and away from street vending. However, income may be endogenous to leadership: many leaders engage in corrupt exchanges and can use their positions to embezzle funds and acquire multiple vending licenses, which can be worth tens of thousands of dollars each, as the next section details.

In sum, administrative, survey, and interview data corroborate the theory's expectation that people with more resources organize more than their colleagues with fewer resources. Street vendors with more education, experience, and material goods are more likely to be in an organization than street vendors with less. This dynamic is particularly clear within street vendor leadership: street vendors actively promote people with college degrees to leadership positions and state that education is an important resource.

5.2 Who Benefits from Organized Street Vendors?

In political science, any discussion of collective action must address the free-rider problem, or why a self-interested person would join a collective effort when they can benefit from others' work without contributing. In the case of street vendors in La Paz, why would a street vendor contribute to a street market organization when they can free ride on the order and certainty that the organization brings?

In La Paz and many other places, street market organizations address the free-rider problem by offering things to members that members want and need, like dispute resolution, representation at the Markets Office, and security. In collective action research, these benefits are called selective incentives – private benefits only available to people who contribute. Officials encourage organizational membership by supplying selective incentives like licenses and access and channeling them through organizations. Providing resources to civil society groups raises other questions, namely, why would officials give resources to civil society groups that could then use those resources to challenge them or demand more (Nelson-Nuñez and Cartwright, 2018)?

Officials address this conundrum by using other incentives to manage the power and demands of leaders and organizations, as this section details. This section also documents the benefits beyond compliance that officials receive from organized street vendors. The section shows that street vendor leaders use their positions for private gain. The stories and quotes in this section demonstrate that officials and street vendor leaders wield selective incentives in ways that primarily benefit themselves. These strategies also exclude free-riders and encourage rank-and-file street vendors to participate in organizations.

When officials pay street vendors to form organizations that monitor and enforce, officials do not necessarily give up control to organizations. Officials can manipulate the number of organizations and their leadership by offering incentives only if organizations unify or only to a preferred leader and her followers. If officials do not want to negotiate with a unified and therefore more powerful sector, they can fracture existing organizations by offering incentives to breakaway groups. Unifying or dividing street vendor organizations curtails an organization's potential to benefit its members. Officials can limit the power of organizations by favoring leaders who are dependent on officials and therefore reluctant to bargain hard, or by cleaving an organization and therefore reducing its potential bargaining power.

Luisa, a prominent street vendor leader, explains, "The parties divide us with money. And then there's the government, the Markets Office, they give things to one (organization) but not others." Luisa described these tactics while recounting how the city government had encouraged La Paz's one street vendor federation to fracture into several competing federations in the mid-2000s, as mentioned at the beginning of this chapter.

Officials readily confirm that they placate or divide street vending organizations with incentives. Markets Office officials elaborated on the many ways they manage organizations and street vendor leaders, corroborating Luisa's and others' statements. Officials deploy access and favors to reward the leaders who comply with their directives and punish those who do not. For example, former Markets Office Director Nicolás Medeiro detailed the different relationships he maintained with different leaders and the level of preferential access that they were granted.

> Of these (leaders), Jaime Santana is the one who gets along with us best and has always worked closely with us, but obviously at this level of negotiation and support, we have the kind of meetings where we touch on specific issues ... This office maintains two weekly meetings with the federation of Jaime Santana and once a week with Choque's federation. With Mavel Machicado, we permit meetings but she must talk directly with me and we don't have the formal relationship that we have with the other two federations.

Medeiro reiterated that he gave more attention and access to Jaime Santana as an incentive to maintain a cooperative relationship. Furthermore, he elaborated that the "specific issues" that they discuss in the meetings are favors and exceptions to the rules that the Markets Office grants in exchange for specific instances of cooperation. Other former directors echoed Medeiro's preferences and strategic management of the different federations and other street vendor organizations.

Officials explained that they split up powerful or problematic organizations by cutting off incentives and inducing mid-level leaders to leave and become the heads of their own organizations. Former Markets Office Director William Hernandez put this most succintly, "You divide and you try to generate an adequate level of governance for the city with this sector ... divide and you will prevail."

"Divide and conquer" was a phrase that I heard over and over again in interviews with officials in La Paz during 2014, 2015, and 2018. Former directors Hernandez, Medeiro, and Gómez all used the phrase and many variants, occasionally multiple times in the same interview. Hernandez put the practice in context when discussing how he dealt with a particularly contentious series of street vendor protests by one organization. The protests prevented officials and street vendors from working for weeks because protesting street vendors blockaded the Markets Office instead of working their stalls.

> We endured (the protests) as a city government until they were spent, because a person who does not work cannot endure ... (the leadership) lost credibility with their people and so we won at dividing them, and now the people believe that we are imposing order.

Other officials and street vendors confirmed that during this series of protests, there was disagreement within the protesting organization. Many street vendors asserted that continuing to protest went against their interests: they wanted to work and they wanted to preserve a working relationship with Markets Office officials. As a result, many street vendors left the organization and split off into smaller associations that now deal directly with the Markets Office instead of going through a larger organization. Current officials and street vendors confirmed that the associations had remained independent from the larger organization, and officials lauded the divisions within the larger organization.

To maintain a compliant and governable street vending sector, officials strategically offer revocable favors to street vendor leaders. Both officials and street vendors confirmed this practice. Fabiana, a former leader, explained how officials can use incentives to control organizations as well as encourage them.

> The city and national government buy off leaders; they get extra stalls. If you're complaining a bunch they take you aside and say, look, why don't you be quiet and we'll give you another spot.

Multiple Markets Office officials confirmed this practice and expanded on the occasionally shady incentives that they use to push leaders and their organizations in the directions that they want. For example, one former director explained how he used a combination of favors to cajol, entice, or reward leaders who cooperated with him and Markets Office projects. These favors included verbal agreements, bending the rules, and making exceptions.

> More or less this is how we manage (the organizations) and in some cases favors come in, for example, with longer hours or permission (to sell) on additional days ... Then I authorize the change verbally. Not formally, in case there is some kind of legal inquiry or evaluation.

Other officials confirmed these strategies. I regularly went on foot patrols with the municipal guard where we would check street vendors' licenses. Municipal Guard commanders and rank-and-file guards explained on several patrols that the licenses we were checking stated place, time, or size restrictions that they were not going to enforce because the association in that area had an informal verbal agreement with the Markets Office, the district administrator, or the mayor. For example, on Sanchez Street, the street's association has an agreement with the Markets Office to let their members sell until 9 a.m., though their licenses state 7 a.m. A nearby market association has a verbal agreement with the mayor to sell in the street outside of the covered market, though they do not have physical licenses and are not registered in the street vendor database. On Avaroa Avenue, shop owners and street vendors have a verbal agreement with the district administrator to nearly double their official stall sizes and sell over the sidewalk and into the street.

The directors', mayors, and others' extensive use of informal, verbal agreements with street vendor leaders support Holland's (2017) arguments about revocable incentives. Officials use the initial verbal offer of an extra stall or extended hours as a positive incentive, and then the threat of revocation serves as a continuous negative incentive to maintain compliance. Samuel explains that revocable incentives are necessary in a city where informal work exceeds enforcement capacity.

> They are a little afraid of the only administrative instrument that we have right now against the street vending sector, which is the revocation of stalls. This is the fear that they have and if they did not, to be sincere, we would lose the battle.

Verbal, revocable incentives are less costly to officials than formal ones, because officials do not have to record and justify these offers in databases, budgets, or in debates with opposition parties. Verbal agreements offer very real benefits to street vendors: temporarily extended hours and stall dimensions vastly increase a street vendor's sales volume. In sum, officials use a wide array of administrative, material, and informal incentives to encourage organization and compliance within the informal sector. Officials carefully manipulate these incentives to keep civil society organizations manageable and governable because their jobs depend on it.

In the theoretical model, street vendors and officials exchange incentives. The theoretical model does not consider whether those incentives are legal or normatively desirable. Empirically, corruption is one way to supply or manipulate incentives. Street vendor leaders and officials allegedly participate in corruption – the misuse of public office for private gain (Rose-Ackerman, 1999, p.91) – when officials use public funds to illegally pay leaders, break the rules to give leaders extra stalls, or when leaders bribe officials for favors. Officials frequently insisted that they do not violate the rules, instead they simply wield their discretion strategically. However, the prevalence of informal agreements and one director's claim, detailed in the previous section, that he made verbal agreements "in case there is some kind of legal inquiry or evaluation," validate street vendors' allegations of illicit inducements like extra licenses and cash.

Street vendors often state that federation leaders are on the city and national governments' payrolls, and these accusations are repeated in the national press (Columba, 2015). No street vendor leader admitted to me that they had received money this way – which is illegal – but elected officials confirmed in interviews and in print that political parties and past administrations made extensive use of this practice. For example, Hernandez alleged that the MAS pays street vendor leaders to campaign for MAS and not for MSM, and that the MAS provides financial support for street vendor organizations. City Council President Pedro Susz alleged that past city officials used this tactic as well.

Street vendor organizations do not officially pay their elected leaders. Instead, leaders develop an array of accepted or suspect strategies to make money from their positions. I observed street vendor leaders accepting taxi rides and lunch from members who they were helping and routinely taking small amounts (10–30 *bolivianos* or U.S.D.$1.50–4.50) for typing up supplemental documents and letters on official letterhead. Rank-and-file vendors, leaders, and officials agree that this is common and acceptable. However, rank-and-file vendors, leaders, and officials allege that most leaders ask for more from members or embezzle association funds, which members and officials do not deem acceptable. One association member waved away questions about electing clean leaders with the Aymara word for stealing, "They all *lunthatapjje*." Juanita, a former vendor leader, followed up with, "They are all extortionists ... The problem isn't the extortion, everyone does that, but how it is handled."

Discretion and legally dubious arrangements between officials and street vendors sometimes veer into the clearly illicit. Street vendor leaders broker corrupt deals between their members and officials, and develop illicit relationships with specific leaders, who collect, bundle, and deliver bribes. These relationships shield officials from corruption allegations and advance the careers of officials and street vendor leaders (see Hummel (2018a) for a thorough treatment of this dynamic).

Silvia, a former street vendor leader who occasionally brokers corrupt deals, explains that the collusion is too profitable to denounce: "Everyone knows, but they make money off of this." Juanita agrees and states that, "All of the leaders take money." Agreements between leaders and officials block rank-and-file vendors from bribing bureaucrats directly, which is why they give money to an established leader to resolve their issues with the Markets Office, as Juanita explains.

> Members give money to their leader to do a specific thing. And this leader will pocket part and give the rest to the official. They have an agreement ... They will not accept just anyone.

In private, street vendors confirm that most of them pay bribes to resolve problems, especially legally dubious problems, at the Markets Office. For example, licensed street vendors are legally allowed to transfer their license to another person only if the vendor can no longer work or died, their family can demonstrate hardship, and the new license holder is a family member. In practice, street vendors treat licenses like real estate deeds and sell them to unrelated people for thousands of dollars. A license's value depends on the stall's location and the status of a license: officials and vendors reported that a centrally located stall with a full-day license and no outstanding license issues can sell for $40,000 dollars or more, while licenses in peripheral markets sell for a few thousand dollars to a few hundred. Officials accept bribes to rubber stamp these legally dubious license transfers as officially sanctioned changes to the license. Street vendors resent corruption and extortion in their organizations and the Markets Office, but most prefer paying a bribe for a favorable and illegal decision, like selling a license, to receiving an unfavorable legal resolution.

State intervention in collective action is not restricted to one ideology. In La Paz, officials and leaders from across the ideological spectrum participate in programmatic negotiations as well as corruption. The leftist and centrist La Paz city governments of the 1980s and 1990s delegated enforcement to and worked with street vendor organizations, a process which continues today under a different administration. Of the three federations in La Paz, one was affiliated with the MAS party, one with MSM, the elite, centrist party in control of the city government, and one is unaffiliated with a party. The federation that I worked with was openly Marxist, but worked with the centrist MSM. In El Alto, the leftist MAS government worked extensively with the street vendor organizations as well. When an opposition party won in El Alto, it made overtures to the El Alto street vendor organizations.

While I observed officials making clientelist offers to street vendors and organizations, most vendors brushed those offers aside as either petty, in the case of party-branded clothing, or suspect, in the case of promises of expedited licenses. Clientelist offers did not appear to drive organization; instead, they existed as a byproduct. For example, one organized vendor that I talked with at a rally for the city government's party during the 2014 presidential elections said, "I have my stall and well, they need more people ... I'm here because there are so few, look. It makes me sorry for them. It's pitiful, isn't it?"

When street vendor organizations and officials participate in a clientelist logic in La Paz, they follow the informational logic identified by Paula Muñoz in Peru (Muñoz, 2018). Officials do not encourage street vendors to form or join organizations – a years-long process in many cases – in order to mobilize their votes. Officials do cajole existing organizations to bring their members to rallies during election season to portray an image of grassroots support to other voters. Most members do not attend rallies. Leaders ask people to attend but do not enforce attendance or apply large amounts of pressure. The informational role that organized street vendors play at rallies is particularly important in the context of local elections in small media markets like La Paz: where polls are infrequent and unreliable, rallies communicate the depth and breadth of a candidate's support.

Officials elaborated on the informational dynamic in interviews, explaining that votes are important but that public, mass suppport at rallies was much more important and possible to monitor. Hernandez, who has mobilized votes for the MSM and aspires to run as a candidate, elaborated.

> First, the vote is secret, you don't know, you can't really measure, if they really voted for you. Second, it's the mass support. A leader that has 3000 people that follows them gives a certain image that they have support, and beyond that, the support of a humble sector.

Other party appointees echoed Hernandez. For example, Medeiro stated, "We need to show strength sometimes and it's easy to get (the street vendors) to march." Importantly, this dynamic is not restricted to the MSM or one side of the ideological spectrum: all major political parties who have competed for power in La Paz and El Alto have sought the support of street vendors. Adding in national politics as well, Hernandez states,

> The (street vending) sector is sought after by all ... They are very flexible and don't think that because they aren't educated they are not intelligent. They see the statistics and when they see that the statistics favor one political group, they join that political group. They wait until the end as well, they are not stupid about mobilizing.

During the 2014 and 2015 national and local election cycles, I saw the promise of favors in exchange for rally attendance increase. Street vendors did not take these promises seriously. The street vendors grumbled, and I observed that few of these favors materialized. The street vendors who I saw at rallies fell into two categories: first, leaders with regular working relationships with city officials who did not want to lose those relationships under a new administration. Second, street vendors with open cases at the Markets Office who were hoping to curry favor and did not want to restart the appeals process under a new administration. Street vendors did not attend rallies because of clientelist promises; they attended rallies because rebuilding interpersonal relationships under a new administration would be a hassle.

After the 2014 election, an older Aymara street vendor leader confirmed Hernandez's uncertainty about votes. She scoffed at the Markets Office's offers and said that even people like her who went to rallies for MSM would then vote for someone else. She stated that she voted for the Green Party because she supports TIPNIS, a national park that the national government was trying to build a highway through.

After the elections, meetings and negotiations at the Markets Office returned to business as usual, with officials primarily negotiating for compliance, especially around infratructure projects. Thus, street vendor organizations, once formed, can be politically useful to officials and may follow an informational logic during election cycles. Only a minority of street vendors respond to officials' promises and requests to attend rallies. Those that do attend do so because they do not want to rebuild relationships with new officials. For officials, this is yet another benefit that they can wring out of the organizations, not the logic behind why informal workers organize.

The quotes and stories in these sections illustrate the theoretical model's second and third implications: officials target informal workers with incentives, including cash, to induce organization, and informal workers increase organizing activity when offered more incentives. Officials materially and politically encourage informal workers to form self-regulating organizations because officials and the administrations they serve benefit from delegating monitoring and enforcement. Organizations give street vendors greater certainty, dispute resolution, and institutional support, which allow them to plan for and invest in their businesses. These benefits outweigh the costs of joining an association and dealing with manipulative leaders and officials.

Street vendor leaders and officials can extract favors and rents through the organizations and benefit much more than rank-and-file street vendors, or than unaffiliated free-riders. Additionally, officials divide organizations and stoke internal conflicts in order to manage the bargaining power of organizations and leaders.

On paper, all of La Paz's street vendor organizations have a strong commitment to democratic practices and respect for consensus-based decision-making. In reality, some organizations live up to deliberative democratic ideals, but many do not. Many vendors benefit materially and politically from state intervention in street markets, but officials' involvement creates many opportunities for manipulation and corruption. As a result, the primary beneficiaries of La Paz's impressive street vendor unions are the street vendor leaders and public officials who manipulate collective action for private gain.

This chapter brings together ethnographic, administrative, historical, and survey evidence from La Paz's street markets to illustrate the dynamics theorized in Chapter 2's game theoretic model. The theoretical model generates several observable implications that should exist in empirical data if the model is useful for explaining informal workers' organizations. The empirical evidence in this chapter shows that street vendors in La Paz embody the model's range of equilibrium outcomes, and do so in the ways that the theoretical model implies. As conditions have changed over time and for individual street vendors, officials have changed what they offer to potential organizers and joiners, and street vendors update their cost–benefit analyses in predictable ways. The theoretical model's mechanisms and implications help explain the variation that street vendors and their unions experience across time and neighborhoods, and from person to person. In the following chapter, case studies from El Alto, Bolivia and São Paulo, Brazil examine additional geographic and individual variation.

6

How to Make Money while Running from the Cops

Renato started working as a street vendor and pickpocket in São Paulo's Vila Velha street market when he was 14 because he wanted spending money. Renato is from a poor family and grew up in a poor neighborhood on the city's periphery, 1.5 hours away from Vila Velha by bus. Renato and his high school girlfriend had a daughter when he was 17, and her birth changed his behavior and plans for the future. He stopped stealing in order to avoid arrest and started working as a street vendor full-time to provide for his daughter. Years later, he works as a street vendor most days and picks up odd jobs to make extra money for birthday parties and Christmas. Renato and his colleagues in the Vila Velha market are poor Brazilians with high school diplomas. The jobs available to them are largely informal or minimum wage retail or service jobs. Renato and other unlicensed street vendors in high traffic areas make slightly more than minimum wage and work *na correria*, or on the run, from military police patrols. While working as an unlicensed vendor in Vila Velha, I hid from military police patrols with Renato and other vendors an average of 7 times per hour, or every 8.5 minutes.

Renato taught me how to make money while frequently running from the military police: we would buy a small amount of merchandise in the morning, usually 5–10 pieces, and buy more after we sold half. We bought a cardboard box and a cheap tablecloth for $1, and made a stand with them. This was our *loja* or shop. We would arrange the products carefully, so that the few pieces looked crowded on the stand. If the police came, we would grab the merchandise up in the tablecloth, pick the box up, and run or walk away. The small amount of merchandise and infrastructure made it easy to get away from police and minimized losses to about a day's profits if we were caught by the military police.

This chapter introduces street vendors, officials, and organizations in three places: El Alto, Vila Velha, and Princesa Isabela. El Alto is in the La Paz department of Bolivia, adjacent to the city of La Paz. Vila Velha is a district in

Why Informal Workers Organize. Calla Hummel, Oxford University Press.
© Calla Hummel (2021). DOI: 10.1093/oso/9780192847812.003.0006

the center of the São Paulo metropolitan area, while Princesa Isabela is on the eastern periphery. I compare the La Paz and El Alto municipal governments and street vendor organizations. I then compare the Vila Velha and Princesa Isabela district governments and the street vendors within each. In the La Paz department, street vending policies, decisions, and enforcement are made at the city government level and large cities centralize these decisions in a city Markets Office. In São Paulo, street vending policy is made at multiple levels of government, while district governments carry out decisions and enforcement relevant to individual street vendors. The subnational government comparisons hold many national-level variables constant while adding useful variation on officials, incentives, and available resources (Seawright and Gerring, 2008, p.296).

São Paulo host tens of thousands of Bolivian immigrants, some of whom worked as street vendors in Bolivia and now work as street vendors in Vila Velha and Princesa Isabela. For example, Isabel, a Bolivian clothing vendor introduced in Chapter 4, worked as a street vendor in Buenos Aires and São Paulo before returning to La Paz. Bolivians' experiences as street vendors in multiple countries enable an assessment of one alternative explanation: that Bolivians organize because they have a history and a culture of civic participation, while people of other nationalities are less inclined to work together.

Pairing La Paz with neighboring El Alto and then Vila Velha with Princesa Isabela holds many state- and national-level variables constant. In the La Paz–El Alto and Vila Velha–Princesa Isabela comparisons, local governments differ in their administrative capacity. While demographic statistics in each place differ (Lazar, 2007b, p.237), many of the street vendors in the Bolivian case studies work in both La Paz and El Alto. In the Vila Velha–Princesa Isabela comparison, the demographics of street vendors in each place are similar, according to an original survey (Hummel, 2018b). The La Paz–El Alto and Vila Velha–Princesa Isabela comparisons are imperfect most-similar comparison of subnational cases (Seawright and Gerring, 2008, p.298).

Pairing La Paz and São Paulo adds a more representative case of street vendor organization. Individuals in São Paulo come from a wider range of backgrounds and bring a wider range of resources to their work than in La Paz. São Paulo's city government has more resources and options than La Paz's government, as well as more administrative capacity, but is still far from being able to enforce and regulate as well as its administrators would like. Street vending in São Paulo is also more representative of street vendor experiences in Latin America, and appears to be similar to street vending in large cities around the world (see Bhowmik 2010, pp.256–274, for a global survey of street vendors and vending policy around the world, including São Paulo).

This chapter focuses on local administrative capacity instead of state capacity writ large because the cases are of local governments instead of countries. I use several different measures to approximate capacity in each case, because different types of data are available in each place. At an estimated $388 billion a year, São Paulo has a higher GDP than all but a few cities and many countries, according to PricewaterhouseCoopers.[1] São Paulo's annual GDP is more than 10 times Bolivia's GDP and its tax base is much larger and much wealthier than La Paz or El Alto's. However, there are vast inequalities across São Paulo's districts (Caldeira, 2000). Those inequalities are reflected in the enforcement capacity, resources, and governing conditions that each district government faces.

Comparing La Paz and El Alto, Arbona and Kohl (2004) claim that La Paz collects five times as much tax per capita as El Alto (p.262). These numbers have likely changed in intervening years, but we can observe the infrastructure, services, and new projects in each place, as well as partially observe the corporate and real estate tax base. These suggest that Vila Velha has more resources than Princesa Isabela, which still has considerably more money than La Paz, which in turn continues to generate more tax revenue than El Alto.

Turning to enforcement costs and law enforcement capacity in markets, São Paulo contracts one military police officer per 50 vendors, while La Paz employs one municipal guard per 400 vendors. The São Paulo average hides large differences in deployment: in Vila Velha, military police have run near-constant patrols on major market streets since 2009. Princesa Isabela received the option to contract military police more recently and their patrols are less frequent. I do not have data on how many municipal guards or other officers El Alto has, but I rarely saw any law enforcement in any market in El Alto.[2] Additionally, El Alto is infamous for vigilante justice, especially lynchings of suspected lawbreakers. Community leaders attribute vigilantism to residents' expectations that the police will not respond to calls or investigate reported crimes (Derpic and Ayala Ugarte, 2013, Rivas, 2016). By comparison, lynchings are rare in La Paz. Throughout the case studies, I use additional

[1] Page 22: http://pwc.blogs.com/files/global-city-gdp-rankings-2008-2025.pdf. I found an unsubstantiated claim that São Paulo collected R$90 billion in taxes in 2015 and that the city budget was R$15 billion. If that is true, São Paulo's annual tax revenue would be on par with Bolivia's entire GDP.

[2] I also started a collection of photographs of street vendors selling under municipal signs prohibiting street vending.

information, such as how often officials showed up to work, to further establish the degree of local administrative capacity in each case.

6.1 El Alto

Hundreds of thousands of people work as street vendors in El Alto and virtually all belong to one of 538 street vendor unions (Lazar, 2007a, pp.12, 53). The National Confederation of Street Vendors claims that 400,000 of El Alto's roughly one million inhabitants work as street vendors and that virtually all belong to unions affiliated with the Confederation (Bolivia, 2013). This would mean that most of El Alto's adult population and many of its teenagers work in the markets. The claim is likely inflated, but not by much: all neighborhoods in El Alto have a neighborhood market where many residents work a stall once a week[3] and the city hosts the largest market in Bolivia (Ikemura Amaral, 2019). Additionally, most teenagers and many younger children in El Alto work at least part-time to supplement their households' incomes (Shahriari, 2014, Rojas, 2014).[4] The massive 16 de Julio market, or *jach'a qhatu*, takes over the city center on Thursdays and Sundays, with over 300,000 vendors covering most of the city center (Tassi et al., 2013, p.207).

La Paz and El Alto differ in their administrative capacity (Arbona and Kohl, 2004, pp.255, 258, 260): the La Paz city government has a clear organizational structure staffed by career bureaucrats who keep the city functioning on a constrained budget. In contrast, the El Alto city government struggles to convince employees to show up for work, and its offices are scattered around the city in unmarked, rented buildings and lack fixed addresses. Both cities rely on civil society organizations to enforce local laws, but lower capacity El Alto delegates more to groups like street vendor unions.

The La Paz city government encourages street vendors to form and participate in unions by offering licenses and bureaucratic access to organized vendors. Association leaders frequently reported that they formed an organization when an official or colleague told them to, often after the municipal

[3] The Confederation, the city government, and many *alteños* claim that almost everyone works a stall somewhere in the city. While I was not able to verify this for the entire city, every *alteño* I know – from career street vendors to housekeepers to my rugby teammates to hip-hop artists – worked at a neighborhood market or the 16 de Julio market at least once a week.

[4] Bolivia passed a controversial child labor law in 2014 that legalized child labor for minors of 10 years and older. Lawmakers and child labor activists – many of whom are unionized minors with the Union of Child and Adolescent Workers, UNATSBO – support the law on the grounds that it legalizes and regulates an economic reality that will exist as long as working parents cannot cover household expenses with full-time jobs (Shahriari, 2014).

guard issued warnings for selling without a license, as the champagne ladies' association's and Amelia's union's founding stories illustrated in the previous chapter. Once organizations form, the La Paz city government delegates enforcement and encourages street vendors to participate as union members in order to boost compliance with local laws.

The La Paz city government does not have the resources, personnel, or political capital to enforce vending regulations on its own and works with street vendor organizations to achieve basic compliance or policy goals. Jorge, a former city bureaucrat, details the extent of the city's negotiations with street vendor organizations:

> To do these (infrastructure projects), we have to go to the federations and lobby them ... The other way is bottom up: We approach the vendors at their stalls and see how everything is, what they are missing, to know how we could frame something so that it's favorable to them ... And if we reached an agreement with them, we would go to the federation with the agreement so that the federation could approve it. From the smallest thing, like moving a stall a meter to avoid blocking a garage, we have to negotiate.

Jorge explains that the city government must negotiate with street vendor organizations; it does not have the capacity to implement policy unilaterally. As a result, the city government offers incentives to induce policy compromises with the organizations. The city also offers individual members benefits like stall improvements for participating in ways that benefit the city government.

Street vendor organizations finance and construct infrastructure projects like public market buildings and roads that governments usually provide (Tassi et al., 2013, pp.122–124). In La Paz, these projects follow a template set out by the city, called a *usufructo* agreement. In La Paz, an organization can propose improvements to public infrastructure, sign an agreement with the city, and finance and complete those improvements themselves. The city retains ownership of the infrastructure and issues a long-term lease to the organization in exchange for paying for improvements. In La Paz, *usufructo* agreements help the city upgrade infrastructure without paying for it and let market organizations make changes to the infrastructure that they use every day without waiting years for the city to budget and complete the same project.

In El Alto, organizations build new infrastructure as well as improve existing structures. Organizations retain ownership of the market buildings that they finance and they build or improve roads so that shoppers can access the new market buildings, because the city government cannot (Tassi et al., 2013, pp.122–124). In El Alto, these agreements are often the only way for market associations to create or upgrade infrastructure because the city cannot or will not complete or even start the project. Goldstein (2016) documented similar agreements around infrastructure improvements in Cochabamba, Bolivia (p.76).

In El Alto, the city government signed a 10-year agreement with the Federation of Street Vendors of El Alto that went much further than any agreement between street vendors and the La Paz city government. The agreement codified monthly coordination meetings and low annual vending fees while offering significant incentives for working with the government and internally enforcing local vending laws. In the 19-point agreement, the city agreed to return 50 percent of vending fees to the sector in the form of public works, finish infrastructure projects that affect vendors within 60 days, and never remove stalls, among other things. In return, civil society organizations like street vendor unions enforce dozens of local laws.

Several of the agreement's points were never implemented, especially the ones that required more planning and resources from the city government. In particular, the fourth article promises a new street vendor headquarters and the seventh article reserves city land for a publicly funded Street Vendors' Hospital. These structures were never built. Likewise, the city routinely spent years on dubious infrastructure improvements that displaced street vendors, instead of the agreed upon 60 days in Article 3. Article 14 of the agreement freezes annual licensing fees for a decade and pledges that the city will return 50 percent of those fees to the sector. The city collected the fees, but how they were spent was part of a public scandal and debate that was never fully resolved.

The city did implement many points in the agreement, to the material and political benefit of the Federation, its leaders, and many of its members. Vendors had much more success getting benefits from the city that required little action or passive non-enforcement. As in La Paz, this is evidence of forbearance (Holland, 2016, p.232) as well as regular working relationships between the city and street vendors, whereby the city provides incentives and delegates to street vendor organizations. As previously stated, the agreement froze licensing fees at pocket change levels for 10 years: the most profitable zone paid 20 *bolivianos*, or less than $3, a year while the peripheral zones paid less than $1.

Additionally, the city worked closely with the Federation and street vendor leaders on a daily basis. The coordinating meetings between the city and the Federation set out at the end of the agreement happened on a mostly regular basis, according to interviewees. Participant observation at the El Alto Markets

Office and interviews with vendors and their leaders demonstrated that the city did pass local ordinances that the Federation requested. For example, the Federation requested and received ordinances that streamlined and centralized processes at the Markets Office.

However, by largely delegating street vendor requests and centralizing requests, authorization, and representation in the Federation and its leadership, the El Alto city government handed the Federation a monopoly over street vending in the city. This centralized an incredible amount of authority in Braúlio Rocha,[5] the leader of the El Alto Federation and the National Confederation. For 10 years, any street vendor making any request to the city had to get a letter from Rocha. Rocha faced constant accusations of corruption, and he has been arrested on corruption charges several times over 15 years.

Officials at the El Alto Markets Office and the Collections Office volunteered examples of how they frequently worked with the Federation. The offices relied on the Federation much more than the La Paz city offices. On multiple occasions, officials recommended that I go to the Federation for information on local laws, data, and street vending practices because the Federation, not the city's Market Office or officials, was the clearinghouse for information on the city's street vending regulations. Additionally, the Federation appeared to have more administrative capacity and certainly a longer institutional memory and paper trail than the city government.

The El Alto Healers' Association is one example of how the city's delegation to the Federation presents trade-offs for street vendors in El Alto. The association of (self-identified) witches, healers, wisemen, and fortune tellers monitors and regulates a high-traffic area in the center of El Alto. The association organized decades ago and coordinates with the city and the Federation. Members pay annual licensing fees to the city as well as association dues. In return, the city maintains their licenses, which allow a cabin-like concrete stall where they can store merchandise and conduct business. With this infrastructure, each member of the union holds a license worth tens of thousands of dollars on secondary markets. In this sense, the city pays potential violators to participate in civil society organizations that regulate members and markets. While an association representative stated that they benefit from the organization and their licenses, he also stated that they *had* to affiliate with the Federation in order to work with the city government. Unlike La Paz, rank-and-file vendors and small organizations have little to no choice in who they affiliate with in El Alto.

[5] I am considering him a public figure because he is an elected union representative and his name and picture frequently appear in national newspapers.

Both the La Paz and El Alto city governments turn to civil society organizations like street vendor unions to internally enforce local laws. Both city governments strike compromises by offering incentives to organizations and their members in exchange for self-regulation. Neither government has the capacity to unilaterally enact even basic policy objectives. However, lower capacity El Alto delegates more power to civil society than La Paz and sustains higher civil society participation.

6.2 Vila Velha and Princesa Isabela

In São Paulo, street vending organizations are a recent and fragile phenomenon (Itikawa, 2006, p.342). Only a dozen organizations exist, representing 1–2 percent (Itikawa, 2006, pp.344–345) of the city's 100,000 street vendors (Pamplona, 2013, p.226). Organizations rise and fall with their founders, have a largely absent member base, nonexistent bylaws, and infrequent meetings. Most street vendors do not participate in work-based organizations (Itikawa, 2010, p.82). The few street vendors who are unionized belong to the one small category that the city government does negotiate with – disabled license holders – or have exceptionally high resources relative to their colleagues (Cuvi, 2016, pp.396, 404–405). São Paulo has the resources and administrative capacity to imperfectly enforce its laws and it does, even against petty violators like street vendors. As the city's administrative capacity and financial resources have improved in the last two decades (Pamplona, 2013, p.237), successive administrations of different ideologies have ramped up law enforcement in street markets (Itikawa, 2010, p.254).

The São Paulo city government started a licensing program in the 1950s that granted licenses to disabled street vendors (Itikawa, 2010, p.250). The city institutionalized street vending in 1991 with Decree 11039, which recognized street vendors' right to work in public space and established a licensing procedure. The city government periodically opened registration for new licenses in the 1990s, coinciding with periods of low growth and high violent crime rates. The timing of these licensing programs suggests that city governments may have been more willing to distribute licenses as enforcement capacity declined. As economic and administrative indicators improved, both conservative and leftist administrations increased enforcement and revoked licenses: in 2001, at the beginning of Marta Suplicy's leftist Workers' Party administration, 23,000 street vendors had licenses but by 2004, only 6000 licensed vendors remained (for Human Rights, 2014, pp.35–37). Between 2006 and 2013, José Serra and

Gilberto Kassab's conservative administrations revoked nearly 4000 licenses and then declared the rest invalid. A court overturned the decision, but leftist Mayor Fernando Haddad attempted to revoke all licenses again in June 2015.

The Brazilian state's and the city government's interventions in street vending are largely punitive. The federal government offers limited tax incentives for informal workers to formalize, but few workers know about or are able to access these programs. The federal government does not work with informal workers' organizations to promote its formalization programs, nor does it conduct much outreach to educate workers about new programs. On the other hand, the federal government has spent millions of dollars to cut off supply chains of counterfeit, off-brand, and improperly taxed consumer goods by sending federal police into street markets and on supply routes throughout the country, with mixed success (Pinheiro-Machado, 2011, pp.290–292).

Pinheiro-Machado (2011, pp. 27–34) conducts research in street markets and along supply routes in Shenzen, China, Ciudad del Este, Paraguay, and throughout southern Brazil, including São Paulo. She finds that federal police successfully interrupted supply routes across Brazil, following stricter tax compliance policies in the 2000s (Pinheiro-Machado, 2011, pp.290–292). However, they did not stop informal retail: some people rerouted or charged higher prices to reflect a higher risk of confiscation. Many street vendors turned from legal goods that lacked a complete paper trail to higher margin counterfeits, reasoning that if all products faced higher scrutiny and a chance of confiscation, they might as well sell more legally dubious but more profitable products.[6] Street vendors whom I interviewed in 2015 reiterated this logic.

The São Paulo city government employs thousands of military police, hundreds of Metropolitan Police, and dozens of inspectors to police street vending. Mayor Gilberto Kassab drastically increased the number of police dedicated to street vending by signing an agreement with the military police in 2009 (Cuvi, 2016, p.403). The agreement assigned 3900 off-duty military police to patrol street markets throughout the city from 7 a.m. to 10 p.m. every day (Cuvi, 2016, p.404). Mayor João Doria renewed the agreement, called *Operação Delegada*, in 2018. At the city level, heavy enforcement has persisted across changes in power between conservative and leftist administrations. Despite campaign promises to social movements representing street vendors, the leftist Suplicy and Haddad administrations maintained levels of policing similar to their conservative predecessors (Itikawa, 2010, p.254), though they backed off the

[6] Pinheiro-Machado presentation at the Latin American Studies Association annual conference, May 30, 2015 in San Juan, Puerto Rico.

conservative administrations' goal to eradicate street vending in the city of São Paulo (Cuvi, 2016, p.407).

Officials in central São Paulo made it clear in interviews that they view street vending as a problem to be controlled, preferably with law enforcement. "Within all of the attempts to control (street vending) that we have here, we know that it's a big problem. It's not a secret," stated one district administrator. The language that officials use to describe their work with the informal sector is highly oppositional: with the help of the military police, officials and inspectors "combat" street vending with "beatdowns" and "operations."

Tiago Moura leads a team of city inspectors and directs military police patrols from *Operação Delegada* in one populous São Paulo district. He explained how he sees street vendors in his district.

> They are many. And they have nothing to lose, they're not worried. They are very simple people that sell from their little stalls. For one of them, if he loses the stall one day, he gets another ... and they have a very hard life, so, for them, if they get beaten up one day, and I say beaten up as in, in a confrontation (with the military police), he's not going to be intimidated, he's going to come back the next day. So, control here is very difficult.

Moura's words illustrate the view of many city officials in São Paulo: street vendors are defiant, and not even violent repression deters them. Moura, his boss, his subordinates, and his colleagues in other districts justify their heavy and often violent enforcement stances by pointing out that unlicensed street vendors are breaking laws. Officials also justify their severe responses with examples of street vendors and other informal workers engaging in more costly illicit activities, like piracy, counterfeiting, smuggling, laundering, or fencing stolen goods. For example, Moura continued, "These street vendors start to bring criminals, people who sell stolen goods, pirated goods."

To Moura, anyone who breaks a law is a criminal, like Renato and Julião. Julião is an older, recovering addict who works on the same corner as Renato and watches out for the younger people near him. He replaced addiction with religion and often prays for the younger men around him or counsels them. Renato and Julião sometimes sell off-brand toys around Christmas or pirated jerseys at sporting events, and use the profits to buy gifts for their daughters. Contrary to Moura's assertions, Renato, Julião, and the other Vila Velha vendors are intimidated by military police patrols and carry psychological and physical wounds from police beatings. Multiple vendors told me of near-death experiences at the hands of military police. Vendors will stop working for days or weeks after these traumatic experiences. Many do not want to return to street vending after experiencing police brutality. Those who do return to street vending come back because they need money and do not have better employment options.

Despite over a decade of heavy policing and the publicly stated goal of removing unlicensed street vendors from Vila Velha and other central São Paulo districts, tens of thousands of street vendors still work in these areas. Many street vendors sell the counterfeit, untaxed, or uninspected goods that officials have tried particularly hard to curb. The Brazilian state and its officials have the resources and organizational capacity to sustain a heavy level of enforcement across multiple administrations. Officials who oversee and implement heavy enforcement policies are aware that they cannot fully eradicate informal work, though they see eradication as the ideal. With the significant but imperfect law enforcement resources that they have, Moura explains:

> We are not going to be utopic and think that we are going to end street vending now, there's no way ... What do we do? Control. This is what we do. What we can do is control it so that this doesn't turn into chaos.

Police attempt to deter newcomers and confiscate unlicensed vendors' goods. Licensed vendors report that the Metropolitan Police come by once or twice a day to verify licenses and ensure that street vendors follow regulations. This is a high level of policing: it means that even the 1–2 percent of vendors in full compliance with city law must maintain that compliance daily. Even licensed, fully compliant vendors reported during interviews that they were harassed on a daily basis by police looking for any excuse to fine them or revoke a license.

Officials and unlicensed street vendors in residential neighborhoods outside of Vila Velha – typically individuals selling food on street corners – reported in interviews that military police or the Metropolitan Police came by once or twice a day as well, and that they run or hide when this happens. One snack vendor admitted that she bribes a police officer monthly to call her ahead of time and then hides in the shop where she stores her wares overnight; she suggested that this is a common practice. An elderly fruit vendor on a quiet street corner reported giving up his former, more lucrative spot to a younger vendor during the Kassab administration because, at 70, he could no longer run away from the police on a daily basis. He lamented that even in his new and quieter spot, he occasionally has to run from the police while pushing a heavy fruit cart. He recounted one instance in which a military police officer pulled a gun while chasing him and his 50-pound cart of unlicensed guavas and pineapples.

Conversely, unorganized and unlicensed street vendors working in Vila Velha contend with constant policing. As previously mentioned, I recorded military police patrols passing by an average of seven times per hour on the market street where I worked. The patrols varied from groups of officers passing every two minutes to breaks between patrols of 20 minutes at a time. The street vendors who I worked with had adapted their routine to the constant policing.

Street vendors noted that they developed these strategies during the Kassab administration and that, prior to the increase in policing under Kassab or in less policed areas, they invested in more product at a time and more expensive wooden carts and tables to sell from. In the month that I worked as a street vendor in São Paulo, only one of the 10 unlicensed vendors with whom I worked had merchandise confiscated, though I saw police confiscating wares from less experienced street vendors almost daily.

For many street vendors in São Paulo, stringent enforcement keeps their resources low by discouraging those with other options from entering that line of work and draining persistent street vendors' resources through frequent confiscation and repression. On paper, policing street vendors means confiscating excess, improperly documented, or unlicensed goods, which inflicts financial losses on petty violators. In practice, as Moura mentioned and I witnessed, many military police use arbitrary force while confiscating merchandise. Police brutality can be fatal; while confiscating merchandise in 2014, a military police officer shot and killed a street vendor selling counterfeit CDs at point blank range (Globo, September 9, 2014).

Contrary to Moura's earlier statement, confrontations with police and confiscations leave significant physical, psychological, and economic scars on street vendors. While working as a street vendor in Vila Velha in June and July 2015, I regularly saw military police draw their guns while chasing street vendors, and three of the 10 unlicensed street vendors with whom I worked had scars from police beatings. Most street vendors, licensed and especially unlicensed, had stories of police brutality. Additionally, younger street vendors told me about colleagues who had stopped working as street vendors because the constant threat of confiscation and violence was too much for them. Older vendors told of colleagues who had worked for years as street vendors and left after the city revoked their licenses or police confiscated a particularly large amount of product. Both actions can erase years of hard work and leave a street vendor destitute. Cuvi (2016, p. 410) documented similar accounts, including street vendors who died after suffering psychological or physical trauma upon losing their licenses or wares.

Under conditions of heavy and often brutal policing, the vast majority of São Paulo's street vendors do not organize. Walter, a middle-aged street vendor in the Princesa Isabela district, links the majority's lack of organization to the city's refusal to delegate or negotiate, "Why don't unlicensed vendors organize? Because it's very difficult to get anything out of the authorities." Talking about his unlicensed colleagues, Benedito, a licensed street vendor working in Vila Velha, agrees, "They don't organize because the city government won't meet with them, it will never give them (licenses)." Paulo, an older street vendor leader with decades of union experience, links the government, the economy, and street vendor disorganization explicitly, "We will always have illegal vendors because the state ... the state is not interested in organizing them."

These quotes explicitly connect the city government's actions and street vendors' calculations about the potential costs and benefits of participating in work-based organizations. Street vendors discuss how licenses function as important incentives: Benedito suggests that if organizations could secure licenses from the government, people would form or join street vendor organizations. In the absence of this state-supplied incentive, organizations have little influence over street vendors and most street vendors, as well as other informal workers in São Paulo, remain unorganized.

The São Paulo city government has succeeded in curtailing unlicensed street vending and deterring many newcomers. However, it has not eliminated street vending and essentially plays a massive game of whack-a-mole[7] with unorganized street vendors. The individuals that these policies target are overwhelmingly poor and have little formal education. As a result, few São Paulo street vendors participate in work-based organizations. Across the border in Bolivia, the conditions reverse: weak city governments actively encourage street vendors to participate in unions, and experienced vendors form and maintain these organizations to capture state incentives.

There is one exception to the São Paulo city government's strict enforcement policies. Princesa Isabela is a working-class peripheral district about two hours away from Vila Velha by public transportation. The district has hundreds of neighborhood street vendors and several street markets. One of these markets is a weekend barter market where residents bring used goods to trade. In Princesa Isabela, a district administrator started issuing licenses to street

[7] Whack-a-mole is an old American arcade game where the player uses a mallet to hit plastic moles that pop out at random from holes in a board.

vendors on the condition that they form an association and help the district assert control over the barter market. Why do officials encourage street vendors to organize and work with the city in Princesa Isabela, while repressing them in other districts? In interviews, District Administrator Isak da Souza and his subordinates enthusiastically elaborated on the pilot program, its logic, and its history. Da Souza summarizes,

> In Prinesa Isabela, there was a market that was out of control. When I got here, you had around 150 licensed vendors, around 600 unlicensed, and maybe 80 marginals working in this so-called barter market. These marginals were selling guns, drugs, animals, snakes, parrots, and all that. This is what we had there. We entered, separating the wheat from the chaff. Regularized vendors to one side. Of these nearly 600 unlicensed, we separated the unlicensed from the marginals. For the marginals, we sent the police in to deal with them and these 600 we started to regularize.

The district administration called in the military police when they received reports of local gangs dealing drugs and weapons in the market. At first, da Souza pursued an eradication strategy and ordered the military police to sweep the area and post patrols. However, during joint raids on the market, da Souza saw the military police chasing older food vendors and artisans along with local gang members. He recalls,

> When we got there with the inspectors, everyone took off running and what grabbed my attention was a woman who must have been 68, 70, who sold little empanadas and she fell literally on her face in them ... From behind, she looked exactly like my dead mother. In that moment there, I told myself that this business is insane, it's not OK. It's one thing when a marginal is selling guns, drugs, and such. It's another thing when it's this woman, she's an entrepreneur, not a marginal. She made the little empanadas, prepared them, put them on a tray and went out to sell ... so I stopped everything and said "No, I'm not going to treat these people like marginals." And I called them to the office and we negotiated.

Da Souza proposed a pilot program: the district would license hundreds of street vendors operating in the area, on the condition that they form an association, formalize, and assist the district administration in eradicating black market activity. Da Souza explained that he required the street vendors in the barter market to organize because dealing with them collectively made his job easier.

> Author:"Why did they form an association?"
> De Souza:"So that we can deal with them collectively ... As individuals I would have to deal with them one by one. So put them together as an entity and I can deal with them as an entity."
> Author:"You told them to organize?"
> De Souza:"Yes, it was the first thing I did."

A year into the program, Princesa Isabela had a new street vendor association with roughly 300 members. Unlike São Paulo's other street vendor associations, the vendors in this association are fully formal in the sense that they have all relevant licenses, pay applicable taxes and social security, and obey a range of local laws. The organized street vendors have registered as micro-entrepreneurs with the national government, registered their association, enrolled in the national tax and social security systems, hold licenses from the city, sell only tracked, registered goods with a paper trail, and have city-issued name tags and vests – they meet more extensive conditions than the rest of the licensed vendors in the city. They also assist the district officials and, with their help, the city government has regained control over that corner of peripheral São Paulo.

Princesa Isabela's pilot program and street vendor association is the exception that proves the rule. In a pocket of São Paulo with lower enforcement capacity than other parts of the city and where informal activity was increasing and imposing higher costs on the city government, ambitious officials tried a new strategy. A career bureaucrat appointed by a center-right mayor explicitly intervened in the informal sector with organizing incentives in order to regain compliance. A group of unorganized informal workers then seized on these incentives to quickly form an association, formalize, and work with officials.

6.3 Individual Differences

In La Paz, El Alto, Vila Velha, and Princesa Isabela, some street vendors found multiple unions while others are joiners and some actively refuse membership. What explains this individual-level variation? In all four cases, informal workers with more resources – especially education – are much more likely to participate in informal workers' organizations than their colleagues with less.

Additionally, the more education a street vendor has, the more likely they are to be licensed, and university-educated street vendors are particularly likely to reach leadership positions. In other words, education appears to correlate with deeper forms of participation.

Bolivian street vendors come from many demographic groups: street vendors come from different indigenous communities, speak multiple languages, and come from all age groups. While many street vendors have only a few years of formal schooling, others hold law degrees. Many street vendors barely subsist on their earnings while others have multiple cars and houses. In line with research that finds that people with more resources participate more than people with less, leaders tend to be better off relative to other street vendors. In the La Paz survey, union members were twice as likely as unaffiliated vendors to own a car, and also more likely to own a house. Assets and income could be endogenous to leadership positions, as discussed in the previous chapter. Education, however, is not endogenous to leadership positions, as most street vendors complete their education before working full-time or before moving into leadership roles.

Education is particularly important: in the La Paz survey, street vendors who had attended college were several times more likely to be union members than people who had not. Furthermore, rank-and-file vendors actively promote leaders with a college education (Hummel, 2016, pp.340–344). Fabiana, a former vendor leader who works in both La Paz and El Alto, points to education to explain why a federation leader will continue in his post, "Jaime Santana is the only one with the academic background, the diplomatic education, to do it." Likewise, Lazar points to the founding of the Universidad Pública de El Alto and its subsequent training of young leaders, many of them street vendors, and support of social movements and civil society groups as a driving force behind El Alto's politics (Lazar, 2007a, p.52).

In Vila Velha, organized vendors like Benedito are better off in terms of education and income than their unorganized colleagues. Most street vendors in an original survey (see appendix for survey protocol and instrument) and Pamplona's citywide study (2013, pp. 237–240) make roughly minimum wage and did not finish high school. From the 1700s until today, street vendors have primarily been migrants to the city with low levels of education relative to other workers (Itikawa, 2010, pp.249–250). In fact, Pamplona (2013, p. 240) finds that as education levels for most Brazilians and most categories of workers in São Paulo steadily increased over the second half of the twentieth century, street vendors retained low levels of education and in some decades the average level of education decreased.

Despite these trends, I find that organized street vendors often come to the profession with more education and earn higher profits from their work. For example, Lourenço is blind and from a poor family in rural Brazil. As a child, he was sent to São Paulo to attend a school for the blind, where he completed high school and initially found a formal office job. When he was laid off during a recession, he became a street vendor and, with more experience than most of his new colleagues, he became a street vendor union leader. Another union leader, Augusto, attended university and used his advantages to start a union.

> I took advantage of my secure situation ... That's where I went after more information, investing time and money out of my pocket. I researched and discovered (The Workers' Trade Union Central) and started to get involved. And, at the time, I started a union.
>
> Augusto, quote from interview transcription (for Human Rights 2014, p.19).

To facilitate the comparison between La Paz and São Paulo, the latter has a large population of Bolivians who migrate to work in textile and construction jobs, especially around Vila Velha. Many Bolivians working in São Paulo, including several whom I interviewed, also work as street vendors, and many worked as street vendors in Bolivia before migrating. Most do not belong to a street vendor organization in São Paulo, even if they belonged to one in Bolivia. Their experiences as street vendors in both countries allow an assessment of one alternative explanation: that Bolivians organize because they have a history and a culture of civic participation, while Brazilians are less inclined to act collectively. However, for Bolivians living in São Paulo, the main difference is in the government's capacity and resulting street vendor policies, not their culture or social capital. Edwin, a street vendor from La Paz working in São Paulo, contrasts the two environments.

> Bolivia and Brazil are extreme opposites. In La Paz, any group can block the highways and the city ... The government gives too much power to social organizations. But here? Nobody does anything.

Edwin points to the governments' positions relative to the organizations and their willingness to delegate as deciding factors between how civil society operates in Bolivia versus Brazil. Interviews in Bolivia confirmed Edwin's experience: one street vendor with relatives in São Paulo stated that her relatives and their associates did not organize or participate in existing street vendor organizations, in contrast to La Paz. Isabel, who worked in São Paulo and Buenos

Aires before returning to La Paz, stated that she had not joined any organizations in Brazil or Argentina, but had quickly joined one in La Paz to get a license.

In summary, street vendors operate under vastly different conditions in La Paz, El Alto, Vila Velha, and Princesa Isabela. In La Paz, El Alto, and Princesa Isabela, individual street vendors have several options about how and where they work. To a certain degree, street vendors also have choices about their legal status and relationship with the city and federal governments. In the Bolivian cases, individuals typically join autonomous street vendor organizations that offer services to members, represent their memberships' interests to the state, and enforce local laws. The cities delegate regulation to these organizations because the cities' limited administrative capacities preclude adequate law enforcement. While the work and organizations are far from ideal, street vendors benefit from having options and, on average, from belonging to organizations that work with the government.

Conversely, street vendors in Vila Velha, São Paulo face starker choices: work illegally or find a different job. Street vendors can choose where they work and what they sell, but their options end there. In greater São Paulo, 98 percent of street vendors work without a license and under constant threat of being stopped by the military police. The city has plenty of resources to spend on law enforcement and urban development, and it has chosen a punitive strategy toward street vending, other types of informal work, and the urban poor more generally. Most street vendors do not belong to a union or other association and see participation as futile, precisely because the city largely refuses to negotiate with street vendor organizations. Organizations occasionally form, but without any benefits to offer members, they rarely grow or endure.

Across the four cases, individuals with more resources participate more than their less well-off counterparts. Individuals with more education, time, and money use those attributes to access or create more options for themselves. For example, street vendors with more money have more choices about what they sell, where they work, and how much to formalize their business, because they have more money to buy different types of products in bulk, pay stall fees in prime markets, or purchase a license or a lawyer. Street vendors with more education and time more readily turn to joining or starting a work-based organization. Street vendors with more education and other experience see organizations as a powerful way to approach governments and their agents. They are also more likely to know or learn the logistical and legal steps necessary to establish an organization. More educated people are also more likely to know how to navigate the bureaucracy and convince politicians and bureaucrats to listen to their demands, in part because of officials' biases (Hummel, 2016). Finally and crucially, officials are more likely to listen to individuals with educational credentials, and because of that, other vendors elect them to leadership positions.

The four cases demonstrate the different conditions that street vendors face when working with local governments of varying administrative capacity. The cases also demonstrate that the options available to street vendors and, consequently, their participation decisions, depend in part on the resources available to a given individual. These conditions explain why some informal workers, like the champagne ladies in La Paz, have stable, licensed businesses and working relationships with local officials through their unions. These dynamics also explain why other informal workers, like Renato and his colleagues in Vila Velha, have an unstable income, no representation, and scars from police brutality.

7
Conclusion

Half of the world's workers hold informal jobs (Ronconi, 2010, p.719). In countries like Bolivia, India, and South Africa, massive informal workers' organizations represent millions of people and make their members' livelihoods more secure (Agarwala, 2013). In cities across the globe, from La Paz to Lagos to Bangkok, citywide associations represent thousands of informal workers and frequently lobby local governments to improve their members' working conditions (Bhowmik, 2012; Grossman, 2021). Why do informal workers form and join organizations?

The answer to this question has implications for the well-being of hundreds of millions of people. This book advances the argument that informal workers organize where their activities exceed officials' enforcement capacity, where officials are under pressure to meet governance goals and advance in their careers, and where informal workers know how to mobilize their colleagues. The project demonstrates that under these conditions, officials may offer private incentives to informal workers who organize self-regulating groups. Aspiring civil society leaders use official incentives to convince their colleagues to join and participate in informal workers' organizations. These benefits help informal workers organize where they otherwise would not. Officials then negotiate with informal worker organizations and the organizations enforce local laws.

Why don't more informal workers organize if membership brings clear benefits? In line with past research on informal markets, this book shows that informal workers face challenges when they mobilize. Most informal workers are poor and work long, grueling hours in order to support their families on low and unpredictable incomes. Every hour spent organizing is an hour of lost income or rest. Additionally, most informal workers do not have experience organizing or extra resources to dedicate to activism. Informal workers often compete with their closest colleagues in many jobs, like street vending, unlicensed transportation, and recycling. This means that an informal worker's coworkers are fierce competitors, not natural allies. With these significant barriers to collective action, many informal workers never form or join a workers' organization, even when they know that they could benefit from one.

Why Informal Workers Organize. Calla Hummel, Oxford University Press.
© Calla Hummel (2021). DOI: 10.1093/oso/9780192847812.003.0007

Unorganized informal workers create problems for local and national governments. Informal workers typically do not pay taxes and ignore dozens of health and safety laws, which creates costly problems for governments. Many informal workers, like street vendors, scavengers, or gypsy cab and mototaxi drivers, work on public land or use public infrastructure in the course of their business, which generates conflicts over public space. Officials can choose to intervene with positive incentives in informal workers' organizing decisions. The theoretical model in Chapter 2 establishes when officials intervene or choose not to. First, where informal workers can organize on their own, the official free rides on their efforts and does not offer any additional help, and we consequently see small organizations. Second, if incentives cost more than the problems that unorganized informal workers create, the official does not intervene and we see no organizations. However, if the official can save money by providing an organizing incentive, they offer an incentive to the informal workers. This incentive helps informal workers create large organizations.

The theoretical model replicates established findings by Olson (1965) and Ostrom (1990) while adding novel results. The model demonstrates when and why a simple state intervention can influence people who will not overcome collective action problems on their own. Most importantly, where unorganized people create problems for officials and will not overcome barriers to collective action on their own, officials benefit by stepping in with organizing incentives. Where possible, officials will free ride on individuals' contributions: if citizens can produce public goods without external help, officials readily free ride on those efforts.

Informal workers organize in nearly every country for which we have data. In the Americas, on average, 20 percent of informal workers join an organization at work. Lower capacity countries like Bolivia, Haiti, and Peru have more organized informal workers than higher capacity countries like Uruguay, Costa Rica, and Chile, and highly educated informal workers are particularly likely to organize. I use machine learning and public opinion data to estimate a data set of informal workers across the Americas in Chapter 3. I analyze this data set alongside a data set of known informal workers, a data set of self-employed workers, and a data set of likely informal workers from 42 countries around the world. With these data, I analyze which informal workers join organizations and where informal worker organizing happens. I find that levels of democracy and political competition do not help explain where informal workers organize. I use these broad trends to select cases for further research: street vendors and officials in two cities in the metropolitan region of La Paz, Bolivia and two districts in the metropolitan area of São Paulo, Brazil.

The qualitative chapters show how the game theoretic and statistical models work on the ground. City officials in La Paz and El Alto delegate enforcement to large civil society groups and report that they cannot regulate sufficiently without these organizations. Lower capacity El Alto delegates more than La Paz. Civil society groups in both cities regulate their members remarkably well – and much more effectively than the police could hope to. Civil society groups attract members with incentives like licenses and government access, which the groups receive from officials. These interactions can become contentious when leaders use state resources to challenge the very officials who supply them. Officials manipulate incentives to manage civil society organizations and demands.

Local and national governments that have sufficient administrative capacity and resources choose to enforce laws against informal work. For example, the United States has one of the lowest rates of informality in the world. This is in part because robust labor markets and clear self-employment regulations give workers many formal employment options. The U.S.'s powerful enforcement agencies also discourage informality and are relatively successful at catching people who persistently skirt the law. Unlicensed street vendors spend much of their time dodging police. Getting caught can have fatal consequences. Police across the country kill street vendors during on-the-job altercations: New York City police killed Amadou Diallo in 1999 and Eric Garner in 2014, and Baton Rouge police shot Alton Sterling to death in 2016 (Baker et al., 2015; Cooper, 1999; Fausset et al., 2016).

Starting in the mid-2000s, Brazilian officials followed suit and used increasing resources to ramp up enforcement against informal markets and workers. The enforcement campaigns put thousands of federal and military police in street markets and disrupted supply routes along the Paraguayan border as well as unlicensed markets throughout the country (Pinheiro-Machado, 2011, pp.287–312). As a result, Cuvi (2016) found that tens of thousands of street vendors in São Paulo left vending after the city government started an eradication campaign (pp.404–406). In interviews with officials and street vendors, city officials state that they prefer to use their increased resources to hire more military police. Officials do not regularly discuss anything with the few informal workers' organizations that do exist, much less delegate law enforcement roles to them. The one exception to this pattern – a pilot program where an official offered licenses on the condition that unlicensed vendors organize and help regulate – occured in a peripheral neighborhood of São Paulo where the city government had lost control to black market actors.

This book contributes to research on collective action, civil society, and informal economies by demonstrating that officials can encourage informal workers to organize and regulate each other. Where unorganized people create problems that an organization could resolve, officials can intervene and promote organization. In places like Bolivia, where national and local governments do not have many resources to increase enforcement, officials have implemented positive and negative incentive structures to encourage informal workers to form, join, and participate in civil society organizations that enforce local laws.

The incentives that officials use to encourage self-regulating civil society groups are cheaper than increasing law enforcement. Officials can implement them within existing administrative structures and without significant budget allocations. For example, in La Paz and El Alto, Bolivia, local authorities use licenses as a positive incentive to encourage informal workers to organize. Only organization members can receive licenses. If an organization does not exist in the area that a person works or if they do not like existing groups, they must form a new one. Licenses give informal workers certainty and enable investment and planning, and can be resold on unofficial secondary markets for thousands of dollars. Governments also encourage organization by granting organized workers access to the bureaucracy. Access can be a powerful incentive for individuals, and it has no direct impact on the city's budget. The La Paz city government has paid street vendor leaders to work with officials in the past, and even cash payments can be cost-effective compared to additional police salaries.

7.1 Informal Sector Policies

Practitioners can develop policies that delegate regulation to informal workers and their organizations. This book demonstrates that officials increase monitoring and enforcement when they work with informal workers. Officials can formalize workers when they co-produce monitoring and enforcement, as the case of the Princesa Isabela district government in Chapter 6 demonstrates. Many lower capacity governments already delegate to civil society (Post et al., 2017). Policymakers elsewhere, including in higher capacity cities and countries, could delegate as well. Delegation increases citizen engagement, can decrease incarceration, and saves money.

Policymakers can use the logic of state intervention to help informal workers formalize and incorporate them into policy processes. Officials around the world frequently launch formalization programs for informal and self-employed workers, but these programs rarely hit their enrollment targets (Bruhn and McKenzie, 2014). Yet this study and others document informal workers going to extensive lengths to acquire documents or resources for formalization, such as licenses and loans, and flocking to easier opportunities for either.

For example, Agarwala (2013) documents informal workers' unions that successfully demanded health cards from the government and ID cards certifying them as informal workers (pp.3–4, 16). Agarwala (2013) claims, "As a result of this strategy, informal workers are ironically pulling the state into playing an even more central role in their daily lives than it has traditionally done for members of formal workers' movements" (p.15). Street vendors in La Paz, El Alto, and Princesa Isabela echo these demands. For all of their frustrating experiences with the bureaucracy, most street vendors with whom I work seek out officials and demand more attention and resources from officials.

With this level of interest from informal workers, why do officials struggle to enroll workers in formalization programs? Conversations with street vendors and officials in Bolivia and Brazil reveal that officials rarely design programs that match the needs of informal workers because many officials do not coordinate with informal workers or their representatives. Existing programs often put a heavy burden of proof and documentation on informal workers while providing delayed or unnecessary benefits. In contrast, when cities or national governments set up formalization programs in consultation with informal workers' organizations and take their needs and resources into account, demand can quickly outstrip supply. For example, any licensing program typically has more applicants than licenses, as La Paz and the Vila Velha district experience. New York City, which has a street vending sector that is smaller but in many ways similar to São Paulo's, has a licensing program for 5000 licensed vendors, a years-long waiting list, and faces frequent pressure from vendors to increase the number of licenses (Schmidt, 2016).

The case of the Princesa Isabela district demonstrates how officials can co-produce formalization and enforcement with informal workers. A local administrator approached street vendors and offered them a clear path to licenses – an incentive that the street vendors all wanted. The administrator offered this incentive on the condition that the street vendors follow several steps to formalize and cooperate with local officials to enforce laws in the district. The approach worked: half of the street vendors formalized, the city directed enforcement at persistent black market actors, and formal, organized street vendors now assist local officials to maintain compliance in the district. The program worked because officials offered street vendors' theirpreferred outcome – to legally work in their local market, as their own bosses – in exchange for help with the officials' goal, which was to regain control over the market.

As in Princesa Isabela, formalization can happen through a carrot-and-stick approach. Officials can give people a path to formalization that eases some of their problems with the government. This option could involve things that local informal workers state that they want, which often includes licenses, safe workplaces, or healthcare. Officials can make these incentives available to most people and within a reasonable amount of time. Officials can then make this option conditional on cooperation, paying taxes, or following local laws. Once people have begun the process, officials can then direct enforcement at persistent noncompliers. Often, as in the case of Princesa Isabela, newly formalized workers help local officials monitor and enforce against more serious violations. Thus, effective formalization policies offer an incentive that people want, follow that incentive with conditions and enforcement against persistent noncompliers, and over time, co-produce formalization and more effective law enforcement.

When designing formalization policies, policymakers may recognize that informal workers have many competing demands for their time and resources. Policymakers can approach informal workers and any existing organizations, instead of waiting for workers to approach them or find programs on their own. Policymakers could seek out and incorporate the input of informal workers and their organizations multiple times during the policy process. Quick, clear, and simple enrollment guidelines and concrete, immediate benefits may help policymakers achieve enrollment targets. Formalization measures – for example, business registrations or micro-business tax brackets – could minimize paperwork and offer clear, material incentives. For example, a micro-business tax could require minimum proof of income for individuals to enroll and governments could assume the responsibility for investigating businesses that might hide in the lower tax bracket. Requiring individuals to provide extensive proof that they run a micro-business at the outset discourages those individuals and does not remove the incentive for larger businesses to hide in a lower tax bracket. Additionally, informal workers are much more likely to participate in formalization policies if they receive concrete incentives like licenses, business loans, or healthcare for participation.

For a mixed success example, Bolivia has a simplified low tax bracket for self-employed people and micro-enterprises, virtually all of which are informal in the country. The *Régimen Tributario Simplificado*, the Simplified Tax Regime or RTS, started in 1987 as part of a tax reform package and in 2015 had 49,452 enrolled contributors.[1] In an interview, an official stated that the program's purpose is to slowly formalize the sector, not to extract significant revenue.

Of the hundreds of street vendors with whom I spoke in Bolivia, I met one who was enrolled, one who had tried, and many who did not know about the RTS. The vendor who tried to enroll said she gave up because the proof of income and other required documentation was more than she had and because she realized that the regulations attached to complying with the RTS once enrolled were too onerous. The one who had enrolled was an older, prosperous street vendor who enrolled with help from a lawyer to receive additional documentation proving her business's legitimacy. She had left her union over a disagreement with leadership and retained a lawyer to help her navigate the bureaucracy. To her, the incentive for enrolling was not a lower tax bracket, but documentation. She used the documentation when dealing with the state and banks, in lieu of the legitimacy that union support provides for other street vendors.

On one hand, the RTS is a success because tens of thousands of informal workers have used it to voluntarily enroll in the tax system. The program's success appears, in part, to come from providing an incentive that informal workers seek out – official documentation – and RTS officials know this. The RTS falls short by enrolling a tiny minority of the country's microbusinesses. This is partially because the bar for enrollment is too high for many, but also because many eligible people are unaware that the program exists. The RTS and other simplified tax programs for informal workers could potentially expand much further if they lowered barriers to documentation and actively coordinated with informal workers' organizations.

The case of La Paz's street vendors comes with a dark side that policymakers should guard against: delegation to civil society groups may increase opportunities for corruption. Importantly, relationships between officials and civil society leaders – which are necessary if a government works closely with civil society – can hide and perpetuate bribery. The ethnographic data demonstrate that leaders become intermediaries between officials and rank-and-file members who need a problem solved. As intermediaries, leaders bundle and deliver bribes to officials, and benefit by taking a cut in the process. This practice advances the careers of officials and civil society leaders at the financial and political expense of rank-and-file members. By mediating corruption, leaders develop working relationships with officials, which makes them indispensable

[1] These numbers are from the official I interviewed, who pulled them from an internal database.

to their members – even as leaders make money off their members' problems. Additionally, when leaders bribe officials, members do not witness the transaction and cannot make an eyewitness denunciation later. This protects officials' careers by reducing their accountability to the people they serve. Governments interested in adopting a delegation strategy can create independent monitoring systems to catch corruption and reduce the incentives for engaging in it.

7.2 Broader Implications

Officials offer organizing incentives to civil society actors in many contexts, not just informal markets. This project argues that where governments cannot directly enforce, they are more likely to incentivize and delegate to civil society groups that can. The theory has implications for contentious politics, corporatism, and enforcement. First, delegation to self-regulating groups carries risk for governments. By empowering civil society groups to develop strong organizational structures and enforcement capacity, governments can inadvertently build organizations strong enough to oppose the state, make onerous demands, and disrupt other projects. Second, the process of state intervention in unorganized markets could launch a process of corporatist state-building. Finally, enforcement decisions have implications for which citizens enter the criminal justice system and which do not.

Delegation to civil society can create new governance problems for officials. By providing resources and empowering civil society, governments can encourage broad-based mechanisms of social control (Ostrom, 1990). However, by building up powerful social organizations instead of state enforcement agencies, governments run the risk of building strong opponents. Civil society groups want outcomes that diverge from what governments, bureaucracies, and officials want (Migdal, 1988). Anria (2018) and Nelson-Nuñez and Cartwright (2018) document this phenomenon in Bolivia: civil society organizations and NGOs frequently groom, select, and support opposition candidates. Hundreds of civil society leaders across Bolivia have developed working relationships with local government officials, taken incentives, and become powerful adversaries of the local government. This includes running for and winning elected officials' seats, as Mavel Machicado's story in Chapter 5 illustrated with the La Paz City Council and as Anria (2018) documented with former street vendor leader and Mayor Edgar Patana in El Alto (p.183).

When officials delegate enforcement to civil society groups, officials set up a principal-agent problem. A principal-agent problem describes a situation where one person, the principal, has the power direct another person, the agent, to do something, but the agent wants to do something different and the principal cannot directly monitor what they do. In delegation, the official, as the principal, wants groups to monitor their members and enforce regulations, and provides incentives to build and strengthen groups that can do so. The organizations, as the agents, benefit from increased resources but may prefer to enforce some regulations and not others, and enforce against some people more than others.

I observed this among street vendors: street vendor unions enforced stall dimensions and selling times, and prevented disputes between street vendors from escalating. However, the organizations rarely enforced other regulations, like paying taxes on goods like alcohol and cigarettes or not selling counterfeit or adulterated goods. Similarly, organizations did not enforce equally. For example, leaders often enlarge their stalls and extend their selling times while preventing rank-and-file members from doing the same.

Civil society organizations may also use their power to demand more from the government. Demands from powerful organizations can put resource-poor governments in a bind: administrations need the support of these groups, but they have limited political and material capital to expend appeasing them (Huntington, 1968). Governments can threaten to cut off incentives, but the groups can also threaten to stop enforcing or actively break laws, quickly creating large and expensive enforcement problems for governments. Civil society groups do this on a regular basis in Bolivia. For example, a common protest tactic is to block highways to stop trade or access to politically important areas (Dangl, 2007). Additionally, government incentives may be crucial for starting and building organizations but less central as groups develop their own bases of support.

The case of the El Alto Street Vendors Federation in Chapter 6 detailed how incentives can build strong civil society organizations that then use their power to demand more from the government, engage in violent contention, and take over the government. In the early 2000s, the El Alto federation burned down city hall, struck an agreement with the city government, and then ran their own candidate for mayor and won. Similarly, in Chapter 4, city council member Pedro Susz discussed how previous administrations in La Paz gave too much to civil society organizations, and that these organizations would use the material resources and political power from the city to demand more. When their demands were not met, the organizations would shut down the city with blockades and violent threats or acts against public officials. Under the *Movimiento Sin Miedo* administration, the city wrested back some power. Civil society organizations no longer blockade the capital for weeks on end. However, civil society organizations regularly blockade city hall and issue death threats to elected and appointed officials. Most Markets Office directors who I interviewed mentioned going home with security details after recieving death threats from street vendors, and one had been kidnapped. During fieldwork in July 2018, the Markets Office director was receiving daily death threats and the Municipal Guard controlled access to the office because the same union that was issuing death threats had attacked another government building and threatened to set the Markets Office on fire. The city government took the threats seriously because street vendors have kidnapped and serverely injured personnel in the past, and unions have shown up at the Markets Office with homemade explosives. Additionally, street vendors have burned down government buildings in El Alto, Cochabamba, and Santa Cruz (Dangl, 2007; Goldstein, 2016).

Resource-strapped governments stand to improve order, compliance, and engagement with civil society by incentivizing organized groups and delegating enforcement roles to them. However, the tactic presents a risky trade-off: by giving money and power to social groups, local governments empower others instead of building up in-house enforcement capacity. Delegation over time can create powerful social groups beyond the government's control.

Under the right conditions, delegation could help officials build government institutions. Andreas (2013) suggests that some early state-building tactics in the United States relied on bringing informal businesses into the state's regulatory system through legalization and limited self-regulation. These businesses were key to the success of early political projects because they gave crucial monetary and in-kind resources to a weak state and held valuable knowledge, like trade routes and locations of foreign operatives. This is similar to a process that scholars call corporatism. Corporatism was a state-building process that brought together guilds, communities, the state, and the church over decades or centuries in Western Europe (Iversen and Soskice, 2009). Neo-corporatism extends further to include some non-European countries (Streeck and Kenworthy, 2005).

Bolivia and India's informal work policies resemble corporatist state-building projects. These policies are part of what Streeck and Kenworthy call neo-corporatism: organized social groups with political representation that recognize the supremacy of the state (2005, p.441). Similar to the dynamics that we see in Bolivia, Streeck and Kenworthy (2005, pp.441, 447) claim that neo-corporatism helps states handle conflict in modern democracies, and these social groups moderate conflict in places where the state struggles to reach, like workplaces.

Delegation to civil society groups can make economic and political sense for weak states, as this project has argued. Scholars studying the co-production of public goods and services have found similar dynamics in water delivery, HIV policy, and more (Nelson-Nuñez and Cartwright, 2018; Post et al., 2017; Rich, 2013). Successful delegation helps politicians and bureaucrats achieve medium-term goals and advance their careers. Voters reward order and predictability and demand deliverables like lower crime, improved traffic, and adequate services, particularly in local elections. Officials tasked with reaching those deliverables face budget constraints and professional rewards that encourage improving governance without large expenses. Cheap or non-monetary incentives, like licenses or access to officials, and delegation to civil society helps achieve goals without straining the budget. Additionally, delegation builds ties with politically active community groups, yet another deliverable that politicians and bureaucrats alike can point to, particularly to their superiors. Returning to the neo- literature, delegation builds neo-corporatist structures by giving organized social groups durable representation in political systems. Additionally, this representation does not necessarily depend on parties and is not limited to election cycles or elected officials.

Broadly, participatory civil societies may return resources to the state over time in the form of tax revenue, savings on law enforcement, and trained personnel (Amengual, 2013; Brass, 2012). Anria (2018) finds that Bolivian civil society leaders use their organizational positions to launch careers in public administration and that the government recruits personnel from social organizations (pp.127–128). Brass (2012) and Rich (2019) find similar personnel trajectories in Kenya and Brazil, respectively. Governments across the world delegate to NGOs and private contractors, often with the explicit goal of saving money and improving service delivery (Besley and Ghatak, 2001, Post et al., 2017). Larger nongovernmental entities, like the United Nations and the World Bank, frequently encourage delegation to NGOs and contractors because they save money, improve outcomes, and reach poorer citizens more than most state bureaucracies (Besley and Ghatak, 2001, p.1365). If delegation increases revenues while decreasing law enforcement costs, then delegation returns resources to the state. Successes with NGOs documented elsewhere and the informal workers' associations documented here suggest that states can build capacity over time by making investments in civil society instead of state-based enforcement mechanisms (Boulding and Gibson, 2009; Rich, 2013).

The argument suggests that governments with lower capacity can encourage participatory civil societies while higher capacity states may track informal and other poor workers into law enforcement systems. The theory implies that higher capacity states track informal workers into the criminal justice system more frequently than their lower capacity counterparts, precisely because higher capacity states can effectively enforce even minor laws. This implication supports recent reports in the United States on modern debtors' prisons (DOJ, 2015) and ethnographic work in urban sociology which finds that heavy enforcement for minor infractions like driving without a license or falling behind on payment plans can trap people in poverty and the criminal justice system (Desmond, 2016; Goffman, 2015). Additionally, the case studies support research in the American context which finds that increased interaction with criminal justice systems decreases political engagement (Weaver and Lerman, 2010; White, 2019).

Local governments with more capacity can reverse this trend by using delegation policies to improve enforcement and community engagement. Several municipalities in the United States have limited delegation policies to integrate particularly marginalized residents into the community. Los Angeles fast-tracked a plan to license and legalize street vending across the city after concerns that increased immigration enforcement could sweep up street vendors cited for minor public space infractions (Branson-Potts, 2017). In another example, Miami, Oakland, and Washington, DC started pilot programs that pay high-risk young people not to commit crimes, and to attend leadership classes (Workman, 2016). These programs give potential violators incentives to follow local laws, while integrating them into the cities' regulatory systems. The programs also increase the local administrations' legitimacy and engagement with the poor communities that the street vendors and young people disproportionately come from. Thus, delegation policies may increase citizen buy-in with local administrations, and bolster parties' electoral success at the local level.

Higher capacity governments may find it easier to avoid some of the pitfalls from La Paz's and El Alto's delegation policies. Higher capacity governments are less likely to encourage corruption by delegating because they are more likely to have effective anti-corruption monitoring systems in place. Likewise, higher capacity governments run a lower risk of empowering civil society groups that can threaten to create larger governance problems because higher capacity governments can resort to direct enforcement if necessary.

Agarwala (2013), Auyero (2001), Holland (2016) and others argue that poor people's votes matter, and as a result, parties and governments try to secure those votes with pro-poor policies, goods, and discretion in the run-up to elections. This project demonstrates that between elections, citizens' compliance matters. Noncompliance can create large and expensive problems for governments, from lost tax revenue to epidemics to spiking crime rates. In contrast to wealthier citizens, many poor people experience governments' interest in their compliance as policing and repression (Scott, 1969, p.1142). Bolivia may offer a less repressive alternative: the government pays attention to poor citizens between election cycles and in some cases works proactively with individuals and groups to achieve compliance. Bolivia's national and local governments increase compliance by materially and politically encouraging self-regulating groups and delegating enforcement to them. Delegation strategies incorporate citizens into communities instead of policing them. Delegation policies improve lives by channeling resources to local organizations while increasing compliance with health, safety, and quality of life regulations.

Governments around the world delegate state roles and responsibilities to civil society groups. Delegation incorporates individuals and communities into state projects. Delegation can also bring previously hidden or illegal activities into state regulatory structures. In Nicaragua, the Supreme Court of Justice designated a sex worker collective as a judicial facilitator (Cabezas, 2019). The collective's members are licensed community mediators, and the official goal of the program is to reduce the police and judicial system's backlog of minor conflicts while integrating sex workers into a regulatory system. The collective has organized over 2000 of Nicaragua's estimated 14,000 sex workers and has affiliated with national union organizations (Cabezas, 2019). In this example, a government with problems tracking and enforcing community conflicts has enlisted a semi-legal group, designated them as intermediaries between the judicial system and their communities, and increased the reach of the regulatory system – all without large budget increases. In doing so, the government has encouraged a semi-legal and largely unregulated group of citizens to organize and become part of the state's regulatory system.

Local governments with shoestring budgets enlist similar tactics in creating new mass transportation, waste disposal, and housing policy. In Kigali, Rwanda, local mass transportation was a hodgepodge of privately owned vans, trucks, gypsy cabs, and mototaxis. Many of these transportation providers had organized themselves into loose cooperatives or business associations that would fight over routes (Goodfellow, 2015, p.132). The local government instituted a new mass transportation policy that banned all mototaxis until every taxi driver agreed to join an association. The association enforces local laws and all mototaxists are now licensed, trained, and wear vests marking them as such (Goodfellow, 2015, p.137). Goodfellow (2015, p.137) states that the government approached the policy with the "rationale of, if you understand something then you will do it better than if someone were to police you." In the example of Kigali, a local government without the resources to institute major mass transportation infrastructure opted to reorganize mass transport in the city by requiring informal transportation workers to organize and regulate themselves. The policy professionalized informal transportation, brought the sector in line with local regulations, and, through licenses, gave thousands of citizens a strong stake in the local government's city development project.

Most examples of government delegation to informal workers or other civil society actors come from low-capacity contexts. I suggest that this is because lower capacity local governments face extreme budgetary pressures as well as pressure from voters who demand improvements in governance by the next election. Higher capacity governments can respond to governance demands by hiring more police, training more bureaucrats, or building new infrastructure, and governments retain more control over these initiatives when they choose not to delegate. On the other hand, lower capacity governments have fewer options, and delegation is cheap, making it more attractive to highly constrained local governments.

Governments around the world struggle to incorporate informal workers into state structures. Workers around the world struggle to cobble together a living from insecure and informal jobs. This book has documented the innovations and trade-offs that local governments and informal workers developed in La Paz and São Paulo to resolve these challenges. The project demonstrates that officials can pay informal workers and others to organize self-regulating groups, and that informal workers take these incentives and organize their colleagues when they have the opportunity. These organizations improve the lives and jobs of hundreds of thousands informal workers while increasing compliance with local laws and citizen engagement in local government. Their experiences have implications for the lives and jobs of hundreds of millions of informal workers around the world. Street vendors and officials in La Paz and São Paulo demonstrate that governments can work with civil society groups to build state institutions where even the most vulnerable citizens demand, participate in, and co-produce the goods and services that they need.

APPENDIX

Theory Appendix

Game Theoretic Model and Proofs

In this finite and complete information game, n informal workers decide whether or not to organize and bargain with an official and j joiners decide whether or not to join the newly organized group. The informal workers move first by playing a public goods game where the moves are organize or defect. The informal workers need k organizers to provide the public good, $g > 0$, and all organizers pay a private cost $c_i > 0$. Every informal worker that defects generates a negative externality, $-e < 0$, for the official. Any organized workers move to a bargaining stage, where the official makes some offer x, where $0 \leq x \leq 1$. The organized workers accept or reject the offer. If the organized workers accept the offer and there are at least k of them, each organized worker receives $g + x - c_i$ and unorganized workers receive g, while the official receives $g - xm - e(n - m)$, where m is the number of organized workers. If the informal workers do not meet the k threshold but still accept the deal, each organized worker receives $x - c_i$ and unorganized workers receive 0, while the official receives $-xm - e(n - m)$. If the informal workers reject the deal, all workers receive a status quo payoff of 0, while the official receives $-en$. Finally, if the initial informal workers form an organization, other informal workers j_i can pay a cost c_{ji} to join after the fact and receive the selective incentive.

Table 1 Model notation

v_i	a given worker; informal worker i.
s	the official.
j_i	a given joiner; joiner i.
x	the official's offer, where $0 \leq x \leq 1$.
n	total number of workers.
k	the number of workers needed to provide the public good, where $0 < k \leq n$.
m	the number of workers who organize.
g	the public good, where $0 \leq g \leq 1$.
e	the official's cost of enforcement where $0 \leq e \leq 1$.
c_i	the cost of organizing to worker$_i$, where $c_i \sim U[0, 1]$.
c_{ji}	the cost of organizing to joiner$_i$, where $c_{ji} \sim U[0, 1]$.

The founding informal workers face two choices: Organize or defect, and then accept or reject the official's offer. The official makes one choice: how much x to offer. The joiners make one choice: join or abstain.

Moving into equilibrium analysis, the game has a unique pure strategy subgame perfect equilibrium. This means that for a given set of parameter values, all actors choose the same strategy set in equilibrium.

Why Informal Workers Organize. Calla Hummel, Oxford University Press.
© Calla Hummel (2021). DOI: 10.1093/oso/9780192847812.003.0008

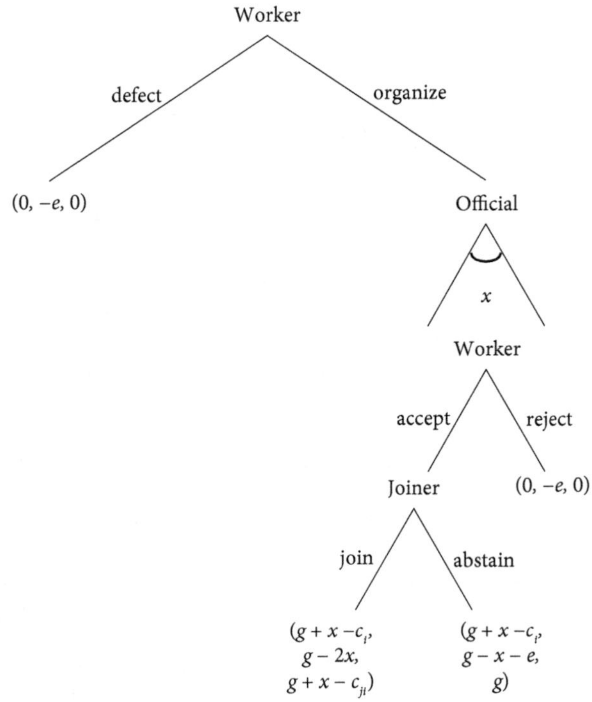

Fig. 1 Stylized representation of the game where $n = 1$ and $j = 1$

Proposition 1 The strategy profiles below constitute the subgame perfect equilibrium:

$$V_i = \begin{cases} \text{organize, accept when } c_i \leq x \text{ and } m \neq k \\ \text{organize, accept when } c_i \leq x + g \text{ and } m = k \\ \text{defect, reject otherwise} \end{cases}$$

$$J_i = \begin{cases} \text{join when } c_{ji} \leq x \\ \text{abstain otherwise} \end{cases}$$

$$S = \begin{cases} \text{offer } x^* = c_m \text{ when } e > c_m \text{ and } m \neq k \\ \text{offer } x^* = c_m - g \text{ when } e > c_m - g \text{ and } m = k \\ \text{offer } x^* = 0 \text{ otherwise} \end{cases}$$

To prove that the stated strategies are in fact equilibrium strategies, we start at the terminal nodes of the game tree. We will establish that in equilibrium, no actor has an incentive to deviate from the strategies stated above. In the final stage of the game, joiners decide to join or abstain. In doing so, a given joiner i compares $g + x - cji > g$. Solving for c_{ji}, a given joiner i will accept when $c_{ji} \leq x$ and reject otherwise. No joiner has an incentive to deviate from this strategy. Accepting when costs are higher than the benefit requires the joiner to accept an avoidable loss, and rejecting when benefits are more than costs requires the joiner to forgo a sure gain.

At the third node, organized vendors decide to accept or reject. In doing so, a given vendor i compares $g + x - ci > g$ if $m > k$. Solving for c_i, a given vendor i will accept when $c_i \leq x$ and reject otherwise. If $m < k$, a given vendor i compares $x - ci > 0$ and will accept when $c_i \leq x$ and reject otherwise. In the special case where $m = k$, a given vendor i compares $g + x - ci > 0$ will accept when $c_i \leq g + x$ and reject otherwise. No vendor has an incentive to deviate from this strategy. Accepting when costs are higher than the benefit requires the vendor to accept an avoidable loss, and rejecting when benefits are more than costs requires the vendor to forgo a sure gain.

At the second node, the official chooses an offer x^*. In making its choice, the official compares their payoff for an accepted offer to a rejected one, and makes a positive offer if $g - xm > -em$ which can be rewritten as $x < e + \frac{g}{m}$. When making a positive offer, the official sets x at the highest organized vendor's cost, c_m (and in the special case where $m = k$, $c_m - g$). The official has no incentive to set x higher because the previous step demonstrated that vendor i will accept any offer at $c_i = x$ or above, thus setting x above the highest reservation value lowers the official's payoff (note that the vendor with the highest cost is vendor m, so if the official sets x at her cost, x is above the reservation values for all other vendors). Likewise, the official has no incentive to set x lower than c_m because lowering x even slightly below vendor m's reservation value triggers vendor m's rejection, saving the official x but adding $-e$ to their payoff.

At the first node, vendors decide to organize or defect. Vendors know the parameter values and payoffs of other players. Therefore, they can anticipate the value of x and base their organizing decisions on it. Vendor i organizes where $x > c_i$ (or in the special case where $m = k, x > c_i - g$) and defects otherwise. Vendor i has no incentive to deviate from this strategy: If she organizes where $x < c_i$, she receives a negative payoff when she could choose to lose nothing. If she defects when $x > c_i$ and at least k other vendors organize, she receives g and saves c_i, but forgoes a larger x.

The equilibrium strategies lead to several different equilibrium outcomes, depending on the values of the parameters. Under the conditions $e < c_m$ and $c_k < g$, no informal workers organize, joiners have no organization to join, and the official does not intervene. A given joiner i at the final node has no organization to join and thus her only choice is to abstain (even if she had a choice, she would choose between paying c_ji and receiving nothing or abstaining and receiving nothing and would still choose to abstain). A given informal worker i in the next node of the game compares $-c_i$ to 0 and opts to reject. The informal worker has no reason to deviate because accepting an offer of 0 and no public good incurs a negative payoff instead of rejecting and taking 0. At the second node, the official offers $x^* = 0$. The official has no incentive to make a higher offer because setting x at informal worker m's reservation point costs more than accepting the externality e. At the first node, informal worker i chooses not to organize because her participation will not generate g and the official will not offer the $x^* = c_i$ that would change her calculation.

Conversely, where $e < c_k$ and $c_k \leq g$, resulting in $m = k$ and $x^* = 0$, exactly k informal workers organize and the official does not intervene. In this case, we look at informal worker k's decisions because she is the pivotal organizer whose actions decide if the public good is provided or not. At the final node, joiner i does not join the nascent organization because $g + x - c_ij < g$. Joiner i enjoys the public good whether she organizes or not and $x^* = 0$ does not offset her organizing costs. Under these conditions, joiner i abstains. informal worker k accepts the offer $x^* = 0$ because $g + 0 - c_k > 0$ or $g > 0$. At the second node, the official sets $x^* = 0$ because g provides enough of an incentive to the organized informal worker to accept in order to keep g. The official has no incentive to increase x^* above c_k and attract additional informal worker because $e < c_k$. At the initial node, informal worker k organizes because $g - c_k > 0$; deviating from this strategy would require her to forgo this gain in favor of 0.

Under the conditions $e > c_{m<k}$ and $c_k \geq g$, less than k informal workers organize but only with state intervention. The conditions $e > c_{m<k}$ and $c_k \geq g$ result in $m < k$ and $x^* = c_{m<k}$. At the final node, joiner i does not join with the few coorperating informal workers because $-c_ij < 0$. Informal worker $i < m$ accepts $x^* = c_{m<k}$ in the next node because $x^* - c_{i<m} > 0$. She has no incentive to reject the offer and take 0 over a positive payoff. In the second node, the official sets $x^* = c_{m<k}$ to incentivize informal workers to organize in the absence of a public good, by offsetting their organizing costs. The official has no incentive to set $x^* < c_{m<k}$ because lowering x^* below any informal worker $i < m$'s reservation point adds an e to the official's payoff and in this case $e > x^*$. In the initial node, informal worker $i < m$ organizes because $x^* - c_{i<m} > 0$, even though worker $i < m$ anticipates that the public good will not be provided.

Where $e = c_k$ and $c_k \leq g$, resulting in $m = k$ and $x^* = c_k - g$, exactly k informal workers organize and the official subsidizes them. In this case, we look at informal worker k's decisions because she is the pivotal worker whose actions decide if the public good is provided or not. At the final node, joiner i joins the new organization if $x > c_ij$ and abstains if not. Next, informal worker k accepts the offer $x^* = c_k - g$ because it is set at her reservation value (she compares payoffs $g - c_k + c_k - g > 0$). At the second node, the official sets x^* at informal worker k's reservation value: $x^* = c_k - g$. The official has no incentive to increase x^* above $c_k - g$ and attract additional informal workers because $e = c_k$. At the initial node, informal worker k organizes because $g - c_k + c_k - g = 0$, and we assume that she organizes at her reservation value.

Where $e > c_{m=n}$, resulting in $x^* = c_{m=n}$ and $m = n$, everyone organizes. At the final node, joiner i joins the new organization if $x > c_ij$ and abstains if not. The informal worker with the highest costs (worker $m = n$) accepts the deal because it is set at her reservation value (she compares payoffs $g - c_{m=n} + c_{m=n} > g$). All other informal workers with lower costs accept and have no incentive to deviate and take 0 over a positive payoff. At the second node, the official sets x^* at informal worker $m = n$'s reservation value: $x^* = c_{m=n}$. Because $e > c_{m=n}$, the official has no incentive to lower the offer and substitute x^* with a more expensive e. At the initial node, informal worker $m = n$ organizes because $g - c_{m=n} + c_{m=n} > g$, and we assume that she organizes at her reservation value.

Overall, equilibrium outcomes depend on the size of g relative to other parameters. If g is large relative to the kth informal worker's costs, the official free rides when k people organize. The intuition behind this is that once organized, the informal workers will not reject any offer because they do not want to lose g. As a result the official offers 0. Consequently, the official may want to pay informal workers more to always organize, but they cannot commit to changing that offer once informal workers pass the k threshold. On the other hand, if g is small relative to the kth informal worker's costs, the official makes a positive offer to all informal workers, and that offer is based on k's costs. Once informal workers organize, the official will make an offer that will keep everyone organized who has orgaizing costs that are lower than the externality they generate (there is some nonlinearity here if that number passes the k threshold, because then g offsets how much the official needs to offer when $m = k$).

We can now explore the comparative statics of the model. The partial derivative of the official's cut point x' with respect to g is $\frac{\partial x'}{\partial g} = \frac{1}{m} > 0$. The partial derivative is positive because negative numbers of participants cannot exist. Therefore, the official's cut point is increasing in g. This means that as g increases, the official's indifference point for making a positive offer also increases; therefore, there is a larger range of parameter values for which the official will make a positive offer. Note that this is because the official and the informal workers enjoy g. Therefore a larger g allows the official to spend more on x. Additionally, where $m = k$, the official can discount her offer by g.

The partial derivative of informal worker i's reservation value x' with respect to c_i is $\frac{\partial x'}{\partial c_i} = 1$. As costs increase, a given informal worker requires a higher offer to offset increasing costs and make organizing worth her while.

The partial derivative of the official's cut point x' with respect to e is $\frac{\partial x'}{\partial e} = 1$. Therefore, the official's cut point increases as the externality increases. This means that as the number of organized informal workers m increases, the official's indifference point for making a positive offer increases and there is a larger range of parameter values for which the official will make a positive offer. In other words, as e increases, the official is willing to accept more values of x in order to avoid e.

Robustness Checks and Extensions

How much do the model's results depend on individual modeling choices? The model produces equilibrium strategies and comparative statics that, as with any model, are a function of its assumptions. Many of these assumptions are critical and directly model the strategic interaction that the case illustrates. For example, linking unorganized informal workers to the official's payoff with $-e$ captures the negative externality and gives the official an incentive to intervene in the informal workers' collective action decisions. Likewise, modeling the initial step as a group decision to contribute or not captures the dynamic that many informal workers face when deciding to band together with workers around them and found a union, as discussed in the main text. While the evidence in the main text grounds many of the model's assumptions in empirical evidence, it also suggests a plethora of other factors that the model either simplifies or ignores. In this section, I discuss how relaxing assumptions or extending the model to include new features affects the results.

Here we examine two assumptions in more detail: private versus public costs and the k threshold. For private costs, we will think through the change but not solve a new game, whereas we will walk through the k threshold example in more detail.

The model assumes that organizing costs are public information, meaning that all players know each others' costs. Empirically, this is not strictly the case. Informal workers may have an idea of the free time, money, education, contacts, and past organizing experience that other workers have, but they almost definitely do not have a complete picture of every potential organizer's situation. We can also think of situations or personalities that may want to misrepresent their costs. For example, someone who does not want to contribute may pretend to be busier than they are or pretend that they have less disposable income than they actually do. We can model private organizing costs by giving all informal workers beliefs about what others' costs are. In a private information set-up, each informal worker knows their cost, and knows the distribution of other people's costs but not exactly what every individual has. This is much more realistic: People are generally aware of their resources and have some idea of their colleagues' that allows them to estimate. We will not solve the model with private costs in this appendix because the result for n-person public goods games is well established and used as an example in many game theory textbooks (the example I am working off of is from McCarty and Meirowitz 2007, pp. 140–145). In the complete information game presented above, we see a low-contribution equilibrium outcome in which no one contributes and a high-contribution equilibrium outcome in which exactly k people contribute. If we move to private costs, we see a similar low-contribution equilibrium in which fewes than k people contribute and the good is not provided, and a high-contribution equilibrium in which at least k people participate and the good is provided.

In the chapter's model, I assume a k threshold, which means that if a certain number of people participate, the good is provided and if that number is not reached, the good is not provided. This assumption has empirical grounding in the case of Bolivia. In Bolivia, a group needs a minimum of 24 members to register as a union. If we conceptualize the union as a public good, then $k = 24$ in this case. However, we can conceptualize the public good in other ways. For example, if the organization provides market security and internal regulation, we might think of the public good as incremental, where every vendor who participates and pays dues incrementally increases the value of the good by contributing to security and following laws.

We can also try a different cost assumption. For example, we can assume that everyone has the same cost. This is realistic if we take a much stricter view of what constitutes a cost and conceptualize costs as dues, which are the same for everyone, or other material costs for founding an organization, which many union founders split between them. I adopt this cost assumption in the example below. The following game has the same set-up as the main model, except there is no k threshold and costs are the same for everyone:

Proposition 2 The strategy profiles below constitute the subgame perfect equilibrium:

$$V_i = \begin{cases} \text{organize, accept when } c \leq x \text{ and } m \neq k \\ \text{organize, accept when } c \leq x + g \text{ and } m = k \\ \text{defect, reject otherwise} \end{cases}$$

$$J_i = \begin{cases} \text{join when } c \leq x \\ \text{abstain otherwise} \end{cases}$$

$$S = \begin{cases} \text{offer } x^* = c \text{ when } e > c \text{ and } m \neq k \\ \text{offer } x^* = c - g \text{ when } e > c - g \text{ and } m = k \\ \text{offer } x^* = 0 \text{ otherwise} \end{cases}$$

In the final stage of the game, joiners decide to join or abstain. All joiners join if $c < x$ and abstain otherwise. At the next node, organized informal workers decide to accept or reject. In doing so, a given informal worker i compares $gm + x - c > gm - g$. Solving for c, a given informal worker i will accept when $c \leq g + x$ and reject otherwise. No informal worker has an incentive to deviate from this strategy. Accepting when costs are higher than the benefit requires the worker to accept an avoidable loss, and rejecting when benefits are more than costs requires the worker to forgo a sure gain.

At the second node, the official chooses an offer x^*. The official sets x at the minimum that all organized informal workers will accept, provided that minimum is less than e, which is what the official receives if they offer 0 and a given informal worker defects or rejects. To achieve this, the official sets x at the organized informal workers' cost minus the public good, $c - g$. The official has no incentive to set x higher because the previous step demonstrated that informal worker i will accept any offer at $c = g + x$ or above, thus setting x above the reservation value lowers the official's payoff. Likewise, the official has no incentive to set x lower than c because lowering x even slightly below the informal workers' reservation value triggers rejection, saving the official xm but adding $-em$ to the official's payoff.

At the first node, informal workers decide to organize or defect. Informal workers know the parameter values and payoffs of other players. Therefore, they can anticipate the value of x and base their organizing decisions on it. Informal worker i organizes where $c < x + g$ and defects otherwise. Informal workers i has no incentive to deviate from this strategy: If she organizes where $c > x + g$, she receives a negative payoff when she could choose to lose nothing. If she defects when $c < x + g$, she accepts 0 over a positive payoff.

These simplifications in the public good and cost terms lead to similar equilibrium outcomes. Three of the five equilibrium outcomes in the main game remain: These strategy profiles contribute to an outcome in which no one organizes under the conditions that $e < c$ and $g < c$, that all informal workers organize without state intervention under the condition that $g > c$, and finally, that all informal workers organize with state intervention under the conditions that $e > c$ and $g < c$. Importantly, players reach these outcomes for the same reasons in each model; therefore, the insight does not change, but the simplification reduces the explained variation.

We will now examine how club goods change the model. Empirically, organizations often provide club goods to their members as an additional selective incentive to recruit members and sustain participation. For example, street vendor unions can offer dispute resolution or legal services for their members. We can introduce a term, h, for association club goods into organized informal workers' payoffs and see if and how the overall results change:

Proposition 3 The strategy profiles below constitute the subgame perfect equilibrium:

$$V_i = \begin{cases} \text{organize, accept when } c_i \leq x + h \text{ and } m \neq k \\ \text{organize, accept when } c_i \leq x + g + h \text{ and } m = k \\ \text{defect, reject otherwise} \end{cases}$$

$$J_i = \begin{cases} \text{join when } c_{ji} \leq x + h \\ \text{abstain otherwise} \end{cases}$$

$$S = \begin{cases} \text{offer } x^* = c_m - h \text{ when } e > c_m - h \text{ and } m \neq k \\ \text{offer } x^* = c_m - g - h \text{ when } e > c_m - g - h \text{ and } m = k \\ \text{offer } x^* = 0 \text{ otherwise} \end{cases}$$

In the final stage of the game, joiners decide to join or abstain. Joiner i has an extra incentive, h, to offset her cost c_ji in this version of the game. She joins when $c_ji < x + h$ and abstains otherwise. At the next node, organized informal workers decide to accept or reject the official's offer. In doing so, a given informal worker i compares $g + x + h - ci > g$ if $m > k$. Solving for c_i, a given informal worker i will accept when $c_i \leq x + h$ and reject otherwise. If $m < k$, a given informal worker i compares $x - ci > 0$ and will accept when $c_i \leq x$ and reject otherwise. In the special case where $m = k$, a given informal worker i compares $g + x + h - ci > 0$ and will accept when $c_i \leq g + x + h$ and reject otherwise. No informal worker has an incentive to deviate from this strategy. Accepting when costs are higher than the benefit requires the informal worker to accept an avoidable loss, and rejecting when benefits are more than costs requires the vendor to forgo a sure gain.

At the second node, the official chooses an offer x^*. In making her choice, the official compares her payoff for an accepted offer to a rejected one, and makes a positive offer if $g - xm > -em$ which can be rewritten as $x < e + \frac{g}{m}$ (note that the club good only enters the official's payoff through its effect on x^*). When making a positive offer, the official sets x at $c_m - h$ (and in the special case where $m = k$, $c_m - g$). The official has no incentive to set x higher because the previous step demonstrated that informal worker i will accept any offer at $c_i = x + h$ or above, thus setting x above the highest reservation value lowers the official's payoff (note that the informal worker with the highest cost is informal worker m, so if the official sets x at her cost, x is above the reservation values for all other workers). Likewise, the official has no incentive to set x lower than $c_m - h$ because lowering x even slightly below informal worker m's reservation value triggers informal worker m's rejection, saving the official x but adding $-e$ to the official's payoff.

At the first node, informal workers decide to organize or defect. Informal workers know the parameter values and payoffs of other players. Therefore, they can anticipate the value of x and base their organizing decisions on it. Informal worker i organizes where $x + h > c_i$ (or in the special case where $m = k$, $x > c_i - g - h$) and defects otherwise. Informal worker i has no incentive to deviate from this strategy. If she organizes where $x + h < c_i$, she receives a negative payoff when she could choose to lose nothing. If she defects when $x + h > c_i$ and at least k other informal workers organize, she receives g and saves c_i, but forgoes a larger x and h.

In summary, adding a club good leads to the same equilibrium outcomes as the main model. Importantly, players reach these outcomes for the same reasons in each model. Introducing h to account for club goods adds an additional benefit to organized informal workers' payoffs and lowers the official's offer by h, but does not lead to different equilibrium outcomes or explanations.

APPENDIX

Quantitative Appendix

The appendix includes supplemental coding, descriptive, and procedural information for the data and analyses presented in the main text. The appendix includes supplementary information for the statistical models presented in the main text as well as robustness checks.

Survey Data

How do we measure informal work? Self-employment and informal work overlap extensively (Vanek et al., 2014, pp.34–35). Globally, most self-employed people are also informally employed (Fiess et al., 2010, pp.211–212). Survey researchers often use self-employment as a proxy for vulnerable or informal employment (Hussmanns, 2004, pp.2–10). The World Bank estimated that in 2017, 36 percent of people working in Latin America were self-employed. The United States had the lowest rate of self-employment at 10 percent of economically active people, while Haiti had the highest rate at 88.5 percent. The World Bank 2017 estimate of 36 percent self-employment is close to the ILO's 2018 estimate of 40 percent informality in Latin America's workforce. The ILO considers self-employment to be one component of informal employment. The ILO's data suggests that, if anything, using self-employment as a proxy for informality undercounts informal employment.

Other researchers suggest more precise ways to measure informal work. Baker and Velasco Guachalla (2018) identify informal workers in the LAPOP data using employment and social security questions in the 2006 and 2008 survey waves. Their designation of informal workers as people who work but are not enrolled in social security structures matches widely accepted definitions of informal work in other research as well as the definition in Chapter 1. Using Baker and Velasco Guachalla (2018)'s definition, 57 percent of working respondents in the 2006 survey wave and 56 percent of working respondents in the 2008 survey waves worked informally. This yields a total of 15,783 informal workers in the 2006 and 2008 survey waves.[2]

In Chapter 3, I use survey data from LAPOP and CSES because their enumerators ask thousands of people in countries across the world comparable questions about themselves, their jobs, and their political participation. The LAPOP data set contains 127,864 respondents, including 30,515 self-employed respondents from 2006 to 2012 and 15,783 informal respondents from 2006 and 2008. The CSES Module 4 and 5 data set contains 73,388 respondents across 42 countries from 2011 to 2018, including 7081 respondents who reported

[2] These numbers are considerably higher than the ILO and the World Bank's 2018 and 2017 estimates. The LAPOP rates may be higher because they are 10 years older and informality has decreased in Latin America in the intervening years.

Why Informal Workers Organize. Calla Hummel, Oxford University Press.
© Calla Hummel (2021). DOI: 10.1093/oso/9780192847812.005.0002

that they were self-employed and worked in often informal jobs like street vending, domestic work, recycling, subsistence agriculture, and construction. These respondents comprise 15 percent of workers in the CSES data set.[3]

LAPOP asks people across the Americas about their work lives, their demographics, their organizational memberships, their political participation and their opinions. Between 2006 and 2012, LAPOP enumerators asked people in Argentina, Bolivia, Brazil, Chile, Colombia, Costa Rica, the Dominican Republic, Ecuador, El Salvador, Guatemala, Haiti, Honduras, Jamaica, Mexico, Nicaragua, Panama, Paraguay, Peru, Trinidad and Tobago, Uruguay, and Venezuela comparable questions about their work lives as well as their political and social participation. These 21 countries are in the data set that this project analyzes. I use these data to establish patterns of informal work and organizational participation in different countries from 2006 to 2012.[4]

LAPOP has expanded the survey to more countries, including the United States and Canada, but enumerators did not ask comparable questions about work for these countries between 2006 and 2012. As previously discussed, in 2006 and 2008, LAPOP asked questions about social security that identify informal workers. Survey administrators have asked questions about self-employment since 2006. LAPOP asked about union membership through 2008 and about professional associations through 2012.

The Comparative Study of Electoral Systems gathers public opinion surveys from countries during their election years. Public opinion teams submit surveys that use a common battery of questions and meet CSES standards. Teams in 42 countries submitted data in different years: Argentina, Australia, Austria, Brazil, Bulgaria, Canada, the Czech Republic, Chile, Finland, France, Germany, Great Britain, Greece, Hungary, Iceland, Ireland, Israel, Italy, Japan, Kenya, Latvia, Lithuania, Mexico, Montenegro, New Zealand, Norway, Peru, the Philippines, Poland, Portugal, South Korea, Romania, Serbia, Slovakia, Slovenia, South Africa, Sweden, Switzerland, Taiwan, Thailand, Turkey, and the United States of America are represented in the data set. Argentina, Mexico, and Peru are in both the LAPOP and CSES data sets.[5]

The CSES background battery includes a self-employment question and a question about organizing at work, which I use in the analyses in Chapter 3. The detailed occupational question assigns a specific occupation from a list of hundreds to every respondent. The list includes occupations like "street and related sales and service workers," "cleaners and helpers," "refuse workers," "subsistence farmers, fishers, hunters, and gatherers," "assemblers," and "car, van, and motorcycle drivers." I coded these respondents into street vendors, domestic workers, recyclers, transport workers, laborers, pieceworkers, subsistence farmers, trades, and service. For street vendors and subsistence farmers, I assume that everyone in this category works informally and code anyone responding to that question as an informal worker. I do this because even in countries with low rates of informality like the United States or France, people selling goods and services on the street and engaged in subsistence activities are largely outside of regulatory and social security systems (Duneier and Carter, 1999, Gowan, 2010, MacGaffey and Bazenguissa-Ganga, 2000). For the other often informal occupations, I code people who reported that they are self-employed and work as an

[3] The CSES data primarily comes from OECD countries with lower rates of informal work, which I suspect explains the different rates of informal work across the two data sets.

[4] I do not include data on informal workers from the 2018 LAPOP surveys because those surveys do not include comparable questions on professional association or union participation.

[5] Brazil is in both data sets, but respondents in the CSES data for Brazil did not answer the occupational questions that I use to identify potential informal workers. Thus, Brazil is not in the CSES analyses.

assembler, recycler, domestic worker, laborer, or driver as informal workers. For example, a refuse worker in Mexico or the United States who is employed is likely a city employee, but a self-employed refuse worker is probably an unlicensed recycler (Gowan, 2010, Rosaldo, 2016, Feldman, 2018). I also code people who are in services and self-employed but not in a professional category as informal. This excludes the few lawyers and consultants in the self-employed category while capturing the beauticians, sex workers, cooks, landscapers, blade sharpeners, delivery people, and more who work outside of social security systems in most countries and make up the majority of the self-employed.

The survey data come from the Version 15 LAPOP release that covers 2004 to 2012. That version contains the ocup1b1_06 question on firm size that Baker and Velasco Guachalla (2018) used to code informality in 2006. LAPOP does not host the Version 15 data set anymore. I received the data and the variable coding from Andy Baker and Ximena Velasco Guachalla, who generously shared their work and answered my questions. I dropped the 2004 respondents from the data set because LAPOP did not ask comparable labor or participation questions that year. Likewise, the data set stops at 2012 because LAPOP stopped asking about professional associations after 2012.

For participation, Baker and Velasco Guachalla (2018) recoded the ordinal professional association participation variable cp9 – attended a professional association meeting once in the last 12 months, attended once a month, attended once a week, didn't attend – into a binary participant variable, where 1 signifies that the person attended at all and 0 signifies a nonparticipant. I added a binary coding for cp10, union participation, which was only asked in 2006 and 2008. I added these together, so that a given individual who reported having attended a union meeting or a professional association meeting in 2006 or 2008 would receive a 1 for organizational participation, while anyone who reported attending an association meeting in 2010 or 2012 would receive a 1.

The Varieties of Democracy 9 data set supplies GDP per capita, life expectancy, and cybersecurity capacity for the state capacity index, as well as polyarchy, political competition, civil society, and vote buying. I rescaled continuous variables for the mixed effects estimators.

To create the state capacity index, I conducted a principal component analysis (PCA) and created an index from those scores. The PCA demonstrates that one dimension, which we will call capacity, explains 68 percent of the variance across three variables in the LAPOP data and loads similarly on the three variables. In the CSES data, one component explains 66 percent, but the component loads similarly on two variables and considerably less on one.

To create the wealth variable, I conducted a PCA and created a wealth index from those scores. The PCA demonstrates that one dimension, which we will call wealth, explains 44 percent of the variance across seven variables. The one component loads similarly across the seven variables.

Random Forest Models

I initially ran a larger random forest model that predicted informality with all of the individual wealth variables, crime victimization, and city size. I have recreated this model in the replication data and in the error matrix and variable important plot below. Table 2 and Figure 2 demonstrate that adding these variables does not meaningfully improve the model's accuracy. In the name of parsimony, I cut them from the main model.

Table 2 Error matrix for the larger random forest model

Prediction	Other	Informal	Error rate
Other	37,864	3,147	8%
Informal	2,186	12,756	14%
Overall accuracy	90.5%		

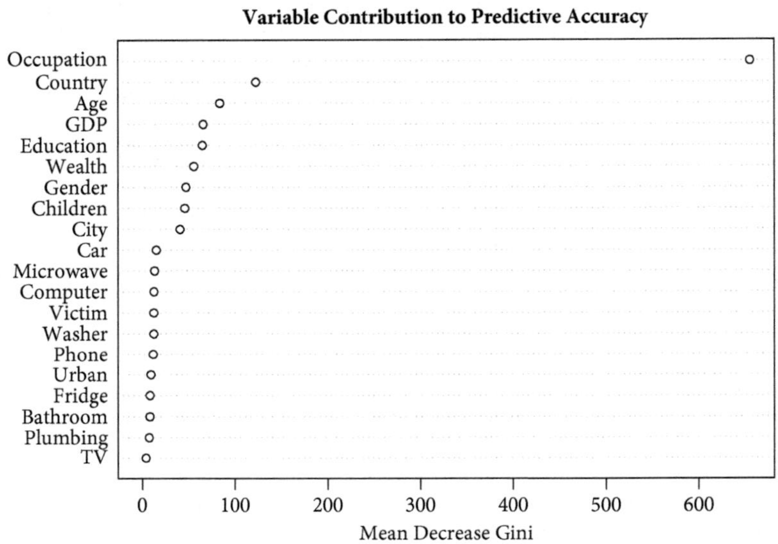

Fig. 2 Variable importance in the random forest model, ranked from highest to lowest predictive power, as measured by GINI score

Table 3 Sparse random forest model error matrix

Prediction	Other	Informal	Error rate
Other	37,319	3692	9%
Informal	2453	12,489	16%
Overall accuracy	89%		

Again, as mentioned in the main text, an extremely sparse random forest model is surprisingly accurate at predicting informal work. If we go from the 20 variables in Figure 2 to the three variables with the top GINI scores, occupation, country, and age, we get very similar predictions. Table 3 summarizes the performance of the sparse random forest model.

Conversely, running the large model or the model in the main text without the occupation variable severely weakens the predictive accuracy of the model. Table 4 summarizes the

Table 4 Random forest model error matrix without occupation data

Prediction	**Other**	**Informal**	**Error rate**
Other	37,518	3493	8%
Informal	9062	5880	61%
Overall accuracy	78%		

performance of a model without occupation data. The model does a terrible job at predicting informal workers, though it can correctly classify formal workers. Clearly, occupation or labor data does the heavy lifting in these predictive models.

To summarize, the alternative model specifications presented above indicate that researchers do not need many variables to accurately predict informal work. However, researchers do need some data about individuals' jobs or work status to build a valid model.

APPENDIX

Fieldwork Appendix

This appendix describes my fieldwork rationale, approach, and design. I discuss methodological and logistical issues here, including unforseen problems and things I wish I would have known when I started. The section also describes participant observation, interview, and original survey protocols and the IRB's confidentiality guidelines. Anonymized field notes and interview transcripts are available on request.

Fieldwork Protocols

Everyone was briefed verbally on informed consent, the project, and the confidentiality procedures. The IRB granted verbal instead of written consent because many street vendors are illiterate and wary of official documents (particularly if a foreigner asks them to sign anything). The University of Texas IRB prohibited me from recording interviews because I asked about illegal activity, though those regulations that the people I worked with break are typically minor local ordinances. I took notes in a notebook during interviews and typed them up within 24 hours.

For follow-up interviews in 2018, the University of Miami IRB granted permission to record interviews. I recorded interviews with officials after we had gone through the consent process and I asked them not to state their names in the recording to keep the recording anonymous. These audio files were recorded on a password-protected iPhone and uploaded to a password-protected Dropbox immediately. Officials did not express any issue with the recording device. I continued to take handwritten notes with street vendors and with street-level bureaucrats like the Municipal Guard. I have made up pseudonyms for interviewees, removed identifying information, and scrambled details like location, wares, and gender in many cases.

In La Paz, I conducted interviews in two batches: informational interviews at the beginning of my fieldwork with academics and street vendor leaders in order to understand the basic structure of street markets and street vendor organizations. After several months of observation, I then started asking officials for interviews and scheduling longer interviews with the ethnographic participants.

I had a standard interview request form for officials in all four cases that included a list of questions. I would use these to guide the interview, and ask follow-up questions as officials introduced points of interest. With street vendors, I would verbally request an interview and offer examples of the questions I wanted to ask. I had a standard list of questions to guide the interview and would follow up to ask for more details about particularly interesting parts of a vendor's story.

Example interview script for a bureaucrat:

How did you get this job?

Why Informal Workers Organize. Calla Hummel, Oxford University Press.
© Calla Hummel (2021). DOI: 10.1093/oso/9780192847812.003.0010

What are the street vending regulations that you deal with?
How do you work with street vendor organizations? Individual street vendors?
There seem to be a lot of street vendor organizations. What are the advantages to having a lot? What are the disadvantages?
How do you manage conflicts between the city and vendors? Between vendors?
What things do you think this office does well? What could be improved?

Example interview script for a street vendor association leader:

How did you start selling?
When and how did you get a license?
How did you become a leader?
(Follow-up questions depending on what they say)
What are your interactions with the (Markets Office/city government/mayor) like? How have they changed?
(Solicit opinions on relevant current events: national elections, municipal elections, threats to revoke licenses)
(Sensitive questions, depending on person: Have you paid a bribe? Why? What are the problems in the Federation? How was the Federation divided? What happens when someone breaks the rules in your association?)

I quickly learned during preliminary fieldwork in 2012 that Bolivian street vendors are extremely guarded. Street vendors who I cold-called in 2012 for interviews did not want to be interviewed. Researchers like Sian Lazar and Nico Tassi had resolved these issues by building up trust and relationships through ethnographic fieldwork; I took the same approach.

Approaching street vendors and officials in São Paulo was much easier. Most street vendors were interested in talking and were curious about why a foreign researcher was in the markets. Officials were less open and many expressed fear that I was a journalist looking for a scandalous story. Officials typically agreed to interviews after I proved that I was from an American university and not a journalist. Military police officials and spokespeople, however, never returned interview requests.

In La Paz and El Alto, I found the federation offices by asking street vendors on the street where they were. Anthropologists who had worked with street vendors had told me that it is crucial to get permission from organization leaders before starting a research project. I approached one of the federation leaders at his office in 2014 with verbal and written descriptions of the project, letters of support from the university I was affiliated with, and assurances that I would not interfere with anyone's work.

I asked to work with the federation for 6 – 12 months, observe meetings, interview leaders and members at their convenience, and visit vendors at their worksites. The federation leaders agreed and asked me to contribute something in exchange for the time and access that I asked for. We consulted a larger group of vendor leaders, who asked for workshops on street vendor policies and organizations in the Americas, which I gave in October. From Monday to Saturday (Saturday is the busiest work day for most street vendors) between September 2014 and May 2015, I went to the federation offices, the Markets Office, or a market to spend time observing and talking with vendors and bureaucrats. I had a notebook with me at all times. I tried not to take notes in the notebook in front of people because many people, especially older women, would start to self-censor once they saw me writing. I also learned basic Aymara after I noticed that people would switch to Aymara to gossip about me while

I was in the room. Basic Aymara is an excellent icebreaker. Many people, especially indigenous women, who were extremely wary of me in the first few months, became very talkative after hearing me stumble out a few sentences.

To my surprise, I received several unsolicited job offers from street vendors who needed an assistant. I did not plan to work as a street vendor, but once I received job offers, I figured it was a good way to get a better understanding of people's work conditions and stressors. It was. A contact asked me to work their stall while they weren't there one day a week, which I did for three months. This involved arriving at 5:45 a.m. every Saturday morning, finding the manager of the warehouse, carrying a 30 – 50 pound bag of clothes and metal grids to the market space, setting up the stall on the sidewalk in exactly the right place (to the tenth of a centimeter), unpacking and displaying wares, answering customer questions and finding the right items in stock, haggling, keeping track of change and what types of wares sold, and preventing robberies. I had a notebook with me where I would mark down all sales, types of items, costs, and notes. I typed up all notes that afternoon. I did not keep the money that I made while working as a street vendor in La Paz or São Paulo. I gave the money I made – which was never more than $50 in profit, and more typically $10 – to the street vendors at the end of every day that I worked.

Original Surveys and Analyses

Towards the end of my time in La Paz, I designed a survey of the city's street vending sector. Over a week in April 2015, I collected 207 survey responses with a team of five administrators. The five survey administrators work for a survey firm started by graduates from the Universidad Mayor de San Andres (UMSA) Sociology Department. All are current or recent sociology students in their twenties, are from La Paz, and have worked with street vendors in prior projects. There were two women and three men, and all identified as either mestizo or white. We conducted all surveys in Spanish. We had an Aymara version of the survey available and two administrators spoke enough Aymara to administer it.

No viable sampling frame exists for street vendors in La Paz, as discussed in the main text. To address this problem, I bought a city map with a grid superimposed from a street vendor and numbered the 61 squares that contained city streets. I then randomized the squares by randomizing 1 – 61 on random.org's list randomizer. We then went down the list until we had 200 respondents, which was a predetermined sample target. When we went to an area, we would go with a map and walk down every street in the grid's square, approaching every other vendor (we flipped a coin every morning to determine if we'd start with the first or second vendor we saw). We went through 21 grid squares representing 16 neighborhoods before reaching the target. The neighborhoods are fairly representative of the city, are in all geographic regions, and range from a high density of vendors – 100 vendors, 49 approached, mostly on one street – to a low density of three vendors, one approached.

While there is no way to know, given existing data, if the sample is truly representative of street vendors in La Paz, the descriptive statistics from the survey match the estimates that vendor leaders and bureaucrats reported in interviews: the average street vendor has worked at their stall for 23 years, is 45 years old, and attended eight years of formal schooling. Eighty percent are women and 45 percent are indigenous, while 75 percent belong to a street vendor organization and 72 percent have a license.

As mentioned in the main text, we can run logistic regression analyses on the survey data to see if these demographic characteristics affect a street vendor's propensity to organize. The analyses take a dichotomous variable for the outcome variable: Did a respondent report belonging to a street vendor organization or not? The main selective incentive from officials is in the model as a dichotomous variable for whether a street vendor is licensed or not. Following the theory's expectation that, at the individual level, resources explain participation, the analyses include several proxies for individual attributes that should contribute to individual organizing costs: whether or not the respondent went to college, whether they have been a vendor leader, and a measure of their assets. Instead of asking for respondents' income, which people often misreport or refuse to report, we asked respondents whether or not they had a cellphone, refrigerator, television, internet access, extra stalls, car, or owned their own house, and then made an index out of a simple count and then a weighted count as a robustness check. Additionally, the analyses include information on street vendors' license status, gender, ethnicity, age, and merchandise. For the ethnicity variable, mestizo is the omitted category and for merchandise, food is the omitted category. Table 5 presents the results of two logistic regression models on the survey data, with and without licenses as a control. Note that the coefficients are exponentiated and presented as odds ratios.

Table 5 Logistic regressions on street vendor survey data

	Model 1	**Model 2**
Past leadership	1.41	1.68
	(.73)	(.76)
College	6.03	3.59
	(7.06)	(3.93)
Assets	1.04	1.28
	(.24)	(.26)
License	11.56*	
	(5.57)	
Gender	2.29	2.69*
	(1.31)	(1.38)
Age	1.0	1.0
	(.01)	(.01)
Aymara	.2*	.76
	(.1)	(.58)
Quechua	.38	.96
	(.33)	(.70)
White	.56	1.31
	(1.01)	(1.82)
Drinks	1.53	1.45
	(1.35)	(1.14)
Clothes & accessories	2.87	2.03
	(2.03)	(1.27)
Books & newspapers	3.06	2.54
	(3.79)	(1.85)
Other merchandise	.95	.60
	(.66)	(.36)

N = 169 Standard errors in parentheses below odds ratios. All tests are two-tailed. $^*p \leq .1$

Table 5 presents trends in the directions that the theory implies: licenses predict whether or not a street vendor is organized. Additionally, people with more resources, like education, assets, and experience, are more likely to be organized (in other words, the coefficients on these variables are positive when predicting organizational membership) but not statistically significant. If the analyses omit license status as a control, gender and ethnicity approach significance.

We can also examine the licensing data in a logistic framework. The logistic regression results in Table 6 portray the location patterns in the license data in another way. Table 6 presents logistic regressions on the licensing data using the district, stall size, stall type, and selling schedule information on the licenses. The outcome is whether a license is associated with an organization or not and the coefficients are log-odds.

Table 6 Logistic regressions on La Paz licensing data

	Model 1	**Model 2**
District		
Cotahuma	– .651*	– .903*
	(.07)	(.07)
Mallasa	– .758	– 1.279
	(.74)	(.83)
Max Paredes	– .013	– .158*
	(.06)	(.07)
Periferica	– .399*	– .476*
	(.10)	(.10)
San Antonio	– .529*	– 1.011*
	(.14)	(.15)
Sur	– 1.458*	– 1.142*
	(.10)	(.11)
Size		.001*
		(.00)
Fixed stall		– .438*
		(.70)
Weekends		.719*
		(.19)
Some days		– .434*
		(.06)
One day		3.146*
		(1.01)

N = 31,904 Standard errors in parentheses below odds ratios. All tests are two-tailed. *$p \leq .05$

The regressions show that the licenses in the central district are the most likely to be associated with an organization. In Table 6, Centro is the reference category and the other district categories are compared against it; the negative coefficients on all of them mean that they are less like than licenses in the Centro to be associated with a registered group. Most of these differences are significant. Conversely, people with fixed stalls and larger stalls are more likely to be independent. This goes against the expectations of the theory, since fixed and larger stalls are more valuable than temporary or smaller stalls. Finally, schedule and days do not appear to have a clear relationship with organization; people who weekends and one day are more likely to belong to an organization than people who sell all days, the reference category, and people who sell some days are less likely.

The survey also had an embedded experiment designed to prime anger about work in the treatment, and mildly positive feelings about work in the control. I do not include the experimental results in the main text because the experiment was underpowered and hastily designed. We used a bottom-up prime, where we asked respondents to tell us an experience that they had at work that made them angry or that they liked. Most respondents complied, but about 15 percent of respondents did not answer the question, responded to the control prime with a negative experience, or responded to the treatment with a positive experience. Following the prime, we asked a series of questions about future political participation (for example, will you participate in a protest in the next year?) and included behavioral measures (for example, we are starting a street vendor health fund, would you like to donate?). When we look at the differences in means between treated and control responses, we see null results whether we drop or include that 15 percent, with one exception, as we can see in Table 7.

Table 7 Survey experiment results

Measure	All responses (n = 207)	Excluding NR and failure to treat (n = 177)
Pay dues next year	$p = .99$	$p = .52$
Ask official for help next year	$p = .81$	$p = .60$
Attend protest next year	$p = .90$	$p = .71$
Run for office next year	$p = .55$	$p = .53$
Donate to fund	$p = .78$	$p = .64$
Letter to mayor word count	$p = .07$	$p = .03$*

*$p \leq .05$

For the survey in São Paulo, we divided each district included in the survey into areas that could be covered in a day, randomized the order in which we would visit these areas, and then randomized which researcher would take which streets within these areas (Tourangeau and Smith, 1996). Once in the designated area, each researcher approached vendors with the same script, and if the vendor consented to participate, proceeded to read out the survey questions and recorded answers on a tablet. We interviewed one person at each stall and we did not inquire whether the respondent was the license holder or the owner of the stall so long as she worked as a vendor.

Basic demographic data such as gender, approximate age, and race, as well as merchandise on offer, were filled out directly by the survey administrator. We opted for this method because it shortened the number of questions for each respondent and because questions on some topics, such as gender or age, could lead to bias or negative reactions on the part of respondents. Perhaps the most sensitive item is the attribution of respondents' race by the survey administrator. For the purposes of our study, other people's perceptions are as or more important than self-identification because others' perceptions should significantly affect their decisions to buy from, license, extort from, or harass, the vendor. Additionally, race statistics in Brazil are extremely complex, subjective, and there is no best practice or established protocol (Telles and Lim, 1998).

We used three versions of the questionnaire (extended, main, and short) to administer the survey. The main version is reproduced in English at the end of this appendix and the Portuguese version is available upon request. Prior to starting the survey, we decided to administer the short version to vendors on the city's busiest commercial street, and its immediate surroundings. This decision was based on information gathered during preliminary fieldwork regarding the intensity of trade in this area, which diminished the availability of respondents, as well as the sensitivity of some questions on associative membership. In retrospect, the relatively high response rate obtained in this area suggests a slightly longer version of the survey would have been desirable. The questions used in the short version are indicated in the questionnaire below. Two days after beginning the survey in mid-July, we had covered one-third of the first district. The response rate was 15 percent and many vendors told us that they would not take the 20 – 30 minute survey because they felt it was too long. Consequently, we cut out follow-up questions, but we did not change the order or wording of the remaining questions. Most of the questions eliminated were toward the end of the survey.

Below is the survey instrument for the original survey conducted in La Paz, Bolivia in English. The Spanish and Aymara versions are available on request and are not repreoduced here to conserve space. In the main text, I draw descriptive statistics from the surveys where official statistics are not available.

Good morning/afternoon. My name is X and I am conducting a survey. The survey takes 15 minutes and we give you a pound of quinoa for your participation. The survey is part of an academic study to understand why street vendors organize and is by a (student at the University of Texas). The survey has questions about your work, your opinions, and your political participation. We are academic researchers and we are not affiliated with any NGO or political party. The survey is completely anonymous and you can choose not to respond to any question or stop the survey at any time. If a customer comes, I can wait.

Do you want to participate? (If yes, give a bag of quinoa)

The first questions are about your participation in the last 12 months, your participation in the past.

1. In the last 12 months, did you go to a meeting at any association, union, or other organization?
2. In the last 12 months, did you ask for help from a local official?
3. In the last 12 months, did you pay dues to an association, union, or other organization?
4. In the last 12 months, did you participate in a protest march?
5. In the last 12 months, did you participate in a campaign?
6. In the last 12 months, did you participate in an organized dance event?
7. In the last 12 months, did you run for election in an association, union, or other organization?

Good. Now (ask 1 or 2 at random – flip coin):

1. Can you tell me about an experience that you've had working here that you liked?
2. Can you tell me about an experience that you've had working here that made you angry?

The next questions are about your participation in the next 12 months, your participation in the future.

1. In the next 12 months, will you go to a meeting at any association, union, or other organization?
2. In the next 12 months, will you ask for help from a local official?
3. In the next 12 months, will you pay dues to an association, union, or other organization?
4. In the next 12 months, will you participate in a protest march?
5. In the next 12 months, will you participate in a campaign?
6. In the next 12 months, will you participate in an organized dance event?
7. In the next 12 months, will you run for election in an association, union, or other organization?

We are starting a small fund to help with the cost of medication and that any street vendor can use. As part of the survey, we want to see if people want to help out with the fund. To see if people want to help, we are asking if you want to give part of your pound of quinoa to the fund. We will give the money that we would spend on buying more quinoa to the fund. This is a free choice, contributing is not obligatory.

Do you want to give some of the pound of quinoa to the fund?
How much?

Also, at the end of the study we will write a formal letter to the mayor asking for changes for street vendors. Do you want to add something to the letter? We will not put your name in the letter.

The next questions are about imaginary money.

1. To make an application go faster, would you definitely, maybe, or never pay a bribe to an official?
2. Would you prefer to win 1000 bolivianos now or 1500 bolivianos in a year?
3. And now the opposite. Would you prefer to lose 1000 bolivianos now or 1500 bolivianos in a year?

The next questions are demographic.

1. How old are you?
2. How old were you when you started selling?
3. Do you consider yourself mestizo, Aymara, Quechua, white, Afro-Bolivian, or part of another ethnic group?
4. What was the last year of school you completed?
5. Before vending, did you have another job?
   a. What?
   b. In this other job, were you part of a union?
6. Currently, do you have a vending license?
7. At this stall, do you work all day, part of the day, or only on market days?
8. Have you been a leader in an association, union, or other organization?
9. Are you currently affiliated with a street vendor association, union, or federation?
   a. How long have you been a member?
   b. Are you a leader or a member in the organization?
10. Currently, do you like any political party?
    a. Which?

The next questions are about people you know.

1. Do you know anyone who can:
a. Organize a protest?
i. What is your relationship with this person?
b. Resolve bureaucratic problems?
i. What is your relationship with this person?
c. Start an organization?
i. What is your relationship with this person?
2. Do you have good friends that you feel close to?
a. How many?
3. In a normal day, approximately how many people do you have contact with? Include your customers, everyone you greet, and anyone you talk to face to face or over the phone.
4. Some people have friends that know each other. Other people have friends that don't know each other. Do you think that all your friends know each other, most know each other, some know each other, or none know each other?

The next questions are about your health.

1. Do you have health insurance or free access to a doctor?
2. In the last three months, have you had a health problem?
a. What?
3. When you have a health problem, do you go to the doctor, a hospital, the pharmacy, an acquaintance, traditional medicine, herbs, or do you do something else?
4. If you belong to a vendor organization, what is your association doing to address the health problems of its members?

1. Finally, to get an idea of the economic situation of street vendors in general, can you tell me if you own the following things? Cellphone, television, refrigerator, internet at home, more than one stall, a car, your own house.

   We are at the end of the survey, thank you for your participation. You can find copies of the results of the survey at the CIDES-UMSA office at the end of May, Av. 14 de Septiembre 4913, Obrajes, next to the Catholic University (give my business card).

   Questions for the survey administrator to fill out:
2. Administrator name
3. Survey number
4. Date
5. Street
6. Gender of person surveyed
7. Mobile or fixed post
8. Type of goods sold

Below is the English translation of the São Paulo survey instrument. The Portuguese instrument is available upon request.

Items used or recorded in the short version are marked with a (*).
Introductory script
Hello, my name is X and I'm (name and university). A colleague and I are doing a survey of street vendors in Sao Paulo. The survey asks questions about your work and

your experiences during the World Cup. It takes about 15 – 25 minutes. The survey is anonymous. We are independent researchers and we are not associated with any part of the government or any NGO. You can choose not to answer any question and you can stop the survey at any time. Would you like to take the survey? (If yes) Here is my card. Do you have any questions before we begin?

1. Did you work as a street vendor during the World Cup?

 Yes (1)
 No (2)
 NR (3)

 Answer if No is selected for Q1:
2. Why did you not work as street vendor during the World Cup? (Do not read the options)

 There was too much police surveillance (1)
 Took vacations (2)
 Other (3)
 NR (4)

 Answer if No is selected for Q1:
3. How did you do to make ends meet during the World Cup?

 Savings (1)
 Family help (2)
 Another job (3)
 Other (4)
 NR (5)

 Skip to Q18.
4. During the month of the World Cup, did you sell World Cup merchandise?

 Yes (1)
 No (2)
 NR (3)

5. During the month of the Cup, did you make:

 More money (1)
 Less money (2)
 Or the same as before the Cup? (3)
 NR (4)

 Answer if "More money than" is selected for Q5:
6. By how much did your income increase during the World Cup?*

 10% (1)
 A quarter (2)
 Half (3)
 More than half (4)
 NR (5)

 Answer if "Less money than" is selected for Q5:
7. By how much did your income decrease during the World Cup?*

 10% (1)
 A quarter (2)

Half (3)
More than half (4)
NR (5)

8. During the World Cup, do you believe that police repression against street vendors:*

   Increased (1)
   Decreased (2)
   Or remained the same? (3)
   NR (4)

9. Have the police ever confiscated your merchandise?

   Yes (1)
   No (2)
   NR (3)

   Answer if "Yes" is selected for Q9:
10. When was the last time that happened?
11. Have you ever received a fine for working as a street vendor or paid a fee to recover merchandise?

    Yes (1)
    No (2)
    NR (3)

    Answer if "Yes" is selected for Q11:
12. When was the last time that happened?
13. For how long have you worked as a street vendor?
14. Before being a street vendor, did you have another job?

    Yes (1)
    No (2)
    NR (3)

    Answer if "Yes" is selected for Q14:
15. What was your job?
    Answer if "Yes" is selected for Q14:
16. In this previous job, did you have a formal contract?

    Yes (1)
    No (2)
    NR (3)

    Answer if "Yes" is selected for Q14:
17. In this previous job, were you part of a union?

    Yes (1)
    No (2)
    NR (3)

18. What is the highest level of education that you completed?

    Did not complete elementary school (1)
    Elementary school (2)
    High school (3)
    University (4)
    NR (5)

19. Do you think the government cares about improving the situation of street vendors?

    Yes (1)
    No (2)
    NR (3)

20. What are the two most important things that the city did for street vendors in the past year?

    (1)
    (2)
    3. NR, cannot think of anything (3)
    4. Nothing (4)

21. Can you tell me if you are affiliated with any of the following groups?

    Yes (1) No (2) NR (3)
    Neighborhood association
    Club or sports association
    Church
    NGO
    Other

22. Are you affiliated with any street vendor association or union?

    Yes (1)
    No (2)
    NR (3)

    Answer if "Yes" is selected for Q22:

23. In what year did you enter this association or union?
24. Have you ever held a leadership position in any organization?

    Yes (1)
    No (2)
    NR (3)

25. In the last 12 months, did you participate in any demonstration or public protest?

    Yes (1)
    No (2)
    NR (3)

26. In the last 12 months, did you request help or send a request to any politician, official, or city government?*

    Yes (1)
    No (2)
    NR (3)

27. In the last 12 months, did you participate in any meeting or public hearing with the city or with some politician?

    Yes (1)
    No (2)
    NR (3)

28. Finally, to get an idea of the economic status of street vendors in general, could you tell me if you have/own any of the following items?

    Yes (1) No (2) NR (3)

    1. Cellphone
    2. TV
    3. More than one bathroom at home
    4. Personal computer
    5. Internet at home
    6. Car
    7. House

29. We have reached the end of the survey. Thank you for your participation. You can finish the survey now, or answer one last question. (If the subject agrees) If we were to write a letter to the city council about the problems that street vendors face, what demands or suggestions would you like us to put in the letter?
30. Enumerator*

    1 (1)
    2 (2)

31. Gender*

    Woman (1)
    Man (2)
    Other (3)

32. Age (NR: estimated 20, 40, 60)*

    Less Than 20 (1)
    Between 21 and 30 (2)
    Between 31 and 40 (3)
    Between 41 and 50 (4)
    Between 51 and 60 (5)
    Over 60 (6)
    NR (7)

33. Race/ethnicity*

    White (1)
    Afro-Brazilian (2)
    Mestiço (3)
    Indigenous (4)
    Asian (5)
    Other (6)

34. Nationality*

    Brazilian (1)
    South American (not Brazilian) (2)
    African (not Brazilian) (3)
    Other (4)

35. Any visible physical disability?*

Yes (1)
No (2)

36. Merchandise sold at the stall: *

Fresh/homemade food (1)
Packaged food (2)
Cigarettes/drinks (3)
Electronic and accessories (4)
Clothing (including bags) (5)
Clothing accessories (including shoes, watches, jewelry, belts, wallets) (6)
Tools (7)
Toys / gadgets (8)
Other (9)
Brazil / World Cup – branded items (10)

Bibliography

Rina Agarwala. *Informal Labor, Formal Politics, and Dignified Discontent in India*. Cambridge University Press, 2013.

Matthew Amengual. Pollution in the garden of the Argentine republic: Building state capacity to escape from chaotic regulation. *Politics & Society*, 41(4):527–560, 2013.

Matthew Amengual and Janice Fine. Co-enforcing labor standards: the unique contributions of state and worker organizations in Argentina and the United States. *Regulation & Governance*, 11(2):129–142, 2017.

Krister P. Andersson. Who talks with whom? The role of repeated interactions in decentralized forest governance. *World Development*, 32(2):233–249, 2004.

Krister P. Andersson, Clark C. Gibson, and Fabrice Lehoucq. Municipal politics and forest governance: Comparative analysis of decentralization in Bolivia and Guatemala. *World Development*, 34(3):576–595, 2006.

Peter Andreas. *Smuggler Nation: How Illicit Trade Made America*. Oxford University Press, 2013.

Santiago Anria. *When Movements Become Parties: The Bolivian MAS in Comparative Perspective*. Cambridge University Press, 2018.

Juan M. Arbona and Benjamin Kohl. La Paz–El Alto. *Cities*, 21(3):255–265, 2004.

Adam M. Auerbach, Adrienne LeBas, Alison E. Post, and Rebecca Weitz-Shapiro. State, society, and informality in cities of the global south. *Studies in Comparative International Development*, 53 (3):261–280, 2018.

Adam Michael Auerbach and Tariq Thachil. How clients select brokers: Competition and choice in India's slums. *American Political Science Review*, 112(4): 775–791, 2018.

Javier Auyero. *Poor People's Politics: Peronist Survival Networks and the Legacy of Evita*. Duke University Press, 2001.

Javier Auyero. *Patients of the State: The Politics of Waiting in Argentina*. Duke University Press, 2012.

Robert Axelrod. *The Evolution of Cooperation*. Basic Books, 1984.

Christopher Bajada and Friedrich Schneider. *Size, Causes and Consequences of the Underground Economy: An international perspective*. Routledge, 2018.

Al Baker, J. David Goodman, and Benjamin Mueller. Beyond the chokehold: The path to Eric Garner's death. *The New York Times*, June 2015.

Andy Baker and Vania Ximena Velasco-Guachalla. Is the informal sector politically different? (Null) answers from Latin America. *World Development*, 102:170–182, 2018.

Curtis Bell and Scott Wolford. Oil discoveries, shifting power, and civil conflict. *International Studies Quarterly*, 59(3): 517–530, 2015.

Daniel Berliner and Aaron Erlich. Competing for transparency: Political competition and institutional reform in Mexican states. *American Political Science Review*, 109(01): 110–128, 2015.

Timothy Besley and Maitreesh Ghatak. Government versus private ownership of public goods. *The Quarterly Journal of Economics*, 116(4): 1343–1372, 2001.

Timothy Besley and Torsten Persson. State capacity, conflict, and development. *Econometrica*, 78(1):1–34, 2010.

Sharit Bhowmik. *Street Vendors in the Global Urban Economy*. Taylor & Francis, 2012.

Merike Blofield. *Care Work and Class: Domestic Workers' Struggle for Equal Rights in Latin America*. Penn State Press, 2012.

Cristina Bodea and Adrienne LeBas. The origins of voluntary compliance: Attitudes toward taxation in urban Nigeria. *British Journal of Political Science*, 46 (01):215–238, 2016.

Estado Plurinacional De Bolivia. El gobierno acuerda con los gremiales la modificación de límites del régimen tributario simplificado, 2013. URL `http://www.economiayfinanzas.gob.bo/index.php?opcion=com_prensa&ver=prensa&id=2995&categoria=5&seccion=306`.

Carew E. Boulding and Clark C. Gibson. Supporters or challengers? The effects of nongovernmental organizations on local politics in Bolivia. *Comparative Political Studies*, 42(4): 479–500, 2009.

Henry E. Brady, Sidney Verba, and Kay Lehman Schlozman. Beyond ses: A resource model of political participation. *American Political Science Review*, 89(02): 271–294, 1995.

Hailey Branson-Potts. L.A. city council votes unanimously to decriminalize street vending. *The Los Angeles Times*, February 2017.

Jennifer N Brass. Blurring boundaries: The integration of NGOs into governance in Kenya. *Governance*, 25(2):209–235, 2012.

Leo Breiman. Random forests. *Machine Learning*, 45(1):5–32, 2001a.

Leo Breiman. Statistical modeling: The two cultures (with comments and a rejoinder by the author). *Statistical Science*, 16(3):199–231, 2001b.

Miriam Bruhn and David McKenzie. Entry regulation and the formalization of microenterprises in developing countries. *The World Bank Research Observer*, 29(2): 186–201, 2014.

Amalia L. Cabezas, 'Latin American and Caribbean Sex Workers: Gains and challenges in the movement', *Anti-Trafficking Review*, issue 12, 2019, pp. 37–56, www.antitraffickingreview.org.

Teresa P.R. Caldeira. *City of Walls: Crime, segregation, and citizenship in S ao Paulo*. University of California Press, 2000.

Manuel Castells and Alejandro Portes. The world underneath: The origins, dynamics, and effects of the informal economy. *The Informal Economy: Studies in Advanced and Less Developed Countries*, 1989.

Nissim Cohen and Sagi Gershgoren. The incentives of street-level bureaucrats and inequality in tax assessments. *Administration & Society*, 48(3):267–289, 2016.

Jose Luis Columba. Se abre una pugna entre 2 sectores de gremiales alteños. *La Razón*, April 2015.

Randol Contreras. *The Stickup Kids: Race, Drugs, Violence, and the American Dream*. University of California Press, 2012.

Maria Lorena Cook. *Labor*, pages 262–271. Routledge, 2012.

Michael Cooper. Officers in Bronx fire 41 shots, and an unarmed man is killed. *The New York Times*, February 5, 1999.

Michael Coppedge, John Gerring, David Altman, Michael Bernhard, Steven Fish, Allen Hicken, et al. Conceptualizing and measuring democracy: A new approach. *Perspectives on Politics*, 9(2):247–267, 2011.

Karla Cornejo Villavicencio. *The Undocumented Americans*. One World, 2020.

John Christopher Cross. *Informal Politics: Street Vendors and the State in Mexico City*. Stanford University Press, 1998.

Jacinto Cuvi. The politics of field destruction and the survival of São Paulo's street vendors. *Social Problems*, 63(3):395–412, 2016.

Benjamin Dangl. *The Price of Fire: Resource wars and social movements in Bolivia*. AK Press, 2007.

Christian Davenport. State repression and political order. *Annual Review of Political Science*, 10(1): 1–23, 2007.

Emmerich Davies and Tulia G. Falleti. Poor people's participation: Neoliberal institutions or left turn? *Comparative Political Studies*, 50(12): 1699–1731, 2017.

Hernando de Soto. *The Other Path: The Invisible Revolution in the Third World*. Harper & Row, 1989.

Donatella Della Porta and Mario Diani. *Social Movements: An Introduction*. John Wiley & Sons, 2009.

Jorge Derpic and Alex Ayala Ugarte. Bolivia: Los linchados de El Alto. *Revista Anfibia*, 2013.

Matthew Desmond. Eviction and the reproduction of urban poverty. *American Journal of Sociology*, 118(1): 88–133, 2012.

Matthew Desmond. *Evicted: Poverty and Profit in the American City*. Crown, 2016.

Ineke Dibbits, Elizabeth Peredo Beltrán, and Ruth Volgger. *Polleras Libertarias: Federación Obrera Femenina, 1927–1964*, volume 9. Taller de Historia y Participación de la Mujer, 1986.

DOJ. *Investigation of the Ferguson Police Department*. United States Department of Justice, 2015.

Paul Gandhi Joseph Dosh. *Demanding the Land: Urban popular movements in Peru and Ecuador, 1990–2005*. Penn State Press, 2010.

Mitchell Duneier and Ovie Carter. *Sidewalk*. Macmillan, 1999.

Jennifer Earl, Andrew Martin, John D. McCarthy, and Sarah A. Soule. The use of newspaper data in the study of collective action. *Annual Review of Sociology*, pages 65–80, 2004.

Julia Elyachar. *Markets of Dispossession: NGOs, economic development, and the state in Cairo*. Duke University Press, 2005.

Linda Farthing and Benjamin Kohl. Social control: Bolivia's new approach to coca reduction. *Latin American Perspectives*, 37(4): 197–213, 2010.

Linda C. Farthing and Benjamin H. Kohl. *Evo's Bolivia: Continuity and change*. University of Texas Press, 2014.

Richard Fausset, Richard Pérez-Peña, and Campbell Robertson. Alton Sterling shooting in Baton Rouge prompts Justice Dept. investigation. *The New York Times*, July 2016.

James D. Fearon and David D. Laitin. Ethnicity, insurgency, and civil war. *American Political Science Review*, 97(01): 75–90, 2003.

Germán Feierherd. Courting informal workers: Exclusion, forbearance, and the left. *American Journal of Political Science*, 2021.

Kiera Feldman. Trashed: Inside the deadly world of private garbage collection. *ProPublica*, January 2018. URL `https://www.propublica.org/article/trashed-inside-the-deadly-world-of-private-garbage-collection`.

Oscar Fergutz, Sonia Dias, and Diana Mitlin. Developing urban waste management in Brazil with waste picker organizations. *Environment and Urbanization*, 23(2): 597–608, 2011.

Patricia Fernández-Kelly and Jon Shefner. *Out of the Shadows: Political Action and the Informal Economy in Latin America*. Penn State Press, 2006.

Norbert M. Fiess, Marco Fugazza, and William F. Maloney. Informal self-employment and macroeconomic fluctuations. *Journal of Development Economics*, 91(2): 211–226, 2010.

Elisabeth Fischer and Matin Qaim. Linking smallholders to markets: Determinants and impacts of farmer collective action in Kenya. *World Development*, 40(6):1255–1268, 2012.

Patrick Flavin and Michael T. Hartney. When government subsidizes its own: Collective bargaining laws as agents of political mobilization. *American Journal of Political Science*, 59 (4):896–911, 2015.

Henry J. Frundt. Central american unions in the era of globalization. *Latin American Research Review*, pages 7–53, 2002.

Gaspar Garcia Center for Human Rights. *Street Vendors and the Right to the City*. Gaspar Garcia Center for Human Rights, 2014.

John Gerring. *Case Study Research: Principles and practices. Second Edition*. Cambridge University Press, 2017.

John Gerring, Strom C. Thacker, and Rodrigo Alfaro. Democracy and human development. *The Journal of Politics*, 74(1):1–17, 2012.

Klarita Gerxhani. The informal sector in developed and less developed countries: A literature survey. *Public Choice*, 120(3-4):267–300, 2004.

Rede Globo. Vídeo mostra pm atirando contra cabeça de ambulante em sp. *G1*, September 9, 2014. URL `http://g1.globo.com/sao-paulo/noticia/2014/09/video-mostra-pm-atirando-contra-cabeca-de-ambulante-em-sp.html`.

Alice Goffman. *On the Run: Fugitive Life in an American City*. University of Chicago Press, 2015.

Daniel M Goldstein. *Owners of the Sidewalk: Security and Survival in the Informal City*. Duke University Press, 2016.

Tom Goodfellow. Taming the rogue sector: Studying state effectiveness in Africa through informal transport politics. *Comparative Politics*, 47(2):127–147, 2015.

Jeff Goodwin. *No Other Way Out: State and Revolutionary Movements, 1945–1991*. Cambridge University Press, 2001.

Teresa Gowan. *Hobos, Hustlers, and Backsliders: Homeless in San Francisco*. University of Minnesota Press, 2010.

Merilee S. Grindle Divergent cultures? When public organizations perform well in developing countries. *World Development*, 25(4):481–495, 1997.

Shelby Grossman. The politics of order in informal markets: Evidence from Lagos. *World Politics*, 72(1):47–79, 2020.

Shelby Grossman. *The Politics of Order in Informal Markets: How the State Shapes Private Governance*. Cambridge University Press, 2021.

Shelby Grossman, Jonathan Phillips, and Leah R. Rosenzweig. Opportunistic accountability: State–society bargaining over shared interests. *Comparative Political Studies*, 51(8), 2018.

Basudeb Guha-Khasnobis, Ravi Kanbur, and Elinor Ostrom. *Linking the Formal and Informal Economy: Concepts and Policies*. Oxford University Press, 2007.

Jonathan K. Hanson and Rachel Sigman. Leviathan's latent dimensions: Measuring state capacity for comparative political research. In *APSA 2011 Annual meeting paper*, 2013.

Russell Hardin. *Collective Action*. Johns Hopkins University Press, 1982.

Jaira J. Harrington. A place of their own: Black feminist leadership and economic and educational justice in São Paulo and Rio de Janeiro, Brazil. *Latin American and Caribbean Ethnic Studies*, 10 (3):271–287, 2015.

Keith Hart. Informal income opportunities and urban employment in Ghana. *The Journal of Modern African Studies*, 11 (01):61–89, 1973.

Cullen S. Hendrix. Measuring state capacity: Theoretical and empirical implications for the study of civil conflict. *Journal of Peace Research*, 47(3):273–285, 2010.

Joseph Patrick Henrich. *Foundations of Human Sociality: Economic experiments and ethnographic evidence from fifteen small-scale societies*. Oxford University Press on Demand, 2004.

Katheryn Hochstetler. *Social Movements in Lation America*, pages 237–246. Routledge, 2012.

Alisha Holland. The distributive politics of enforcement. *American Journal of Political Science*, 59 (2):357–371, 2015.

Alisha C. Holland. "Forbearance." *The American Political Science Review*, 110(2), 232, 2016.

Alisha C. Holland. *Forbearance as Redistribution: The politics of informal welfare in Latin America*. Cambridge University Press, 2017.

Alisha C. Holland and Brian Palmer-Rubin. Beyond the machine: Clientelist brokers and interest organizations in Latin America. *Comparative Political Studies*, 48(9): 1186–1223, 2015.

Pierrette Hondagneu-Sotelo. *Domestica: Immigrant Workers Cleaning and Caring in the Shadows of Affluence*. University of California Press, 2001.

Calla Hummel. Vendedores populares y políticas de representación de género. *Umbrales*, 29:331–359, 2016.

Calla Hummel. Disobedient markets: Street vendors, enforcement, and state intervention in collective action. *Comparative Political Studies*, 50(11): 1524–1555, 2017.

Calla Hummel. Bribery cartels: Collusive corruption in Bolivian street markets. *Latin American Research Review*, 53(2), 2018a.

Calla Hummel. Do poor citizens benefit from mega-events? São Paulo's street vendors and the 2014 FIFA World Cup. *Latin American Politics and Society*, 60(4): 26–48, 2018b.

Wendy Hunter and Natasha Borges Sugiyama. Transforming subjects into citizens: Insights from Brazil's Bolsa Família. *Perspectives on Politics*, 12(4):829–845, 2014.

Samuel P. Huntington. *Political Order in Changing Societies*. Yale University Press, 1968.

Ralf Hussmanns. Defining and measuring informal employment. *Bureau of Statistics Paper*, ILO, Geneva, February. URL http://www.ilo.org/public/english/bureau/stat/download/papers/meas.pdf, 2004.

Aiko Ikemura Amaral. *Identity, Work, and Mobility amongst Bolivian Market Vendors in El Alto and S ao Paulo*. PhD thesis, University of Essex, 2019.

ILO. *Women and Men in the Informal Economy: A statistical picture*. International Labor Organization, 2018.

Luciana Itikawa. Vulnerabilidades do trabalho informal de rua. *S ao Paulo em Perspectiva*, 20(1): 136–147, 2006.

Luciana Itikawa. *Trabalho Informal nos Espaços Públicos no Centro de Sáo Paulo*. PhD thesis, Universidade de Sáo Paulo, 2010.

Torben Iversen and David Soskice. Distribution and redistribution: The shadow of the nineteenth century. *World Politics*, 61(03):438–486, 2009.

Nathan M. Jensen and Aminur Rahman. *The Silence of Corruption: Identifying underreporting of business corruption through randomized response techniques*, pages 154–170. Routledge, 2015.

Nathan M. Jensen, Quan Li, and Aminur Rahman. Understanding corruption and firm responses in cross-national firm-level surveys. *Journal of International Business Studies*, 41 (9):1481–1504, 2010.

Colin Jerolmack and Shamus Khan. Talk is cheap: Ethnography and the attitudinal fallacy. *Sociological Methods & Research*, pages 1–32, 2014.

Desmond King and David Rueda. Cheap labor: The new politics of bread and roses. *Perspectives on Politics*, 6(02):279–297, 2008.

Herbert P. Kitschelt. Political opportunity structures and political protest: Anti-nuclear movements in four democracies. *British Journal of Political Science*, 16 (01):57–85, 1986.

Benjamin Kohl and Linda C. Farthing. *Impasse in Bolivia: Neoliberal hegemony and popular resistance*. Zed Books, 2006.

Marcus J. Kurtz. The dilemmas of democracy in the open economy: Lessons from Latin America. *World Politics*, 56(02):262–302, 2004.

Sian Lazar. *El Alto, Rebel City: Self and Citizenship in Andean Bolivia*. Duke University Press, 2007a.

Sian Lazar. 'In-betweenness' on the margins: Collective organisation, ethnicity and political agency among bolivian street traders. *Livelihoods at the Margins: Surviving the city*, Routledge, pages 237–56, 2007b.

Lehm Ardaya Lehm, Silvia Rivera Cusicanqui, and Victor Hugo Ricaldi. *Los Artesanos Libertarios y la Ética del Trabajo*. Ediciones del THOA, 1988.

Steven Levitsky and Lucan A. Way. *Competitive authoritarianism: Hybrid regimes after the Cold War*. Cambridge University Press, 2010.

Steven Henry Lopez. Efficiency and the fix revisited: Informal relations and mock routinization in a nonprofit nursing home. *Qualitative Sociology*, 30(3):225–247, 2007.

McCarthy, John D., and Mayer N. Zald. "The trend of social movements in America: Professionalization and resource mobilization." (1973). General Learning Press.

Janet MacGaffey and Rémy Bazenguissa-Ganga. *Congo-Paris: Transnational Traders on the Margins of the Law*. Indiana University Press, 2000.

Raúl Madrid. *The Rise of Ethnic Politics in Latin America*. Cambridge University Press, 2012.

Gerald Marwell and Pamela Oliver. *The Critical Mass in Collective Action*. Cambridge University Press, 1993.

Lindsay Mayka. *Building Participatory Institutions in Latin America: Reform Coalitions and Institutional Change*. Cambridge University Press, 2019.

Doug McAdam. *Political Process and the Development of Black Insurgency, 1930–1970*. University of Chicago Press, 1982.

Martin Medina. The informal recycling sector in developing countries: Organizing waste pickers to enhance their impact. 2008. This is from a World Bank publication, Gridlines, Issue 44 URL https://openknowledge.worldbank.org/bitstream/handle/10986/10586/472210BRI0Box31ing1sectors01PUBLIC1.pdf?sequence=1

Ruth Meinzen-Dick, K. Vengamma Raju, and Ashok Gulati. What affects organization and collective action for managing resources? Evidence from canal irrigation systems in India. *World Development*, 30(4):649–666, 2002.

Joel S. Migdal. *Strong Societies and Weak States: State-society relations and state capabilities in the Third World*. Princeton University Press, 1988.

Amara Moira. *E se eu fosse puta*. Hoo Editora Ltda, 2016.

David Muchlinski, David Siroky, Jingrui He, and Matthew Kocher. Comparing random forest with logistic regression for predicting class-imbalanced civil war onset data. *Political Analysis*, 24(1):87–103, 2016.

Paula Muñoz. An informational theory of campaign clientelism: The case of Peru. *Comparative Politics*, 47(1):79–98, 2014.

Paula Muñoz. *Buying Audiences: Clientelism and Electoral Campaigns When Parties Are Weak*. Cambridge University Press, 2018.

Maria Victoria Murillo. *Labor Unions, Partisan Coalitions, and Market Reforms in Latin America*. Cambridge University Press, 2001.

Robin Thomas Naylor. *Wages of Crime: Black markets, illegal finance, and the underworld economy*. Cornell University Press, 2004.

Jami Nelson-Nu nez and Kate Cartwright. Getting along or going alone: Understanding collaboration between local governments and NGOs in Bolivia. *Latin American Politics and Society*, 60(1): 76–101, 2018.

Carolyn Nordstrom. *Shadows of War: Violence, power, and international profiteering in the twenty-first century*. University of California Press, 2004.

Pamela Oliver. Rewards and punishments as selective incentives for collective action: Theoretical investigations. *American Journal of Sociology*, 85(6):1356–1375, 1980.

Benjamin A. Olken. Corruption perceptions versus corruption reality. *Journal of Public Economics*, 93(7): 950–964, 2009.

Benjamin A. Olken. Direct democracy and local public goods: Evidence from a field experiment in Indonesia. *American Political Science Review*, 104(02): 243–267, 2010.

Benjamin A. Olken and Rohini Pande. Corruption in developing countries. *Annual Review of Economics*, 4, 2012.

Mancur Olson. *The Logic of Collective Action*, Harvard University Press, 1965.

Zaraí Toledo Orozco and Marcello Veiga. Locals' attitudes toward artisanal and large-scale mining: A case study of Tambogrande, Peru. *The Extractive Industries and Society*, 5 (2):327–334, 2018.

Elinor Ostrom. *Governing the Commons*. Cambridge University Press, 1990.

Elinor Ostrom. Collective action theory. *The Oxford Handbook of Comparative Politics*, pages 186–208, Oxford University Press, 2007.

Elinor Ostrom. *Understanding Institutional Diversity*. Princeton University Press, 2009.

Elinor Ostrom. *Governing the Commons*. Cambridge University Press, 2015.

João Batista Pamplona. Mercado de trabalho, informalidade e comércio ambulante em São Paulo. *Revista Brasileira de Estudos de População*, pages 225–249, 2013.

Gobierno Autonomo Municipal De La Paz. *Comerciantes en vías públicas*, 2015.

Elizabeth Peredo Beltrán. *Recoveras de los Andes: La Identidad de la Chola del Mercado*. La Paz: TAHIPAMU, 1992.

René Pereira Morató. Para escuchar las voces de la calle: Las contradicciones entre el derecho al empleo y el derecho a la ciudad. *Tinkazos*, 11(25):49–58, 2008.

René Pereira Morató. *Comercio Popular en Vía Pública: Estudio en el Macrodistrito de La Paz*. Fundación PIEB, 2015.

René Pereira Morató, Eugenia Bridikhina, Jaime Montaño Garcia, and Ramiro Blanco Torrez. *Para Escuchar las Voces de la Calle: El comercio popular en vía pública en La Paz*. Fundación PIEB, 2009.

Guillermo Perry. *Informality: Exit and Exclusion*. World Bank Publications, 2007.

Rosana Pinheiro-Machado. *Made in China: (In)formalidades, pirataria e redes sociais na rota China-Paraguai-Brasil*. S ao Paulo: Anpocs, 2011.

Alison E. Post. Cities and politics in the developing world. *Annual Review of Political Science*, 21:115–133, 2018.

Alison E. Post, Vivian Bronsoler, and Lana Salman. Hybrid regimes for local public goods provision: A framework for analysis. *Perspectives on Politics*, 15(4):952–966, 2017.

Canice Prendergast. The motivation and bias of bureaucrats. *American Economic Review*, 97(1):180–196, 2007.

Robert D. Putnam. *Bowling Alone: The collapse and revival of American community*. Simon and Schuster, 2001.

Robert D. Putnam, Robert Leonardi, and Raffaella Y. Nanetti. *Making Democracy Work: Civic Traditions in Modern Italy*. Princeton University Press, 1994.

Stephen Quackenbush. The rationality of rational choice theory. *International Interactions*, 30(2):87–107, 2004.

Jeffrey Reiman and Paul Leighton. *Rich Get Richer and the Poor Get Prison: Ideology, Class, and Criminal Justice*. Routledge, 2015.

Danielle Resnick. The politics of crackdowns on Africa's informal vendors. *Comparative Politics*, 52(1):21–51, 2019.

Jessica Rich. *State-Sponsored Activism: Bureaucrats and social movements in democratic Brazil*. Cambridge University Press, 2019.

Jessica A. J. Rich. Grassroots bureaucracy: Intergovernmental relations and popular mobilization in Brazil's aids policy sector. *Latin American Politics and Society*, 55(2): 1–25, 2013.

Emily Hencken Ritter and Courtenay R. Conrad. Preventing and responding to dissent: The observational challenges of explaining strategic repression. *American Political Science Review*, 110(1): 85–99, 2016.

Miguel Rivas. Desde 2014, El Alto tuvo 16 intentos de linchamiento y 3 ajusticiamientos. *La Razón*, April 2016.

Sally Roever and Caroline Skinner. Street vendors and cities. *Environment and Urbanization*, 28(2): 359–374, 2016.

Sally Christine Roever. *Negotiating Formality: Informal Sector, Market, and State in Peru*. PhD thesis, University of California, Berkeley, 2005.

Bruno Rojas. *Minoristas en los Procesos Democráticos*. CEDLA, 1992.

Bruno Rojas. El trabajo infantil en Bolivia: Características, causas y desafios, 2014. URL `https://cedla.org/obess/el-trabajo-infantil-en-bolivia-caracteristicas-causas-y-desafios/`.

Lucas Ronconi. Enforcement and compliance with labor regulations in Argentina. *Industrial & Labor Relations Review*, 63 (4):719–736, 2010.

Manuel Rosaldo. Revolution in the garbage dump: The political and economic foundations of the Colombian recycler movement, 1986–2011. *Social Problems*, 63(3):351–372, 2016.

Susan Rose-Ackerman. *Corruption and Government: Causes, consequences, and reform*. Cambridge University Press, 1999.

David Rueda. *Social Democracy Inside Out: Partisanship and Labor Market Policy in Advanced Industrialized Democracies*. Oxford University Press, 2007.

Thomas C. Schelling. *Micromotives and Macrobehavior*. WW Norton & Company, 1978.

Samantha Schmidt. New York City may double number of food vendor permits. *The New York Times*, October 2016.

Ben Ross Schneider. The career connection: A comparative analysis of bureaucratic preferences and insulation. *Comparative Politics*, pages 331–350, 1993.

Ben Ross Schneider. *Business Politics and the State in Twentieth-Century Latin America*. Cambridge University Press, 2004.

Friedrich Schneider, Andreas Buehn, and Claudio E. Montenegro. New estimates for the shadow economies all over the world. *International Economic Journal*, 24(4): 443–461, 2010.

James C. Scott. Corruption, machine politics, and political change. *American Political Science Review*, 63(04): 1142–1158, 1969.

Jason Seawright and John Gerring. Case selection techniques in case study research: A menu of qualitative and quantitative options. *Political Research Quarterly*, 61(2): 294–308, 2008.

Sara Shahriari. How young is too young? Bolivia debates child labor law. *Christian Science Monitor*, March 2014. URL `https://www.csmonitor.com/World/Americas/2014/0326/How-young-is-too-young-Bolivia-debates-child-labor-law`.

Curtis S. Signorino. Structure and uncertainty in discrete choice models. *Political Analysis*, 11(4):316–344, 2003.

David Skarbek. Covenants without the sword? Comparing prison self-governance globally. *American Political Science Review*, 110(4): 845–862, 2016.

Molly Smith and Juno Mac. *Revolting Prostitutes: The fight for sex workers' rights*. Verso Trade, 2018.

Duncan Snidal. Coordination versus prisoners' dilemma: Implications for international cooperation and regimes. *American Political Science Review*, 79(04): 923–942, 1985.

T. A. B. Snijders and R. J. Bosker. *Multilevel Analysis: An introduction to basic and advanced multilevel modeling*. Sage, 1999.

Hillel David Soifer. Measuring state capacity in contemporary Latin America. *Revista de Ciencia Política*, 32(3):585–598, 2012.

Hillel David Soifer. *State Building in Latin America*. Cambridge University Press, 2015.

Hernando de Soto. *The Mystery of Capital: Why capitalism triumphs in the West and fails everywhere else*. Basic Books, 2000.

Susan Stokes. Perverse accountability: A formal model of machine politics with evidence from Argentina. *American Political Science Review*, 99(3):315–325, 2005.

Wolfgang Streeck and Lane Kenworthy. *Theories and Practices of Neocorporatism*, pages 441–460. Routledge, 2005.

Sidney Tarrow. *Power in Movement: Social Movements, Collective Action and Politics*. Cambridge University Press, 2011.

Nico Tassi, Carmen Medeiros, Antonio Rodriguez Carmona, and Giovana Ferrufino. *"Hacer Plata sin Plata:" El Desborde de los Comerciantes Populares en Bolivia*. PIEB, 2013.

Nico Tassi, Alfonso Hinojosa, and Richard Carnaviri. *La Economia Popular de Bolivia: Tres Miradas*. Fondo Editorial de la Vicepresidencia, 2015.

Edward E. Telles and Nelson Lim. Does it matter who answers the race question? Racial classification and income inequality in Brazil. *Demography*, 35(4):465–474, 1998.

Tariq Thachil. Does Police Repression Spur Everyday Cooperation? Evidence from Urban India. *The Journal of Politics*, 82(4): 1474–1489, 2020.

Charles Tilly. *The Contentious French*. Belknap Press, Cambridge, Massachusetts, 1986.

Michael Touchton, Natasha Borges Sugiyama, and Brian Wampler. Democracy at Work: Moving beyond elections to improve well-being. *American Political Science Review*, 111(1): 68–82, 2017.

Roger Tourangeau and Tom W. Smith. Asking sensitive questions: The impact of data collection mode, question format, and question context. *Public Opinion Quarterly*, 60(2):275–304, 1996.

Abel Valenzuela Jr., Lisa Schweitzer, and Adriele Robles. Camionetas: Informal travel among immigrants. *Transportation Research Part A: Policy and Practice*, 39(10):895–911, 2005.

Joann Vanek, Martha Chen, Ralf Hussmanns, James Heintz, and Françoise Carré. *Women and Men in the Informal Economy: A statistical picture*. ILO and WIEGO, 2014.

Ashutosh Varshney. Ethnic conflict and civil society: India and beyond. *World Politics*, 53(03):362–398, 2001.

Vesla M. Weaver and Amy E. Lerman. Political consequences of the carceral state. *American Political Science Review*, 104(04): 817–833, 2010.

Ariel White. Family matters? Voting behavior in households with criminal justice contact. *American Political Science Review*, 113(2): 607–613, 2019.

WIEGO. Wiego organization and representation database. URL http://wiego.org/wiegodatabase, 2016. Accessed: 2016-04-12.

Karen Workman. D.C. crime bill would pay people to avoid committing crimes. *The New York Times*, February 2016.

Deborah J. Yashar. *Contesting Citizenship in Latin America: The rise of indigenous movements and the postliberal challenge*. Cambridge University Press, 2005.

Nieves Zúñiga and Paul Heywood. Cleaning up La Paz: How Bolivia's biggest city freed itself from a ubiquitous culture of corruption. *Foreign Policy*, September 2015.

Index

Note: The following abbreviations have been used: *f* = figure; n = footnote; *t* = table